T0195823

THE INTRUSION OF CANCER IN AN ALREADY HECTIC, UNCERTAIN LIFE

A Story of Our Journey
With Cancer Called
Multiple Myeloma

SHIRLEY BAROODY OBROCHTA

authorHOUSE®

AuthorHouse™
1663 Liberty Drive
Bloomington, IN 47403
www.authorhouse.com
Phone: 833-262-8899

Published by AuthorHouse 03/26/2021

ISBN: 978-1-6655-1955-7 (sc)
ISBN: 978-1-6655-1956-4 (hc)
ISBN: 978-1-6655-1954-0 (e)

Library of Congress Control Number: 2021905042

Print information available on the last page.

Multiple Myeloma (MM) is the rarest type of blood cancer that affects the plasma cells with in the immune system. Plasma cells are the white blood cells that help to fight off infections by producing antibodies that identify and attack foreign invaders.

Multiple Myeloma develops as cancerous cells accumulate within the bone marrow and crowd out healthy blood cells.

MM afflicts over 400,000 people a year.

It is a bone painful cancer that takes over your everyday life is treatable but not curable. You plan your days around your pain and how to live with it and through it.

With MM you have good days, bad days, in between days, but never cancer free days.

Dedicated In Memory of My Husband Sonny
and
In Honor of Our Children
Scott and his wife Lorrie
Douglas and his wife Jill
Eric and his wife Vanessa
Elizabeth and her husband Derick,
Our grandchildren Kylie, Trevor, Ariana, Gavin,
Aidan, Evan, Trinity, Kendal and Jax

Acknowledgment

First, foremost, and always our children. I am so grateful to each and everyone of you. I could never put into words exactly what you mean to me and how swollen with pride my heart is to have you all in my life.

To our extended family of cousins, aunts, uncles, and those who are our chosen family through years of friendship. For all you did for us on this journey I thank you.

Our family physician Dr. Parker at Tri County and his staff. For always being there when we needed you. For the many times you checked up on Sonny and I to see how we were doing.

I am also grateful to Wilmont Cancer Center of Strong Memorial Hospital Rochester New York

More gratitude than I have words for Dr. Ifthi (Ifthikharudin) and his nurse Shari, for the honesty, kindness and compassion through out Sonny's diagnosis and treatment.

Dr. Passero and Cheryl B. You two are an awesome team and coming to Sonny's monthly or weekly visits with you were informative and very caring. You have an amazing talent and soft heart.

Gratitude in over abondance for all those around the country and even around the world who prayed for Sonny and our family. Many times, as we were forever waiting, we felt the warmth and tingle just knowing we were being lifted up in prayer.

Especially grateful to our heavenly Father for all the times our prayers were answered. Though in the end we did not get the answer we wanted, we know that Sonny is the winner. Not hear on earth in our time but there in heaven on Your time.

Introduction

When you have your health even for a day, it is reason enough to celebrate gratefulness every minute!

As I start this journal, we have reached much success in our business over the last 30 plus years. Now our family is carrying on with that success in three locations by our sons Scott, Doug, and Eric.

Our daughter Elizabeth (aka) Libby is working for a local accounting firm, developing an internal business of Office Rehab while holding an accounting position in the firm.

All our children are self-supporting, and raising growing families as well as their responsibilities of being home owners. For that we are grateful and very proud.

Left to right Scott, Eric, Douglas, Elizabeth

We have been self-employed in the auto and truck repair business, with towing service, over the last 30 plus years.

To have someone say "I wish I was as successful as you" is a great compliment. But here's the catch. They too would do anything to be as successful as you, if it were easy.

The reality of our success is not sleeping til noon, you have to get up with the sun, you have to work day, night, and weekends too. Never stop learning, give more than you get, you make other people's problems your own and you fix it right the first time. Work hard no matter the weather. Pour your sweat, tears and sometimes blood into every job no matter how little or how big. If a job is worth doing its worth doing well.

To keep that kind of success for over 30 years, you get up the next day and do it all over again, year after year after year.

Do this and we guarantee you will be successful too. BUT and here's a BIG BUT. Don't do it because you have to, do it because you want to!

At this moment in our life none of the success that we took so much pride in is important. It is rather dull, unfulfilling, and not so bright in the face of a terminal illness. Nothing about our success can make us unhear what we have been told.

In the darkness of the night, lying awake with my mind going to 100 things that in the long run don't really matter, I can feel the God given breath being sucked out of our life and freedoms to live and work as we know it to once have been. My body feels heavy, so heavy I might just sink completely through my mattress to the deep darkness under my bed.

We now know that nonstop pursuit of wealth and a name is just not that important.

God gave us senses that we might feel love and not dwell on the wealth of things accumulated, but sometimes we don't see that until we are faced with the uncertainty of life.

The wealth of things accumulated we cannot take with us when we die.

What we can take is our memories of those we left behind. In turn we can leave memories, just be sure and leave good ones, memories made by thoughtfulness and love for each other. That is life's true treasure and riches. In all honesty, sometimes easier to say than to do.

Only Sonny has learned this much to late. In some sense we all learned to late. He cannot make up for his past, none of us can, but he intends to leave good memories from here on out, until his end, that is his goal.

I imagine like any other life scare that he had in the past that this will be the same. Meaning, he will treat us all kindly until at some point he thinks he has beat this cancer thing then he will go back to treating us like possessions instead of his life's treasure. If the past scares of his health issues are any indication then I already know how this will end too.

Being a workaholic, making a living, and a name for himself is what his life has always been.

That is fine and good, but because he is a hard-core workaholic, he expects everyone to have the same life and work ethic, which is not always the case.

I read these words just the other day "when you are healthy life has no limits. Go where you want to go do what you want to do, it's all up to you, when you're terminally ill all you want is your health, and wish you had traveled when you were healthy"

Steve Jobs once said "The most expensive bed in this world is a sick bed. There you lie alone. You can hire a person to drive you, to take care of your home, to make money for you, but you cannot hire someone to carry your sickness for you, you must lay there alone.

All material possessions lost can be found or replaced, but once you lose your life it's gone, there can never be a do over."

When someone experiences a loss of health and you're at the mercy of God and the doctors, there you are wishing you could open up the book of life and start over, and or at least finish reading it to see how it really ends. Especially the chapter on "Healthy Life Again." Reality is that is never how it ends.

Whatever stage of life you are in right now, know that you have time left to cherish every moment, because none of us really know when that curtain will fall. We don't leave this world alive. So, until the curtain comes down, make things right with your family members, treasure your family, and value others, because clearly life is hard and to damn short!

We all know our end will eventually come, and not just those dealing with a terminal illness. None of us know the day or the time our life on this earth ends.

Not only will the end come, but the end also signifies a new beginning, hopefully in heaven for those that leave us, and for those remaining it will be a new beginning of learning to live without a member of our family and or friend.

God gives all of us only a certain amount of time here on earth. Every day we wake up and we decide and we choose how we are going to live those given minutes and hours.

There are no do overs, no second chances on any moment, that time is spent, it's gone, you don't get it back. The day is over, so make every day count.

This journal started out with my intention of keeping Sonny's medication, treatments, and doctor orders documented so we can just look back and know what was done when and where, and the names of the complicated medical words, hard to pronounce medications, and diagnosis's.

We never knew words like Valcade, Zometta, Prednesone, Stem Cell Transplant, Chemo Cocktail, Morphine, Revlimid, Infusion, and Chemo would ever become a part of Sonny's daily routine. We never thought in our whole life that any of us would ever have need for an "Oncologist, Hematologist, Radiologist, Orthopedic, Cardiologist!"

We were happy enough with our General Physician and Physician Assistant!

We have known a few family and friends who have died because of cancer.

I have tried not to hate because I know that hating is a vicious emotion.

I TRULY HATE CANCER.

I hate what it does to people and those who love them. Cancer steels your present, your future, and your joy. It does it in such a way it will bring you to your lowest ever. It will bring you to your knees and sometimes flat on your face.

Then when you're at your lowest and angriest, and the only way you can see is up but there is no stair case or elevator, you get really pissed and you get really angry and decide screw cancer, it's not going to control us.

Then at times it does just that. You experience so much anger, hate, compassion, like, love, kindness, hope, hopelessness, care, upsets, peace, misunderstandings, explanations, and total brain fog. Sometimes you can have many of those feelings with in the same day, even within the same hour.

This soon turned into a vivid journal of the many chapters in our life's cancer story. I had a nagging feeling in the beginning that this is going to be an important account in a very long journey.

Sonny feels someday our story of how we endured, survived, or didn't, will be someone's else's encouragement, survival story.

It is raw, emotional, reality! It will make you mad and upset at times because of the way we handle things on our own. It is who we are in every sense, yet at the same time it is who we have not chosen to be, yet here we are!

It comes from our heart, our love of each other, family, and friends, and yes even our hate of this hand we have been dealt.

We started this journey actually a few months before the diagnosis when Sonny hurt his ribs at work, probably around September 2013. He was drilling holes with a huge magnetic frame drill, in a truck frame he had been fabricating, and the drill lost contact with the frame and the weight of Sonny's body hit the drill full force on his ribs. The hazards of the job. It was nothing for him to get bruised.

Little did we know at that time that cancer was creeping, or had crept, into our life and would change us all in the way we live.

I'll open this journal with the following statement, to all who have lived with someone who has cancer, to all who have cancer, to all who have known someone with cancer or any other terminal disease.

If possible, don't let the disease steel your joy for today. Don't think about the joys you might miss. Live for today. I know it's an old saying, but it's true: Love with all your heart, for the joys you have are those present with you today. Be grateful you have the opportunity of today

This is our story as it happened

This is hard, damn hard. Though at times we hated each other, we never stopped loving each other. Only a long-time married couple would understand that statement.

This journal and account of our cancer and our life is brutally honest, so forgive me in advance if I offend anyone. This is and was our reality, our fears, our frustrations, our anger, our pain, our love, and even our hate in dealing with Multiple Myeloma.

I call it our cancer because cancer, *any cancer*, does not only affect the person who is diagnosed but it affects every family member in so many ways. One would never know unless you also have experienced this journey.

I have written this book, in the hopes that our experience may help others who have been diagnosed with multiple myeloma. If by chance any doctor cares to read it, I hope that they may know and understand from a family's view point and that of a caregiver's perspective on caring for their loved one with multiple myeloma.

Some entries are day by day, even moment by moment. The ones that go months apart are the best, because the bigger the time lapse without entry the better our life and Sonny's health was.

If you believe in God and answered prayer, and turning your problems, trust, and life over to God to handle. You better also be prepared for life's reality, with your five-point seatbelt tightened. You don't get to tell God what the answer is for you, instead you need to be prepared.

What the answer is not, is damn hard to accept.

Friday the 13th of December 2013

On Friday December, 13th 2013 was when we finally got someone to believe us that the pain is not all in his imagination, yes Friday the thirteenth.

Last night December 12,2013 we spent seven hours in Dansville Noyes Hospital. It was the evening of the twelfth. But we never left until early morning on the thirteenth.

Sonny has had a pain in his lower left abdominal rib area for a few months now. At first, he thought it was because he slipped with a power drill and it slammed against his ribs. After a few weeks' time to let the bruise heal and still no relief from the pain, he went to see our family physician Dr. Parker.

The doctor sent him for a chest and rib area x ray and there was nothing broken or cracked, so they chalked it up to muscular bruising and pain. A few more weeks went by to let his rib area heal, and the pain is now worse and effecting his breathing. He went back to the doctor and was sent for a CT scan.

On Thursday December 12, 2013 he talked to Dr Parker on the phone and was told "there is nothing visibly wrong, and they didn't know why he is feeling so much pain". At this point he was ready to call it quits and resign to the fact it's all in his head.

I would not give up. I know my man he has a high pain tolerance and if he says he's in pain you just know it really hurts. I called his cardiologist that afternoon, on a whim that it might be heart related because of the hard time breathing, even though the pain was in his lower chest and rib area. His cardiologist said to go to the ER and get a second opinion.

We arrived at the ER a little after 5pm and didn't leave until after midnight. They ran blood test that came back showing low white blood count and caused some concern with the ER doctor. Admittedly at that time we didn't know what that meant. The next test ordered by the ER doctor was a CT scan with contrast.

In the meantime, while we were waiting in the ER for all the testing, they gave him some pain medication that helped a little. Sonny told me to go get groceries since that was our plan for the evening. I went to Tops in Dansville and stopped back at the hospital. He was still waiting for both the ER doctor to let him know what he found out, and the CT scan.

It was 9:15p.m. and the ER was so busy that it appeared we were going to be there a few more hours. Sonny told me to "take the groceries home and let Maddie (our dog) out, then come back, hopefully he would be ready to go home by then.

I got back to the hospital at around 11:20p.m. I walked into the ER room where Sonny was. I could tell the news he just got was not good. His face was red, and there were tears in his eyes. The ER nurse immediately came over and stood by me. The ER doctor had a look of concern in his eyes and on his face, as he explained to me what was going on.

The ER doctor said "the good news is, his spleen is fine. A spleen injury was suspect because of the impact on the area of his body when he fell against the drill. But the uncertain news is there is a mass appearing to be tumor of some sort on his lower right side behind his lung and it's pushing on the nerves along his spine. That seems to be the cause of his pain."

There in a split second, our lives have now been forever changed. As well as the lives of our whole family. It was like the very breath we had was sucked out of us, and we melted into and became one with the floor. The cold, cold floor of the ER, so hard so cold, and so lonely. Cold with fear unable to breathe, unable to think. So many questions yet numb and blank at the same time.

3

We are in total shock; we don't know what "it" is.

It's almost Christmas and we don't want anyone to know. At least not til we have more answers to our own questions. After all, we ourselves don't know what it is. How could we even begin to explain it to our kids, our parents, and our siblings? We don't want to worry anyone, and adding more people to worry about the unknown isn't going to solve or help the situation.

It is ironically funny how in a blink of an eye your life can change, yet for all appearance must remain the same. Its Christmas and yet we have to deal with this and pretend we are happy. We wish the holiday was over. At this moment, we find no blessing in Christmas this year.

Friday the 13th of December We have an appointment with Dr Parker at 4:30p.m. because of last night's ER visit and test results.

When we arrive it's very cold and snowing like crazy.

We saw Dr. Parker and he did say we need to find out if the tumor or mass is cancer or not. If it is, he needs to get treatment started. It is too late to set up an appointment in Rochester at Strong Memorial Hospital cancer center. The James Wilmot Cancer Center to be exact. They will call us on Monday. Dr Parker put in an urgent order for Sonny to be seen ASAP.

That tells me if it were not serious then why would he need an "urgent" referral?

Tonight, we will be watching our youngest granddaughter, Kendal while her mom goes Christmas shopping. Life goes on, and it should, but we have no energy to spare. Though it is not a physical type of energy loss. It is an emotional, and mental type of exhaustion.

What is happening to Sonny, to us, to our family, is so unfair. In the long run, our kids and grandkids, who are the ones losing out on precious time. Having a little one here gives us a nice distraction from all that is going through our mind.

Now just like I have done my whole life, I must lift my chin and be everyone's rock, everyone's care giver, researcher, and everyone's strength. When at times I just want to run away from it all to a place where no one can find me, and let them fend for themselves. But I won't, because I am who I am no matter what is going on I get over myself, I continue to love beyond measure, I find hope, I forgive, and move on.

Saturday December 14, 2013 Sonny is not feeling too well today. He went to the hospital for blood test this morning. He was sitting on the couch this morning, and as he got up to get a second cup of coffee, we heard a loud pop followed by severe pain in his lower rib right abdominal side behind his hip. I hope he can be seen this week so we get some answers and he can get some pain relief.

Monday December 16, 2013 Dr. Parker prescribed Gabapentin one hundred milligrams, for nerve pain. It may help him get some much-needed relief from the pain and also to get some uninterrupted sleep. It didn't help very much. Maybe this is one of the medications that has to build up in a person's system before you get relief.

Tuesday December 17, 2013 Dr. Parker called us. The cancer center wants Sonny to have another CT scan of his whole chest and rib area before they will see him. He has an appointment for that tomorrow at 10:30a.m. at Noyes Hospital.

Wednesday December 18, 2013 Today Sonny went to Dansville hospital for another CT scan, that will be sent to Strong in Rochester then they are supposed to set up an appointment for us to go up so we can find out just what is wrong with him, and what the "mass" is.

Thursday December 19, 2013 Sonny went to his heart Dr. To make sure everything is ok with his heart, all was good. Dr Varron looked at all of Sonny's latest test results from Noyes Hospital and was shocked that there had been no blood test was done for his PSA levels. In other words, there was no test for prostate cancer.

He told Sonny prostate problems could cause the kind of pain he is experiencing.

Here he is a cardiologist and he ordered this PSA test for Sonny! He also said if our doctor does not call us by tomorrow morning with the results of the blood test, then to call his office and let him know and he will find out for us. The thing is we don't understand, why would prostate cancer show up as a mass behind his ribs? We are confused.

We find ourselves grasping at straws of information. We want to hear anything else but cancer. We want to hear; here's a pill, and don't worry we can fix this.

December 19, 2013 Dr. Parker's nurse called at 8p.m. and said Dr. Parker does not have the last CT test results and that he will be calling us tomorrow December 20, 2013 to let us know when we are scheduled in Strong to see the "specialists." We just don't know yet what kind of specialist they are sending him to.

I think they called because I sent Dr. Jessica, our physician assistant an e mail. I asked her to please help us. I told her that this not knowing was driving us insane. We have so many unanswered questions, and possibly unnecessary worry. Within twenty minutes of my email the nurse called.

The thing is no one is saying anything, possibly because they don't know either. No one is saying this is or is not serious. The not knowing is really causing, I think too much, unnecessary worry. But it's the nature of the unknow that causes worry.

11a.m. December 20, 2013 Dr. Parker called. There has been no change in Sonny's CT scan. He does however have high protein in his blood. Dr. Parker also told us that Wilmot cancer center in Rochester wanted more information first. That is why we haven't heard from them. They should be calling us today to set up an appointment for Sonny to be seen. To find out what is going on, and why Sonny is in so much pain. Dr. Parker told Sonny he could take Advil 4x's a day. I know he won't, he does not like to take medicine even if it helps. I never can understand that about him.

4:40p.m. Dr. Parker's office just called. Sonny can be seen in Rochester at Strong on January 3, 2014 at 4p.m. by a Dr. Ifthi (this is short for some very long name I cannot pronounce let alone spell)

5:45p.m. Dr. Parker's office just called back Dr. Ifthi had a cancelation and will see Sonny on Tuesday December 24, 2013 at 9a.m.

Since last Thursday, the night at the ER, I have found it very hard to pray day or night.

Believe me, the night of the ER visit words flowed freely to God in petition for my husband's diagnosis, understanding, peace, acceptance, and healing.

From then on, the words don't come, I can't even force them, my mind is numb. I wonder is it Satan, or is it just my faith, or lack of?

The only words that come to me are words of thanks and songs of praise. It doesn't make sense at a time like this. That all I can do is praise and thank God! Why is the Holy Spirit doing this to my mind? Really, thankfulness, praise, and worship for this? The unknown and no definitive answers!

No way am I thankful for Sonny's pain, or the unknown. What the hell is wrong, who is putting those things in my mind? Is it God showing me a way, telling me to trust in Him? Possibly how to cope with the unknown? Or is it Satan? Trying to wear me down spiritually, to plant doubt and fear in me, in us?

It's Christmas and for the first time in my life ever, I just want the holiday to be over with. I have no merriment, no Christmas cheer, no joy in my heart.

Shirley Baroody Obrochta

My heart is as cold as the whole outdoors.

What I express on my face is not what is in my heart. I wear a mask of a fake smile and false confidence. This Christmas I am a phony. Only going through the motions of happiness and Christmas cheer.

I Didn't Say So To Sonny

Today December 24, 2013 Christmas eve. I'm sure this is going to be one of many trips to Rochester. I just feel it in my bones but **I didn't say so to Sonny.**

We arrived at Strong around 8:15a.m. and we were directed to Sonny's appointment. We followed the directions and as we turned down the hall the sign read, James P Wilmot Cancer Center. **I didn't say so to Sonny** but I got a very uneasy feeling when I saw that sign.

We went to the information desk at the end of a very long hall. We were sent to the sixth floor. My first thought was, "must be going through the cancer center is just how to get to the doctor that Sonny is seeing". But that was just self-encouragement, to deny the dread I really felt **I didn't say so to Sonny.**

We get off the elevator and there in front of us at eye level is a sign that says Blood and Bone Marrow Transplant Center. Sonny looked at me and said "I don't think this is going to be good". Little did we know at that moment he was absolutely right.

We saw Dr. J. Ifthikharuddin. So that is why he is called Dr Iftthi. He was very nice, very human, very compassionate, soft spoken and caring. I have a feeling we will be seeing a lot of this Dr. Ifthi, but **I didn't say so to Sonny.**

After meeting with Dr. Ifthi, Sonny had a bunch of tests. Blood test, X-rays, and bone marrow biopsy. We have to go back on the twenty sixth, the day after Christmas. Then he will have a PET scan and to go to the radiation department to talk to a radiologist about the up and coming treatment of the mass/tumor behind his ribs.

Sonny and I are very scared but holding it together for each other. I called all the kids from the hospital after we saw the oncologist, and told them all what was going on. A difficult conversation, because I didn't have answers for them as to how it happened, what can be done, will he be alright or where we go from here.

It's Christmas Eve and I had to say "the doctor thinks your dad has a cancer called Multiple Myeloma" I couldn't explain it all to them because I didn't understand it myself. Nor had I ever heard of this kind of cancer.

My heart was breaking. I didn't want to make those phone calls. But I could no longer keep it from them. We were scheduled up for too many appointments. I could no longer hide that something was just not right.

Naturally, the kids and Sonny's Mom are devastated, and tomorrow is Christmas. As for my mom her reaction was, "that's too bad, will he have to change his diet?" She's a cold-hearted woman, she thinks food fixes everything!

How do you ever prepare to hear the words *"you have cancer"*, at any time much less Christmas?

The first thing that goes through your mind is, this is it, how long do I have? You immediately think it's a death sentence. We were in shock to put it mildly.

Unless you are or have gone through this you could never know the impact it has on you and your family.

Thanks a lot Santa. Cancer is not what we asked for!

Christmas 2013 This is what we are most grateful for: Them and their parents

From upper left clock wise starting at eleven o'clock:
Kylie, Trevor, Ariana, Gavin, Aidan, Evan, Trinity, and Kendal

Don't Turn Around

I heard someone explain a terminal illness this way, I'll try to retell it.

Imagine you're going about your day minding your own business, when someone sneaks up behind you.

You feel something hard, and it's pressed up against the back of your head, as someone whispers in your ear.

"Be very quiet, don't turn around, just listen. I am holding a gun against the back of your head. I'm going to keep it there. I'm going to follow you around like this every day, for the rest of your life."

"I'm going to press a bit harder once in a while, just to remind you I'm here. You need to try your best to ignore me, to move on with your life. Act like I'm not here, but don't you ever forget one day I may just pull the trigger, or maybe I never will.

Isn't this going to be a fun game?"

This is what it is like to be diagnosed with cancer. Any stage of cancer. Any kind of cancer. It will never truly go away. It's always in the back of your mind, like the feel of a cold hard gun barrel.

Once you have been diagnosed with cancer there is no going back to your old life. No matter how badly you don't want to do this, your life has been forever changed.

The change may require just a little adjustment and decisions or it may require life altering adjustments. Suddenly life is very different. Our priorities have shifted, every month, every week, every day, every hour, and every minute. No matter where you go cancer goes with you. You can't put it on a shelf, or pack it away until you're ready to deal with it.

At first you talk about it a lot within your home, you and your spouse, and family. Hoping for some kind of understanding and answers to the unknown. At other times, you may never want to talk about it. Maybe it will all just go away if we don't speak of it.

You may have a friend or friends who have heard you have cancer. They ask "How are you doing?" Some genuinely care, some are nosy and only want gory details. At first when you try to talk to them, the words "I have cancer" choke the breath right out of you and you swallow the sobs coming from your throat to your stomach. Sobs you don't want anyone to know about.

If they, (the one diagnosed) do talk about it, they aren't asking you to make it better. They want you to sit with them in their fear, their sadness, their anger, just don't expect any answers because they have none. Yet there are also people like me who just want to be left alone, to try to figure this out.

How can I fix this? I have to fix this. I am going to fix it!

Don't try to talk them out of how they are feeling, the cancer patient or their caregiver. That doesn't help. It will only make them feel like what they are going through is being minimized or unimportant, that they should not feel like they do. Don't remind them of all the good things they still have in their life. They know. They are grateful.

But some days they are more aware of that gun pressing into the back of their head and they need to talk about it.

As for our life we have always been on the go, independent, very active, and always very busy. We are too busy living to have an *intrusion* of cancer.

Cancer was intruding on our life style. We don't have time for this!

Time, it's always moving forward, never backwards, it never stands still, yet it feels like there is no more time. It feels like we already have run out of so much time.

We are a living together married couple, with children, and grandchildren. We were also strong independent, live our own life type people. We always have something to do, something to fix, and something to make better. Our entire world has been turned upside down, never to be upright again.

Nothing makes sense. We were told, the best you can do is live with *MM* you cannot fix this!

Oh yea MM, just watch us!

TREATMENTS BEGIN
December 26, 2013

We are back at the Wilmot Cancer Center at Strong for a full day of appointments. Seeing the radiologist at 10am. They were very good, we talked to a Dr. Behkall (radiologist) he said he is very confident that he can eliminate the mass that is behind Sonny's ribs.

Sonny had a mapping scan that gave the radiologist the full picture of the mass from every angle, in 3-D. We have to come back at 4pm for the actual radiation treatment.

From seeing the radiologist, we were off to the Science Center, in another part of the city, for the PET scan at 12:30pm. We talked to a nurse who told us all about the procedure and of Sonny being radioactive afterwards.

Then as they checked him in, Sonny's glucose level was 246. Much too high for the PET scan. We had to reschedule for the following Thursday.

The radioactive fluid goes into his body by way of IV glucose water and with his blood sugar numbers being so high he can't do the glucose. His blood sugar numbers are high due to the steroids he is on to reduce the pain. Already it seems as if we are not going to win this war and the battle has just started, but **"I didn't say so to Sonny"**

Back at the radiation department by 3:30pm. Sonny is in extreme pain. He feels like screaming kind of pain. They took him in a little before four. It took about an hour and a half, but the radiologist is very certain this will eliminate the tumor.

Sonny came out of the radiation treatment room in so much pain he was spitting bullets. He was mad because the pain hurt so bad. The radiologist table was so hard and flat which exacerbates the pain in his bones. He just looked at me and said "let's get the fuck out of here."

We got in the van, he turned the heat on in the seat for his back, and we went home. I had to drive; I drive everywhere now.

12/29/13 Bad pain last night. Three days post radiation. He got up about 11:30pm to go to the bathroom and he could not feel his legs and fell against the bed post and had to sit down and wait til he had feeling again. The pain was so severe he had a hard time breathing. Sonny slept in the recliner the rest of the night because it kept the pressure off his spine from the tumor. When he lays flat all his weight is on his spine where the tumor is.

It's very hard to see someone who was always physically strong, who could do anything and everything to suddenly come to a halt. Its very hard to see someone who was physically strong, who could do anything and everything suddenly become so weak. He can no longer carry the forty-pound bags of pellets for the stoves any more. But I can fill that obligation until he is strong once again. It's what we do, help each other.

Now more than ever there is nothing worse than something you cannot do anything about. Right now, we are shocked, especially because the reality is, cancer is nothing we can fix. The fear that grips us is that he might lose this battle.

We are both "fixers" there is "nothing" we can't fix or repair, or so we thought!

The unknown is becoming an unwanted, and the awkward. We want a quick fix, a pill to swallow, but it's not to be. Our regular routine has been interrupted, but not by choice. It's like a pause button has been hit in our lives and from the side lines we are now spectators of fate, weekly appointments, many pills, medicines, and so many doctors that are all 85 miles away.

When Christians hear about someone who has been given a terminal diagnosis such as cancer. Our first thought and concern are do they know the Lord? We want to make sure they are right with God and are going to heaven when they die. After all no one wants the alternative of hell.

I think our youngest son Eric thinks his Dad doesn't love The Lord, but he does.

The thing is, knowing God is a personal relationship for everyone and everyone is different. There are people who go to church their whole lives and don't know God.

There are some who no longer go to church, because of organized religion. They are in a closer relationship with God than those who go all the time.

There is a big difference in religion and God, they don't always go hand in hand but I won't get into that here, not now anyhow.

That Six Letter Word

Cancer it makes you fear the very breath in your body. It makes you mad, scared, confused, and you question every little pain. Sadly, it makes you hate!

It is the worst thing we have ever had to explain to our children, so far. Telling them of your possible impending death through a terminal diagnosis is just not right.

Inside you shudder with fear and uncertainty. You are very scared, but you want to always remain in control and un afraid in all appearances to face what you have to in front of your children.

We are the ones to up hold the family, to protect, to take care of the children, to be there always. We are the parents, "we don't break down."

We never want to show fear to our kids. We want them to carry on with their lives, and not stop living because of their Dads cancer. We have relied on our faith and strength to carry us and them. We vow to always be honest with them about any and all cancer information on Sonny. But I absolutely refuse to let them see my heartache, worry, and fear. We are the parents We will carry them always, not the other way around.

Cancer has a way of turning people's conversation to religion and your belief in God or a higher form, one of which can change your destiny at any moment. That we have no doubt. We are believers and God is our savior. Though we never force our religion or belief on anyone. If you wanted to talk about it I would.

Same being said we don't like others to shove their beliefs or if they have no belief down our throat in order to change what we feel is right or wrong for us.

Many are of the belief that he has sinned or he deserves this cancer because of his past, or because of his fathers' sins. Due to scripture in the Bible that says we suffer due to the sins of our fathers.

We don't go there. It's just wrong, and we believe it is misinterpretation of scripture! Yet some have tried to force that on us because it is what they were taught or believe.

Right now, we don't want to argue religion with anyone. It is between our God and us. We don't need to find common ground with anyone but our selves. We need to protect every ounce of energy we have into getting beyond the pain and taking our worries up with God. Our God keeps us afloat and our head above water and He will see us through this ordeal too, or not.

January 2, 2014 5a.m. We are on our way to Rochester for the day. The roads are covered with snow and its ten degrees. Today at 7:45a.m. he is scheduled to have a PET scan to check for other tumors and other cancers. He seems to be feeling pretty good the last few days, morning are the best times for him.

At 3:45p.m. we have an appointment with the oncologist to get the final results of all the testing that has been done the last couple of weeks. I think I will need a pen and paper for that appointment, my memory from here to there is sometimes sketchy. I'm already on information overload trying to wrap my head around all of it.

7:10a.m. We have arrived at the imagery department. Boy is it cold. Sonny's test will take about two hours start to finish. He is both very brave and nervous. Not from the test but because of what the outcome might be. Waiting on the unknown is very hard. Again, the unknown haunts us like a giant shadow in an already dark as night alley. The unknown, and yet we wonder will having a medical name or label to whatever is wrong make it better? I really don't think so.

11am PET scan done and we are on our way to breakfast at Denny's. We were both starving, Sonny couldn't have anything to eat since supper last night. I had my coffee this morning but that was it. It's snowing very fine snow and the wind is wicked, cold, and bitter.

We arrived back at Strong Memorial around 1:30p.m. and his appointment isn't until 3:30p.m. We parked in the hospital parking garage and waited until three to go in. We left the van running while we were sitting in the garage cause it's so bitterly cold. Sonny had the heat turned on in his seat and the seat reclined back. He napped while I played solitaire on my I-pad.

Time, though it was moving same as any other day, seemed to drag on so very slowly.

Waiting in the doctor office is very nerve wracking. Sonny and I are sitting in the exam room, and have seen the nurse, and one doctor already. The one doctor, Dr Noel who we first saw questioned Sonny about how he was feeling since he was there last week. She instructed Sonny to be taking his pain medicine as prescribed in order to stay on top of the pain. Which is a little more often than he does. She explained to him that if he took it regularly as ordered and not just when the pain got so bad, he couldn't stand it, he would have much better relief and less break through pain. Like I mentioned before he hates to take medicine.

Dr. Noel left us to go "confer" with Dr. Ifthi. Sonny isn't saying anything and neither am I. We are both very nervous, cause if it was good news, we feel that the Dr. would have been in much sooner. Just self-talk and wishful thinking I suppose. It's an awful long time before Dr Ifthi comes in or at least it felt like a very long time. When he does nurse Shari and Dr. Noel come with him.

The news was not good, but not hopeless either.

We are both numb with uncertainty, confusion, fear, and anger. The doctor said "all the test confirms what we suspected." Multiple Myeloma cancer of the blood plasma, and in the bone marrow, terminal but treatable!

How can that be, how can it be both terminal and treatable? We don't understand! We never heard of Multiple Myeloma, who ever heard of this kind of cancer? Not us!

That six-letter word cancer has now and forever changed our lives

I t's hard to believe that we are Sitting here in the Wilmot Cancer Center just observing everyone. The only consolation is that you know everyone else is here because somehow, some way their lives are also affected by that six-letter word.

I use to hate when I heard people talk and they swore using four letter words. Now I know a six-letter word that hurts more!

Cancer is a weird disease because you can have it and not look sick. Even at times when you are sick you can still look pretty good. Confusing at times. He doesn't feel sick, he only has a bad pain in his lower back, rib area. Asking himself is cancer a sickness or a pain?

Some people here look better than others. We have heard some say "today is my last treatment, I am cancer free".

From what we understand so far, Sonny will never be able to say those words. The only comfort we have in being here is to know we are not alone. This is the place where we all find hope, knowledge, security, and some even regain health.

6p.m. We are on our way home. A lot of information was given to us today. Confirmation from all the testing that he does have Multiple Myeloma. A cancer of the blood plasma. It is not curable, but he can have treatments and he can live with it.

Next Tuesday he will begin chemo. A combination of pills, shots, and IV's, (aka) a chemo cocktail.

Just hearing the word *cancer* changes your life and the lives of the people who love and care about you. We all want to remain optimistic and strong even if we are scared to death on the inside.

We will love each other through this no matter what comes up or how hard the road gets.

The oncologist is very hopeful that even though it will be rough, Sonny is a good candidate for much success that this will go into some type of partial remission and he will be back to feeling like himself again. Dr. Ifthi told Sonny "give me a year and I promise you will be back to yourself again."

Dr Ifthi is very hopeful about Sonny's return to some kind of normal health. Because he said everything else about Sonny is strong and healthy. We feel very cared for there. Doctor Ifthi's nurse Shari is very compassionate, and nice. It doesn't matter how simple or foolish our questions seem to us they inform us in a very gentle way. They have a kind heart and informative mind with the ability to put you at ease. You just know she cares. She is a good match with Dr. Ifthi.

Turns out I didn't need paper and pen today because at the end of the office visit, they gave us a summary of today's test, medications, upcoming appointments and over all view of the diagnosis.

From six letter one-word life diagnosis, to two words, *cancer free*, two words we know we will never hear. No one is ever free of Multiple Myeloma. We were told it can be managed and will become dormant, but never eliminated, always present but sometimes nonactive.

2014

January 3, 2014 Friday Sonny is real sick tonight. He has the chills, shakes, and vomiting. He has had chronic hic cups since Thursday night, due to his treatment. I called his doctor and they sent in a prescription of Chlorpromazine to stop the chronic hiccups. It worked.

The chemo shots in the stomach are very pain full to him. We were supposed to go out to fish fry with Scott and Lorrie but he just couldn't do it. We stayed home and went to bed early.

January 7, 2014

We are back at the cancer center today. Sonny had his cancer infusion treatment all went well with the infusion. It was very windy and very cold. The temperature when we got here was minus five and the wind chill was minus 22.

I knew today was going to be a bad day right off the bat. I spilled my coffee first thing before I even got one sip, then I burnt my toast. Sonny didn't want to eat this morning but he did have his coffee. It didn't improve his attitude, he was mad at me soon as he got out of bed, it's as if he hates the sound of my breathing, the way I look, and the sound of my voice. Sometimes his words cut me deeply and all I'm trying to do is take care of him. You know, in sickness and health!

Sometimes when he looks at me, I see/feel hate. Maybe its resentfulness in his eyes, and I don't know why. I am kind to him, I do whatever he needs to have done, I try to make him comfortable.

I try to be compassionate and understanding and put myself in his place.

I often have to stop and ask myself, How angry would I be at the world if I had that kind of diagnosis? How compassionate would he be towards me? I could mention of my life with him and how he treats me when I'm sick, but this is not about me!

The day didn't get any better at the cancer center either. Sonny was so pissed at me because I could not park the van in a few parking spots that he thought I should have. I tried but they were for smaller cars if I did get the van in those spots one of us would not have been able to open our door or gotten out. After the second time around the six floors of the parking garage, and being told how to park, and how "fucking stupid" I am that I'm afraid to park. I finally stopped the van in the middle of the driving lane of the parking garage and said "fuck it and fuck you, you park it," and he did. I walked to the lobby alone and crying!

We both are on edge. I hate myself for saying what I did. I never, ever use that word, never!

What is happening to us? This is not fair.

Suddenly of all the stupid things that suddenly crossed my mind was, I know he won't have the strength to go camping this summer he just won't be able to do it. But hey it's only January why the heck is camping even on my mind? Why are we not just dealing with the here and now everyday, why is my mind so messed up?

January 8 2014

Today is our 42-wedding anniversary. We are grateful for every year of our marriage and over all they have been good years. Naturally some were rough but we didn't give up. This year there will be no celebration just survival of the day. Would we say I do all over again?

Yes we would in a heartbeat.

January 14, 2014

Today was the first time we drove to Rochester without driving in a snow storm. Today was Sonny's second chemo treatment, and his first bone strengthening IV of Zometa. We didn't get out of the center til 4p.m. Again, I was driving after we left the hospital and again, I was not driving the way Sonny approves of. He gets so mad. I never ever have any trouble driving or parking unless he is with me. Then I know I am being judged and tested. I wish he could drive as much as he does, but the medication makes him to sleepy to be able to drive safely.

We get to the restaurant for supper and I can't eat fast enough. He eats so little now that a couple of bites and he is ready to go. I have taken up too much of his precious time. We leave the restaurant; I leave hungry and left most of my meal on my plate. I did get to taste what was on my plate but that is about it. I am not a fast eater.

When we get home, I vacuumed and shampooed the bedroom carpet to get ready for our new adjustable bed that comes tomorrow. Sonny slept in his recliner. I tried to sleep in the other recliner because our bed is no longer set up in order to make room when the new bed is delivered in the morning. I couldn't sleep so I ended up in the spare bedroom around 10p.m. Our little dog Maddie was so upset and confused about our bed being gone. She always sleeps between Sonny and I. Tonight she couldn't settle down she wandered the house. Jumping on Sonny then coming to me, until Sonny yelled at her then she came in and got in bed with me and settled down.

January 15 2014 Today our new bed should arrive this morning. I do hope we both can sleep better now. It is a Temperpedic memory foam mattress adjustable bed. Two separate mattresses in one frame, so we can both adjust our own side of the bed individually.

People keep asking how Sonny is? I don't really know what to say, because I don't want to drag anyone down. Sometimes I can't tell who really cares and who is just being nosy so they have something to gossip about.

We are finding out our real friends are the ones who take time to stop and see Sonny not just ask about him. His cousin Dick, friends John S, Jack T, Dave G, Roy S, Ken S, good neighbor Terry S, and Ken P. and many others call us. All good friends to Sonny and I. They all offer to help around the house and drive us to Rochester if we like.

Then there are others who say "how are you holding up?" I'm sure most of them mean well and are genuinely concerned.

"Well how the hell do ya think? My husband is terminally diagnosed with a cancer neither of us ever heard of" Of course I don't really say that, I just think it.

I am trying to be strong and positive. I hang on to every positive word the professionals tell us. But the truth is, my faith is failing and I live for today and that is all. I don't know what our future holds. I live with a daily concern, worry and heartbreak for my husband.

I sometimes think it is my fault he is so sick because when we would have huge disagreements, I would secretly wish he would take hike. Of this I am not proud.

Do other couples do this or am I just evil?

I have a lot of guilt about my feelings, I am trying to keep buried while I do everything in my power to see to it, he is comfortable and doesn't suffer. I know he is worried about his health, life, and death. Leaving his family.

I see him cry and I know he is scared. I am not much comfort to him. I could be, but he won't let me. He says "leave me alone, I'll be ok" At times he won't talk about some things, he won't let me in his life except as housekeeper, nurse, and caregiver.

Though I am an ordained pastor I was never schooled, trained, studied, advised, or mentored on how to handle a terminal cancer situation with in my own home.

Yesterday he asked me would I do his funeral when he dies. I couldn't believe it. I brushed him off and said yes if that's really what you want. Deep inside of me I know I can't even think about such a thing. I know I'd never be able to do it if it ever comes to that. If it gives him peace of mind at the moment then that much I give him. Did I just lie to him or give him a false hope?

How would I write or preach his funeral and still be brutally honest? How others know him and how I know him is all about two different men. The hero he is to everyone else, the verbally abusive hurtful person he can often be to me. The emotional bruises and hurtful words no one ever see's or hear. Then there is the man he is to everyone else, the man whose reputation with others I promised to always respect. Then as I think about it guess we can all be that way at times. We all have a dark side.

I believe he hates me or at best just tolerates me, and yet I stay and take care of him, simply because at one time we were deeply in love. Before routine life and making a living became priority. He is the father of our children and he has provided very well for all of us.

In 1972 I stood in front of God, my family, and friends. I promised to be there for him through all sickness and health, no matter what. I will keep that promise! We were once deeply in love. Over the years that changed to comfortably in love, and that's what works for us.

No matter what we go through I know he does love me and I love him.

I just love him so much I want to fix this stupid cancer shit and get on with our lives. I get so mad at myself when I act this way out of character. Out of frustration, and fear, and hurt, with upset and anger.

Our New Language

I never dreamed that one day my everyday talk and vocabulary would include words like "chemo treatments and oncologist". That I would have to learn a whole new language of medical terms and medicines. Always with so many confusing and unanswered questions, sometimes not even knowing what questions to ask.

I always considered myself a spiritually good woman of faith in God. Now I'm not so sure what I believe, except that I may be being punished for my thoughts. I feel cheated and challenged at the same time. At times I feel like giving up and running away, other times I want to kick cancers ass!

I am watching the strongest man I ever knew deteriorate right before my eyes. In the last three weeks he has lost twenty-two pounds. He cannot lift a gallon of milk without pain, or even his lap top. Everything is too painful for him to lift.

Things round the house are falling behind because I wait on him all the time for the things he can't do, like put his socks on and tie his shoes, pick things up off the floor. I fill the pellet stoves, fill the water softener, take out the garbage, clean the vehicles, not to mention all my regular house work that I do. Like laundry, meals, house cleaning, and getting groceries, which he cannot even help to carry in the house any more.

We are grateful for our children's help, and neighbors Ken P. and Roy S., who stop by to see if we are ok and if we need help.

I am trying to stay positive, but I don't know how much longer I can hide my angry feelings. Anger I don't want and don't understand. I don't want to lash out at God but sometimes That is exactly what I feel like doing.

Emotionally....I am dead
Mentally ....I am drained
Spiritually ....I am lost
Physically ....I am Exhausted

January 16, 2014 Today was a very bad painful day. He took a lot of pain medicine throughout the day and slept almost all day. The only time he was awake was to go to the bathroom, take more medication, and to eat a little, very little. He does not eat much. As of this day he is under two hundred pounds for the first time in 30 years.

He gets very depressed at times. I am also noticing he is easily confused. I wonder if his treatments effect his brain. Today he started to use a cane for stability and help getting up and down. It won't be forever, soon as his strength returns all will be well. He just cant take a chance on any broken bones while on chemo.

Last night he slept pretty well, but he sweat so much his pillow and sheets were soaked.

He cannot wear jeans because they hurt his back and his skin is so sensitive from the radiation, so he wears pajama pants or sweat pants. He hates them!

January 17 Today I brought our old recliner from the house down to the shop so he can be comfortable when he is here at the shop. He doesn't need to go there but it's what he wants to do. He's in his element when he's at the shop.

Saturday January 18 Doug came over and put a new high-rise toilet for his Dad. The regular one is just to uncomfortable and too low for Sonny to get on and off especially with the bone pain. The new one will serve both of us well in our old age when our knees get bad.

January 21 We are back to Strong Hospital today for his third chemo treatment. He has lost so much weight he has gone down two sizes in pants and shirts. I have lost a couple of pounds too but I can stand to lose a few!

I sometimes get so mad that he can't do things, but I would never tell him that. I get mad cause I know if it were turned around, he would not give me the time of day or help me. I know this because of all the times I ever got sick or had surgery, or even when I was in the hospital having the kids. It was always a bother for him to help me. He would leave me at the hospital, go to work, and not return until it was time for me to go home. He would be mad to take me to appointments when I couldn't drive after surgery. He would get mad if I had to leave the shop for a doctor or dentist appointment. I guess you could say he wasn't so much mad at me, as he was mad, he had to leave his work for me.

Matter of fact I totally quit going to the doctors and dentist for annual checkups for many years because of his whole attitude to me if I took time off for me. I only go to the doctors if I have a problem, I can't fix myself. When I did go, I'd pay for it for days in how he treated me.

Now I have to suck it up and do for him because he is my husband. I can't ever let him know how it breaks my heart to see him deteriorate right before my eyes. I can't let him see that in me. I need to stay positive so he knows all is well with me.

All my married life it's always been all about him and his comfort and whatever he wanted, so, why should this time of our life be any different. It's still all about Sonny, it always will be. I always took care of him and the children and he always worked.

Honestly, I can say this on this paper but not out loud. In my heart and mind I think it's only going to get worse. The way he treats me, his selfishness and his condition.

I am not without compassion no matter how bad he treats me. I always try to put myself in his place. I guess I'd be angry at life too. Truth be known I guess we all would be.

January 21 We went for his chemo infusion and we got so excited because his blood test came back as a slight increase in his healthy blood cells. This after only three rounds of chemo treatments. This news was very encouraging.

Another thing we always noticed is that the second day after his chemo cocktail and infusion he feels fantastic, not much pain and lots of energy.

When we mentioned it, the nurse told us that his good days are due to the hundred mg. steroids he takes on Tuesdays with the chemo. It's all part of the "chemo cocktail".

January 28. Dr. Ifthi and chemo today. Not his regular oncologist appointment but we are here because of his consistent back pain that isn't getting better and he isn't getting any relief from.. Dr Ifthi said Sonny's blood protein numbers are down slightly which is good, it means chemo is starting to work.

They are sending him to have an MRI to see if they can find out what is wrong with his back. He has so much back pain and he shouldn't with the amount of pain meds he is on.

January 31, 2014 I came home early cause things were quiet at the shop. Doug was in a bad mood for a few days now so I told him I did not need him to bring in pellets for me that I could do it. He's under a lot of stress running the shop and employees for us.

I loaded 10 bags on the back of the Kubota and was backed up to the door of the sun room and had started to unload the bags when a neighbor Joyce and Ken P stopped by when they noticed what I was doing and helped me.

After they left Sonny was just moved to tears because of how good our neighbors are. He was also emotional because he could not do the work. He said he was so helpless. I tried to reassure him it was not forever. He was really down, depressed, and just sobbing with heartache of the inability to do the things he used to. My heart breaks too to see him this way, but I fully believe it will not be forever. He will regain much of what he has lost, I just know it. It will take time.

There are days we just sit and stare at the walls of our home. A lot running through both our minds yet not either of us willing to talk about everything yet. All the what ifs, and all the if only's.

Some days we do nothing physical short of breathing. Yet we are so physically drained by the end of the day we fall into bed totally exhausted. Sometimes we are so emotionally drained that even sleep does not restore our energy. We wake up as tired as when we went to bed, because our minds just don't quiet down.

We feel surrounded by love, concern, and help of our family and friends and at the same time we have put up an invisible wall and we let no one in, at times not even each other.

There are boundaries that only we can know. Everyone wants to do something but there is nothing anyone can do. It's our battle it's our problem, everyone needs to get on with their life. I don't say that in a mean way, I'm trying to be respectful and understanding of everyone's need to just be normal.

It's our cancer! I don't mean that in an ungrateful way. We are truly grateful. We just are not used to having someone else wait on us. It's mostly that we don't want our kids or parents to put their lives on hold and stop living because of us. We can handle it, we always do, and if we can't we know your numbers.

February 1, 2014

We are in Rochester at the imagery department for his MRI. It will take about two hours.

I am very concerned about his mental attitude. Some time he just cries because he is no longer able to do much of anything physical. He said he feels so helpless and he feels the pain is driving him insane because it never ends.

We are starting to talk a little more about our future, if there is one. I believe there is and there will be.

He hates taking so much medicine. He wants one pill that will fix everything. He is so heartbroken about his physical shape. I try to keep his spirit up but he is so depressed about his situation. He said he wished he could take a pill and be done with this life.

MRI complete and we are back home. We are not sure when we will have the results.

February 6, 2014 Oncology appointment today, and we got some encouraging news. We saw Dr. Ifthi today, he said he is very pleased with Sonny's progress. Sonny's chemo is killing a great number of cancer cells. Which is very good after only one month of treatments.

The down side is the chemo is also killing his white blood cells (immunity). Those are the ones he needs to fight any kind of illness, especially infections. If his white cells fall to low, he can't have chemo, therefor the cancer grows. If they could only isolate and kill just the cancer cells wouldn't that be great?

Also, we got the results of his MRI. He has two lower discs in his back that have cracks/fractures. This is a situation that can be fixed eventually, but only after his white cells come up, which we know they won't as long as he takes the chemo. It's clearly a damned if you do and damned if you don't.

For now, he has to endure the pain. That just isn't right. Seems he should be able to sign a waiver and take a chance to get his back repaired.

Today, Friday February 7 he woke up and was experiencing light headedness and very weak. He did go to work but was physically exhausted. He went home at noon and slept til 3:30p.m. He came back to the shop and appeared to be a little more alert. I think it may be his medications causing his weakness and fatigue.

Saturday February 8 Sonny is very weak and tired today. He ate breakfast but it came back up. He was up around 6:30am and probably slept in his recliner 10 hours out of the 14 he was out of bed.

He was in bed by 8p.m. He was very emotional after he went to bed. He is very depressed about his situation even after the report he got on Thursday. He doesn't want me to tell the oncologist about his depression because it would mean he will have to take another pill or see a psychiatrist, neither one he is willing to do. I am trying to be very positive and encouraging, and not let him know I worry a lot too. I told him it's just going to take time. He said he doesn't have time he wants his old life back.

When he was awake today, we finally were able to talk a lot about the cancer and how it could impact our lives, and our future. What we wanted for each other should one of us have to go on living without the other. I think that made us both feel better. Though secretly I hope we grow old and miserable together, but loving each other. If you have been married this long then you know exactly what I mean.

We understand depression is normal reaction when you don't know just how much life you have left. But then even a healthy person doesn't know their day to day existence either. When your healthy you just don't think about it as much as someone going through a terminal illness.

I feel bad for Sonny. I don't know how to fix him. How to bring him out of this depression? Do I just help him work it out and get to a point that he is grateful for the moments we are given every day?

I know he feels like he has lost everything, everything that was, Sonny Obrochta. His work, his physical strength, his meaning, his purpose, his reason to get up every day. The only thing he has known his whole life is his work, his business, helping others, and fixing their problems, yet he cannot fix this life sentence! My heart breaks every day to see him go through this.

Sunday February 9 2014

Sonny got up about 5:45a.m. I have been up since 4a.m. I'm worried about Sonny. How to help him today and try to be kind to him no matter how he treats me.

He said he feels a little queasy and at times feels it's hard to breath. He doesn't want to go to the hospital e-room. He took a Mucinex decongestant to see if that helps. Again, he slept most of the day, and ate very little.

I wish I could get him to focus on what he can do and all that he knows. He is only focusing on the physical things he can no longer do. He has more knowledge and experience about so many things that others never gain in a life time.

Others who know him think he's a marvel, a miracle worker, a great guy, but they don't have to live with him. I promised to protect his reputation always, and at times it has cost me my happiness. At times I am only happy on the surface. No one knows the Sonny I live with. When he's not happy none of us are.

He needs to be grateful for his financial security and not so bitter about every dollar that gets spent. In his mind we can't spend a thing because he, wants me taken care of when he dies.

Why now, why does he care if I am left with anything when he's gone?

He needs to look at all he has and be thankful before he pushes everyone away.

He knows a lot of people and could be a good positive influence on many, many men if they knew his story and how he has grown being a self-made and successful business man. Full of knowledge and wisdom from life experiences and hard work.

He knows he is vulnerable and right now his illness is his priority. He wants his health back. I know he talks to God. I know he believes that Christ died for him as well as others who believe. I have no doubt about his faith. Even though he is not a practicing, or a going to church Christian. That was all ruined by some awful church congregation members we experienced at a little church we were attending. He no longer trusts anyone who goes to church and professes they are Christian.

He thinks most go just to be seen on Sunday and the rest of the week they live according to their own ways and no thought of God unless they want something.

I believe he is right!

February 15 Today is a very down sleepy day for Sonny. He has slept about all day except for eating and for our parade of visitors.

We had an actual parade of people from North Urbana Church. They came in their cars and paraded by our house very slowly, honking their horns. When they stopped out front of the house the ladies got out of their cars complete with pompoms and cheered for Sonny. The parade was headed up by my cousin Sissy. It was so nice to see them all. They left us posters they hand made with well wishes and inspirations. They visited for a short time, laid hands on Sonny in prayer and then left. There was Sue, Charlie, Sis, Dwayne, John, Missy, Debbie, and Rich, Uncle Ed and Aunt Nancy. Good people all of them. Really emotional happy time for Sonny and I.

February 19 We are at the cancer center for the weekly treatment. I'm sitting here with Sonny in the waiting room, every seat is taken. As I look around, I see there are many people here who are much worse than Sonny is. You can actually see the damage cancer and or treatments has done to their bodies. Sonny's cancer is invisible, internal, raging within his body with extreme bone pain.

My thought for today is; wouldn't it be a wonderful thing if there was no need for a place like this, if all cancer centers were empty, and nonexistent? How great it would be if all oncology doctors and nurses had no job to come to. It's not that I want people to be out of a job, it's just I wish there was no need for cancer care.

As I said before Dr. Ifthi and his nurse Sheri, are a good team and are very companionate and caring. One day as we were walking down the hall to get labs done, Dr Ifthi was coming the other way, he called us by name and took the time to stop and talk. He's a wonderful doctor. you just know his concern is genuine.

This has happened a couple of times. If you knew just how big Strong Hospital is then you know how important that is and how comforting to know that in such a big place with so much going on, thousands of people there, that a Dr. would remember you and call you by name after only seeing you a few times.

Strong Memorial is so big it's like a city within a hospital. Strong Memorial even has its own zip code!

Chemo Brain: Yes, Its Real!

Chemo brain is the cognitive changes that sometimes occurs in people going through chemo treatments. They don't know why it happens or who is at risk for it. It is scary and can show up at intermittent times, last for hours or even days.

Sunday February 22, 2014

A normal day or so I thought. We got up about 5a.m. We had our coffee and watched the news. Sonny seemed fine just a little slow in his movements, but it takes him a little longer in the morning to get going now days.

We had breakfast and then I went to Hornell to get groceries. I got back around 10a.m. Sonny was sleeping in the recliner in the living room. He woke up when I came in but was acting confused as to who I was. I got the groceries put away and then decided to bake some cookies.

The doorbell rang and it was someone looking for Eric. When I went back into the house Sonny was standing by the corner of the living room where the living room wall meets the hall. He was leaning against the corner with his face into the wall. I asked him if he's alright and he said "it's going to go back together harder than it came apart" I told him he better sit back down that he wasn't awake yet.

He steps over to where his coats are hung and goes through his coat pockets. I'm not sure what he was looking for. Then he stands in front of the hutch and takes his shirt off, his slippers, his pajama bottoms, then his underwear and headed for the sun room naked. I yelled at him "what the heck are you doing? He told me he was going to take a shower. I said you better wake up first and I pointed him in the right direction. I got him headed into the bathroom and went back to my baking.

The heard the water running a long time so I went in to check on him and he was in bed covered up.

The water I heard running was in the shower, and the water in his sink was full blast both hot and cold-water spigots were on. His clothes were in the waste basket instead of the hamper. I shut the waters off and went back to the bed to check on him and asked him if he was ok.

He suddenly threw the covers off and told me he was going to be late. "Why didn't I wake him up?" When I asked him where he had to go he said to see his Dad. It old him his dad has been gone a long time now.

He was very confused. As he got dressed, he grabbed the back scratcher off the top of his dresser and tried to put it on his foot. I asked him if his foot itched and he said no, he was just trying to put his shoes on. He thought he had the shoe horn in his hand.

I helped him with his socks and then he came out in the kitchen and had a couple of cookies and then sat on the bench at the table while I baked the rest of the cookies and fell asleep sitting at the table.

I woke him up and told him to go sit in the recliner before he fell off the bench. He just looked at me and said "the boys will be here soon "I asked him what boys, he told me "the boys and I are going out" I said "ok but for now you go get in the recliner and I'll wake you when the boys get here." Reality was, the boys were not coming to pick him up, but only in his mind.

He slept til dinner was ready at 5:30p.m. When I woke him up to eat, he seemed more lucid and a ware mentally, but just a little off balance physically. He ate a good dinner and went to the sunroom to sleep some more in the recliner. The fatigue and mental exhaustion seem to be a side affect of the chemo treatments.

February 28, 2014 Friday He was very week. This was the day of our closing on the sale of our business, to our middle son Doug and his friend Wayne M.

It was a very sad day for both of us. A lot of emotions going through us. Everything we worked for and built now out of our hands. It's like a hit in the gut with a baseball bat. Forced into an early retirement because of cancer. It really, really stinks! He was very emotional and cried a lot on Friday. He was too weak to go to the closing and I had power of attorney. I had to sign for both of us.

Doug and Wayne took the time to come and see Sonny a few hours after the closing. They all talked a lot about the business and shook hands. Sonny wished them all the best and he sincerely meant it. By evening he had calmed down. He had not had any medicine at all since Wednesday morning because he kept vomiting everything up, so without the medication for pain, he was feeling all the pain of the cancer in his bones today.

Saturday March 1 Today he woke up in extreme pain.

This past week on Wednesday he became violently ill during the night. He vomited about every hour and a half until he had dry heaves. He had chills but no fever. He could not get warm. He had the electric blanket on high and three other blankets on top of that. He finally got threw throwing up Thursday evening, then slept well. We think it was just some kind of stomach flu bug.

This morning he took a long-term oxycodone and a short term, ate some breakfast and then napped on and off all morning. He is very shaky today. His arms and legs have a lot of involuntary movement and muscle tremors. I'm not sure what is causing that. That is something we have to ask the doctor about. In my opinion I thinks it's a reaction of the oxycodone.

Come dinner time he was very confused. He came to the table while I was still cooking. He clearly didn't know what he was doing. He sat there and played with the silver wear. He just sat there and stared at the wall. It took me about another 15 minutes to finish dinner while he sat at the table.

I had taco pie and I fixed him a cheese burger and a tossed salad because he doesn't like tacos. I poured his milk and I sat down. He put ranch dressing on his salad and then just sat there and stared at his plate. After at least a full minute maybe longer he picked up the catsup and put it on his burger. He also tried to put catsup on his salad. When I asked him what he was doing he said he didn't know. He proceeded to drink some milk while he put his fork in his burger and plopped it down on his salad.

I asked him if he wanted help and he said "why, do you think I'm a baby?" I got him his hamburger roll and put his burger on it for him, and he continued to just drink milk. He got mad when I told him he needed to eat. He started to eat his salad, just a couple of bites, then just push it around on his plate.

As he sat there, he grabbed the catsup again and slid the bottle back and forth between his hands on the table, then he picked up the milk jug and put it down again and again each time saying "I can to pour my own milk I'm not a baby."

I asked him "aren't you hungry?" because he wouldn't eat any lunch today either, he said "yes" he was hungry. I told him maybe he should put his drink down and eat something instead of just drinking milk.

When I asked him if he was alright and he said he had to "go pee pee." like a three-year-old child would talk.

I hate seeing him like this. Its awful heart breaking! It just is not Sonny!

When he got back to the table, he said he wasn't hungry. I finished my dinner and he just sat there. I cleared the table and then gave him his evening pills. He was confused about what to do with them. He put them in a napkin, balled them up and was going to throw them away.

I opened the napkin and told him again to take his pills, he did and went in the living room and fell asleep in his chair.

Sunday March 2 Sonny is up and in the shower at 4a.m. I asked him why he was up so early he said he stinks from sweating so much and needed a shower. But then he came to the living room with just his underwear and socks, thinking he had to put work clothes on and go to work. I told him it was Sunday.

It is now 7a.m. so far, he has slept a little, and gone to the bathroom about six times since he got up. We were watching the news and he said,

"I don't know what I'm going to do, with all the science that I know I still don't know who I'm going to send to Russia, it would be like just throwing body's in line and killing them"

I think he said this because of Russia and the Ukraine on the news. He looks at me some times like he doesn't know who I am let alone who he is. Then in a blink of an eye he can be perfectly lucid and alert.

We were invited to Libby's for dinner today He went to our room and got ready to go to Libby's for diner. When he came out with only one sock on, I asked him where the other sock was and he didn't know. I went to the bedroom to looked for it and couldn't find it. Turned out he had them both on the same foot. When I figured it out, he said "this is so fucked up I don't know what is wrong with me." At times when this confusion happens, he is always aware after the fact.

Another thing is he can't keep his hands still he is very nervous jerky movements like an old man. He has a lot of involuntary movements in his arms, shoulders, hands, and legs. I don't know what causes that. It seems to happen within 30-60 minutes after taking the oxycodone. This is something we need to address with his doctor.

We went to Libby's for dinner we got there at 3:30p.m. and were home by five. We could not stay to visit because Sonny was to confused and to tired. It was very hard on Lib to see her Dad like that. He ate one bite off his plate and one bite of bread and drank half his milk. Then he just stared into space and his hands just shook. His eyes would roll back in his head and he could not carry on a conversation. I really think his behaviors have everything to do with his medications.

March 3, 2014 There is no difference. He is very confused and in a lot of pain. He stayed home this morning. He drove his truck to the shop mid-morning. (He should not drive.) Anyhow he was only there for an hour. He left the shop because he was tired, weak, and confused. I watched him from the office window to make sure he got home, we live right next door.

He got home ok, but as I watched him, I see he was trying to back up the drive way to the barn, he tried a few times but he just couldn't do it. He left the truck out by the road and walked to the house. Doug went up later and parked the truck. I went home right after that, and stayed with him.

He tried three times to pour a bowl of cereal this morning and just made a complete mess. He tried to tie his shoes by pointing the tv remote to his foot.

He did not eat any dinner; well, he ate one bite of pineapple and one bite of pork. He only drank half his milk.

This type of behavior is happening a lot. I know its out of his control, but I worry for his safety.

When he was having a lucid day, we talked about trying marijuana and are seriously thinking of trying it. We hear it helps with cancer pain, nausea, and appetite. At bed time he was pretty much out of it. Just talking and talking about such random things.

He told me he and Zach, one of our employees, were building a killer fighting robot out of the man lift and that they were going to Bemus Point to compete against other robots.

One other thing I noticed was even if he showers every day, he has this horrible odor that I just can't put my finger on. It's awful. I think it's all the medicine he's on and it comes through his pores. It smells toxic.

March 4 today started out fine, pretty normal, well our new normal that is.

He had pain in his back when he got up. Nothing out of the ordinary, no worse than other days. He came to the shop and was alert, walking around, and was coherent. He was able to think clearly and carry on conversations.

That all changed by 11a.m. He was talking nonsense and he went home early to take a nap. Again, I watched to make sure he got home. Today he was driving the Kubota RTV. As I watched him, I realized he could not figure out how to get his Kubota into the garage, and he left it in the drive way. I do have to give him credit to know enough to leave the vehicles in the driveway when he cannot maneuver through the garage doors.

I came home in the afternoon and he was still out of his mind. He was talking randomly and telling me he "figured out the problem was not enough hydraulic pressure." He was in some pain and then took a pain pill and laid down. I went back to the shop to do a little more office work. I came back home around 4p.m.

What a mess in the kitchen when I got home. There was sugar, pepper and salt spilled all over the table, benches, and the floor.

Sonny was in the sunroom crying loudly "oh my God no, oh my God no" over and over. I looked in on him and asked him what was wrong and he said it just wasn't right. When I asked him what was not right, he said that "we should not have so much snow when it's the middle of summer, it doesn't make sense why do we have so much snow in July, what is going on?"

He was sitting at the dining room table in the sunroom. He was very confused and didn't know me or where he was. I assured him its ok, not to worry about the weather. Maybe he just needed to relax in the recliner while I get supper ready.

I cleaned up the kitchen and he was still moaning and crying out. I went out to the sunroom to check on him He said he hurt so bad and he couldn't stand up. I went and got both of his canes and helped him to stand. Then I helped him get up the steps from the sunroom to the main part of the house.

He was very confused and was accusing me of making him eat to much when in fact he never ate anything. He got into the living room and screamed out with every step. This is awful because he is a man who has a high pain tolerance and never complained of any pain for as long as I have known him, well that is until this cancer hit him.

He once was working under a school bus out in the middle of a big field, something went wrong and the bus dropped off the jacks dropped on his arm. His arm only bruised but the cinder blocks below his arm broke. That is how strong this man is!

He walked to the bedroom door and then tried to fit between my recliner and the wall, he couldn't figure out how to get to the door way. I got him turned around and back to the couch but he just cried in pain. I said "that's it you need to go get this pain checked out."

Somehow, I got him loaded up in the van and we are now at Noyes hospital in Dansville. They have drawn blood and done a CT scan they started an IV and gave him pain medicine in a shot. We have been here about two hours he doesn't remember why he is here and he wants to leave. He wants to know why I would do this to him since he hates hospitals. About 9p.m. they decided to admit him. He was not happy at all. I left around 10p.m. I went home and took care of the stoves, and our little dog Maddie, and went to bed. I was totally exhausted after the last few days.

I was up by 5a.m. Sonny called me around 6a.m. He seemed very alert and clear minded and wanted me to be to the hospital by 8a.m. He told me he had something to tell me and he sounded like he was crying, or had been crying. He said he was not good.

Naturally I panicked. I called Pam, one of my best friends. It was early and I knew she would be up. I could not call the kids I did not want to panic them, and besides I had no idea what it was he was going to tell me.

I went to work at 6:30a.m. as usual. I told Doug where his dad was and why I took him to the hospital last night.

I told him that I had to leave at 7a.m. to go to the hospital and take him some clothes, because we were hoping he could come home this morning. If they had answers to why he was in so much pain and confusion.

I got here about 8a.m. Sonny did not remember anything about last night in the ER. He didn't even remember calling me at six this morning. He is still in a lot of pain especially in his right knee. He cannot move his right leg much due to the knee pain. The charge doctor came in and we asked to get transferred to Strong and he said he would arrange it.

The charge doctor called Sonny's oncologist and between the two doctors they want to get his pain under control and get him back on his feet before he comes back to Strong in Rochester. Then he will see a spine doctor and have the surgery he needs for his fractured disc in his back.

It is now 3:30p.m. He is sleeping he said the pain in his knee is a little better this afternoon.

He ate a good lunch and is drinking that is a good thing. He was dehydrated and malnourished because he has not eaten good for about two weeks.

He has had plenty of visitors today. Cousin Sis came for an hour this morning, Chip S stopped by then this afternoon Charlie S and Roy S came by. It has been a very busy day for Sonny.

I am so mad at this place. Sonny has not been given his medicines that he was on at home. He has taken a lot of pain medicine here and is now painfully constipated due to the opioids because they have not given him his stool softener or his laxative. You would think these professionals would know opioids cause constipation. I questioned them about it then they added it to his pills but not until this afternoon. Much too late, now he suffers a different kind of pain! Seems never ending for this man!

Friday March 7th. A hospital orthopedic doctor came to see Sonny's leg today because his knee is still swollen and painful, he drew off about two cups of fluid and it tested positive for strep and or staph infection which needs to be cleaned out surgically. Removing the fluid did relive some of the pain.

Before they took him for surgery, he wanted me to know he had been hiding money and where I could find it if he doesn't come through the surgery.

They took Sonny to surgery to flush the infection out and to put a drain in the knee joint to continue to drain the infection. He will be on IV antibiotics, and cannot get any more chemo treatments til the infection is gone.

When he came out of surgery to recovery, they called me into the recovery room. He was very agitated and they didn't understand what he was saying. I went into recovery to help the nurses with him. It turned out he thought he was going to work. When I got in there he said "take these damn thongs off so I can get to work" I said Sonny you don't wear thongs" then he started telling the nurses how to bolt up the transmission after they get it lined up. It was the sedation medication talking.

A few hours later he got back to his room upstairs and in his mind, he was "still under a truck" this time he was putting a rear in Randy J's truck.

The nurse was taking his blood pressure and he was talking to her about gear oil and wanted to know how much gear oil they put in it. He kept telling his mom and I to lower the bed side table and tighten the bolts or the transmission would fall out.

The nurse asked him what his pain level was on a scale of one to ten and his answer was "352, it has 352 rears". Again, the truck mechanic in him was coming out of his mouth.

An hour later the nurse was in and she was doing vitals again he was in mechanic brain mode. He was telling her how to change the AC unit in John S's truck.

It's 5p.m. and he is resting more comfortably, I think the sedated working brain is finally resting. I hope he can sleep well tonight.

Saturday March 8, He seemed in a healthy and determined mood when I got to the hospital. He wanted up and out of bed. I helped him get up and get to the bathroom so he could clean up. It was very painful for him but he did it.

The hospital orthopedic Dr. Capecci came in and told him to move his leg and to keep moving his feet while he laid in bed or sat in a chair, that it will help the circulation and the healing. He did a few times but only at my insisting. He stayed in his bedside chair until after lunch. Then he was in bed for the rest of the day.

He had a lot of visitors.

John S., Roy S., and Dan and Karron H. He was able to stay awake for most of their visit tho his thinking and talking was sometimes confused, and he kept falling asleep as we all talked.

I left after he had his supper. By then he was running a fever and was confused again. The nurses gave him fever medicine and pain medicine so I'm sure he slept most of the night.

I really don't know when he will be coming home. He doesn't seem as determined as he was a day ago. He seems resigned to lying in bed. I cannot move him or lift him if he comes home with this attitude.

I'm not sure who to ask what the truth is about his condition. From where I sit it seems pretty dire right now, because the nurses asked me if I contacted hospice to come in? Not sure why they would ask that! Makes me wonder what we are not being told.

Sunday, March 9 2014 I will go over to the hospital about 11a.m. today.

Turned out to be not a good day Sonny could not think clearly. He slept a lot and is very shaky.

Scott, Lorrie, Kylie, Derick, Libby, Doug, Aidan, my mom, and Eric stopped by.

Not all at the same time but at different intervals. The pastor of the Wallace Wesleyan church Pastor Spencer stopped by. It was a busy day for him and he is still in a lot of pain in his right knee, so he doesn't even want to get out of bed, and the nurses don't make him.

Monday March 10

Today we made some changes. Sonny wasn't, and hasn't been himself. It seems more than the knee pain and I want answers. I needed to get to the bottom of it. I watched hm very closely. His mental clarity and physical reactions.

Today I told the doctor the Sonny has times of mental clarity throughout the day but becomes confused and shaky within an hour of taking the oxycodone. The doctor changed Sonny's pain medicine to morphine and what a big difference. He is able to stay awake longer, he has pain relief without confusion. He is aware of where he is, what is going on, and who everyone is. I see a glimmer of hope and determination in him now. The hand tremors are calm to nonexistent.

He is eating well and he started physical therapy today too. They stood him up with a walker and he took about six steps and sat in a chair for the rest of the morning. After lunch he had a nap, then wanted out of bed again. He got up with help and walked to the bathroom and got washed up then walked to the window across the room and sat up in a chair until bed time. He did really well. He is very happy with his progress and so am I.

Medication can do unreal things to a person's mind. In Sonny's case it was the oxycodone. I am glad I paid attention to what was happening and asked the doctor to change his pain medication.

Eric had a conversation with his Dad tonight about heaven and Jesus. I think Eric thinks that his Dad does not believe. He just wants to make sure his dad gets to heaven. Sonny does believe in God he is just not demonstrative about it.

You don't have to be a Sunday go to church person to have a relationship with God. That is a personal choice. I think I said that somewhere before in this journal.

Tuesday March 11 2014

What a day! The orthopedic came in and had Sonny sit on the edge of the bed with his feet relaxed and not touching the floor. He then took the drain tube out of his knee and immediately Sonny just gushed blood, a lot of blood it literally sprayed out like a faucet. All over the floor, the nurse, and the doctor.

They had him lie back in the bed and raised his feet up. It bled so much it took an hour of ice and constant pressure by the nurses to stop it. Then he had to keep it still for a few hours to make sure it wasn't going to start.

We then found out the bleeding happened because he is on blood thinners. We did not know that he was even on blood thinners. I guess we don't always ask the right questions and trust everything that is being done!

He also had physical therapy at around 1p.m. He walked down the hall to the nurse's station, got into a wheel chair. The nurses took him to the physical therapy stair steps. He went up and down the steps a few times without any issues at all. This was one of the requirements in order to be able to come home. He passed!

They gave him two units of blood today because of the blood loss and his blood iron was really low so he got blood, iron, and sodium, all by IV. He has His fighter determination today. It is so good to see his determination and mental clarity. He may be coming home tomorrow if all goes well.

He will be on IV antibiotics at home and the county in-home nursing will be stopping by once a week to check on him and me because I will be hooking up the IV medicines as prescribed. They are going to teach me how tomorrow.

April 2014

It's been a few weeks since I last wrote. Sonny has come a long way since he got out of the hospital. We have gotten into a care routine of showering, but first wrapping IV ports in Saran Wrap so no water or bacteria can get in through the ports.

Our days are busy with IV dressing, ice packs, pain pills, IV antibiotics, plus his regular daily medications, and eating. At night I'm up every hour emptying his urinal so he doesn't have to get out of bed, because getting in and out of bed is so painful for his knee, but that to will pass when he doesn't have so many fluids running through his system.

It's exhausting because in between I go to work, and take care of everything around the house. I don't know how much longer I can keep this up. I put on a good front so no one knows just how often I cry from exhaustion. I am so physically and mentally exhausted and heartbroken that he has to go through this crap. It's our own fault because either one of us refuse to ask for help. We can do this ourselves! We will do this ourselves!

We do not and will not call anyone for help. This is our personal battle. We agreed right from the beginning we will fight it together with and for each other. Besides that, Sonny won't let anyone else do anything for him but me. Oh, if someone stops by and offers to help or do something, we will let them, but we don't call or ask for any help unless it's absolutely necessary. It's just who we are. Both stubborn, independent asses! Ha Ha

Today is April 7

Sonny has had a few good days. He now walks around the house without the cane but takes it with him when he goes outside just so he doesn't fall.

His friend Roy has stopped by a few times a week to check on him and see what he needs help with. He knows Sonny won't ask for help unless he really has to. Roy always helps in such a way that Sonny's dignity is intact. I guess you could say he's a man's man, he really is quite compassionate and caring for a man. Sonny and I really appreciate that. I guess it takes a compassionate man to know what another man feels.

He has been back to the oncologist and he will start chemo again on April 18. For hopefully one more round then on to stem cell transplant process, with some form of partial remission. Which is the ultimate goal.

He does however need to gain weight. He has lost fifty pounds and Dr. Ifthi said he doesn't want him to lose anymore.

April 10

At times he seems to be doing really good in the last few days. Yesterday we went to Pa. To get parts for Doug, he drove down and back. Sometimes he seems like himself and other times he just lays around and doesn't want to do anything. He has one more week of IV antibiotics then back on chemo.

April 14 What a turnaround, Sonny is doing really well with good energy and healthy appetite. He has been out on the tractor all weekend. He stone raked and rolled the driveway and both sides of the road. He seemed like himself again. I think the sunshine and getting out side has improved his attitude and health immensely.

It also proved to him that he is valuable to all of us.

His cousin and best friend Dick stopped by today. Sonny always enjoys Dicks visits. They laugh talk about vehicles and equipment work, and the times of their wild and crazy youth.

April 17

What a difference a few days makes. Last night Sonny was really sick, and confused. Compared to three days ago when he was near normal. Today he could do nothing but sleep. He had his supper and was in bed by 6p.m.I had to wake him at 6a.m. this morning and make him get up, have breakfast and shower. He had been sleeping for twelve hours, except to get up to use the bathroom.

He is confused about what day it is, he is again having shaking hand tremors, and asking the same questions over and over. Like what day is it, what time is it. He sweats buckets. Every day he has to change his clothes a couple of times a day. I have to change the bed because he sweats so bad at night. Sometimes I have to change it in the middle of the night and again in the morning.

I'm not sure what is going on with him.

April 18

We went to Strong today in hopes of getting his chemo started again. But his white and red blood cells are to low. They told us a normal blood count is over 1000 and Sonny's is under a hundred. His BP was very low 93/61 but his oxygen level was 99, that was the only vital sign he had that was close to normal.

Instead of chemo he got a shot of Neulasta a blood building medicine and they gave him a prescription of steroids to take for the next four days.

I have a bad feeling about this whole thing and what he is going through right now. Especially when the oncologist said to Sonny "I am very worried about you", and all Sonny would do is stare straight ahead with absolutely no reaction or response at all. He had no life in his eyes, no reaction!

The infection disease clinic did take out his IV port today because the antibiotic round was finished. His oncologist thought they should have not; in case he needs more antibiotics.

April 19 Sonny had such bad night sweats we had to change the bed at 1:30a.m. When he got up this morning he was confused. He kept searching for the spark plugs, cap and wires so he could fix the tractor. I told him we could do it later but he kept insisting, so I finally told him NAPA is delivering them, that I'll let him know when they are here. Then he sat in his recliner to wait for the parts to be delivered and fell asleep. When he woke up, he never mentioned fixing the tractor.

He has moments of confusion on and off like this in the last few days.

Yesterday when we were in the elevator at the cancer center, on our way to the 6th floor, he said he is sick of all of this running around from this doctor to that doctor. He hates that this has become his life instead of working.

Monday, we go back to Strong Hospital infusion center for a blood transfusion and hopefully start chemo again. At times he says he just wants to end it all. No more medication, no more doctors, no more anything.

Easter Sunday April 20 2014

All the kids and grandkids came over, along with my Mom, my sisters and their families. It was a beautiful day sunny and nice. We set up the lawn chairs outside and visited while the kids played in the yard.

Sonny was not right today, really not himself. He slept until everyone got here then I woke him up for dinner. He sat out side with everyone but could not carry on a conversation and didn't have a clue about what was going on.

After we had desert, he went to the living room and fell asleep in his chair. He slept there until bed time which for him was 7p.m. He had a very restless night. Up a lot going to the bathroom and wandering around the house. That makes for a very long night for both of us, when neither of us get any sleep.

Monday April 21 2014

We are at Strong. Sonny will get a blood transfusion and then chemo. He is very confused.

On the way here he wanted me to get off at the Avon exit because we were going to miss his friend from high school, Rogers funeral. Thing is Roger is not dead.

When we came into the hospital the volunteers put him in a wheel chair and took us to the cancer center. He was too weak to walk that far. While we were waiting in the waiting room lobby, he tried two times to take the wheel chair apart because he needed to fix the breaks and the steering.

We finally got to an infusion room. They asked him if he wanted something to drink, he said "if you're not going to give me milk don't bring in the cookies either" everyone laughed.

As I sit here watching all the busyness of the cancer infusion center nurses, I wish so badly that we never knew this place existed. The blood transfusion line is hooked up and he keeps messing with the IV lines. His blood pressure is a little low but there is no fever today.

He is sleeping sitting up in the infusion chair. When he sleeps his eyes are half open and he sleeps with his mouth open too. I don't know what causes this.

His pulse is a little high but everything seems to be going as planned. Fingers crossed.

Suddenly at 9a.m. his heart rate just shot up from seventy to one hundred seventy-one alarms went off, nurses came running from everywhere. I had no idea what was wrong. They told me we may be going to the emergency room because the infusion center is not equipped to help him. They are contacting Dr. Ifthi, we are now waiting on Dr. Ifthi's orders to see what he wants the nursing personnel at the infusion pod to do.

11a.m.

We are now in the ER at strong. Sonny is sleeping a lot, or maybe just in and out of consciousness, I'm not sure yet what is going on with him, no one does.

When he opens his eyes, he doesn't know who I am or where he is, I have to tell him. He is hooked him up to fluids and machines are monitoring his BP and heart rate. His BP is 88/63 and dropping, heart rate is now 146 so that is coming down. It appears he is starting to stabilize somewhat.

They have to take him for a CAT scan to check his brain for tumors and cancer, and his lungs for fluids. They also now suspect an infection some place in his body or blood but they don't know what kind or where. He does not have a fever so it makes what is happening a mystery to the staff. Until all the blood test results are back no one has any idea what they are dealing with or why.

They are letting me go to CT with him but I have to wait outside the CT room. When he was in the CT scanner, they had a problem with him. He pulled out his IVs both of them and he wouldn't lay still. He was still very confused at that time.

Alarms went off, intercom went crazy calling for help in the MRI unit, (which is where Sonny was) nurses and doctors came running from every direction.

I just knew in my heart the reason for all of the running was Sonny, but I had no idea exactly what was going on.

I was waiting outside the CT room waiting for them to bring Sonny back out.

I sat there just watching all the activity coming in and going out of the room where Sonny was. Finally, they came and told me what was going on. Sonny was being very combative and uncooperative. They thought if he saw me or I could talk to him he'd calm down.

They were right. He did calm down after I went in there, then he let the nurses and doctors do their job. I was not prepared for what I saw. Blood everywhere because he had pulled out the IV tubes.

We were back in the ER after CT scan episode.

2:15p.m. a nurse came from ICU and said they will be taking him to ICU. They want him stay on IV antibiotics for a few more days. It may take a day or so for all the test to come back to determine what was going on. At this point they really don't know what viral or bacterial issues are going on in his body. In the meantime, until they can identify it, he will be on very strong antibiotics that will help with any kind of bacteria that may be in his body.

He finally got up to a bed in ICU. He is now hooked up to a few IVs of fluids, saline, bicarbonate, antibiotics, and I don't know what else. It's been a very stressful day. My butt is sore from hard chairs. I am very worried about Sonny, but I know this is the best place for him to be.

Poor Sonny he doesn't have a clue about what is going on. The nurses told me to go home that he would be sleeping soon because of the sedation and pain medication. He really needs to give his body a rest and they promised to take good care of him. I left about 6:30p.m. I was so tired and relieved Sonny was stable and finally resting comfortably.

Tuesday April 22 rainy day about sixty degrees outside. I got to the hospital about 10:00a.m. He seems much better frame of mind but he does not remember anything about yesterday, the infusion center, the emergency room, or the CAT scan episode. I'm so glad to see he is thinking clearly now, but I'm worried because he doesn't remember yesterday.

The nurse said he is doing so much better and will be moved out of ICU today and down to the cancer floor. Right now, he is getting an echo cardio gram to see if the infection has gone to his heart.

Wednesday April 23 Sonny was taken out of ICU last night and put in a regular hospital room. An awfully small room with another man who clearly has mental issues and stays up all night with tv on very loud!

1:30p.m. we are just waiting for a room to become available on the 7th floor cancer care center.

He worried out loud a lot today. About his situation and not being able to do the things he wants to like take care of our property, and going camping with me. In general, just living the life we always knew. He just wants to be a productive human being once again. He is worried that his body just can't take anymore. He is worried about putting me through all of this. I assured him we will be fine, that we will get through this together. Just like every other obstacle we ever come up against in our 30+ years together. We faced it together no matter how bad it was and we always came out on top.

Funny thing is he has never ever worried for anything in his life ever, especially about me. I am always the one to worry about everything and everyone. Worry was just never in his vocabulary. Lord knows I do enough for both of us!

59

Life As We Knew It Has Drasticly Changed

Our rolls have changed somewhat. Now I am the one to go off to work while he is home sick. The difference is I take care of him, and whenever I was sick or had babies or had surgery, he went to work and never gave my condition or health another thought, or maybe he did. Could be working was his way of handling things that were uncomfortable for him.

He never had compassion, he did the only thing he knew, work!

The only thing ever on his mind was his job, he knew I would somehow struggle to take care of myself, the kids, and what needed to be done around the house. Like he always says to me "you're a big girl you'll figure it out"!

I can't say I hold a grudge, but then again maybe I do, as wrong as it is, even resentful at times but it's not in my nature to do to him what he did to me. I know how that feels and I wouldn't do that to him. I never give up and I always give chances. Again, and again to infinity!

Today Wednesday April 23......he has been in the hospital since Monday. Today they have identified the bacteria infection it is called Enterococcus. It comes from the intestines and or gall bladder. It's has responded to the antibiotics that he is on but they want to run another test tomorrow where they put a scope down his throat to look at his heart from the inside to make sure the heart valve is not infected. I believe it's called and IEG, TEE, or EEG! Not sure I can't keep up with the medical alphabet terms anymore.

When they get that test result, they will know what kind of antibiotic to send him home with and for how long. Over all he is doing good and wants to come home. I want him home as well.

He has been talking a lot about his situation and how our life has turned out. All I can do is try to be positive for him and let him know I am not worried that I believe all will be ok. He has his faith and the best doctors in Multiple Myeloma at Strong Memorial Hospital.

I cry for our situation sometimes, I cry for him a lot, but never around him or anyone else. I have to stay strong, I'm the mom, I'm the rock, the foundation of the family. I have to keep it together. God has my hand and is by our side. I will "trust the Lord in all things" maybe!

The IV antibiotics he is getting now are vancomycin and gentamicin I'm not sure what one he will come home with. Everything is pending on the other blood tests results.

April 24 Sonny had his TEE

Ahh haa I finally got the right letter sequence, internal echo cardio gram.

Everything is good, no infected heart valve. Now he will only have to be on antibiotics for two weeks and he can get back on the chemo soon.

Tonight 8p.m. he got moved to the cancer floor. Oh, my goodness, what a treat this is for him. A very nice room, better than a hotel. He definitely will sleep better tonight. He deserves this.

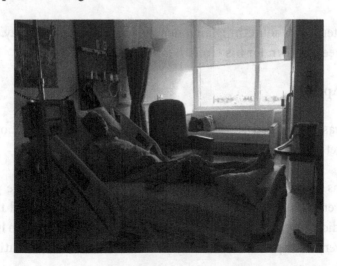

I didn't get home til 9:30p.m. it was a very long and trying day. Our poor little dog she doesn't understand why she's left alone so much.

I know it's not right to hate and God says not to hate, but I do feel hatred in my heart. I hate cancer! I am sorry, it is not fair that good people like Sonny to have to suffer such awful health issues when there are so many worthless scum bags deliberately on the drugs of their choice. There are others also who in my opinion are a waste of breath, still free loading off others or the government, never worked a day in their life and in perfect health.

I get so angry at times. When no one is around I have screamed at God like I have never screamed before. I'm just so angry at what cancer has taken from Sonny and his life as it once was.

True we don't always get along; we are not the perfect married couple with no problems. I have never met a couple that was perfect. Only those who think they are. However, we do love each other with all our hearts, and no one ever wants to see your loved one, or anyone go through all this cancer shit!

I keep thinking this shouldn't be. **Not Sonny.** Not a man who is for the most part always been very healthy and the physically strongest man I've ever known.

That statement is something anyone who knows him would say. He has always been known for his Goliath strength.

Friday April 26

Sonny was discharged at 5p.m. We were so glad to go home. I hope now he can get on with getting better and recovering his strength.

He seems to be doing good and is very glad to be home. He gets up about every hour to go to the bath room, but we understand that the new medicine he is taking for his heart is what is causing this to happen. He has very little pain, and is hungry most of the time. He is eating well and he is able to carry on a decent conversation and not loose trac of his thoughts. I must admit I didn't think on Monday he would be coming home for a very long time.

This whole cancer journey so far feels like an uphill ride with the brakes on. Going up, always moving, getting nowhere. Who knows where we will get off, or even if it will ever stop.

Right now, he seems to be trapped in a body he doesn't want. Who am I kidding he is trapped in a body where no one ever wants to be. Weak, frail, broken, and at times helpless!

When Will Healing Happen
Or Will It Never Happen?

What can I really say to put everyone at ease when it seems as if we are on a very slow boat that never stops to port and we can never depart from? The trip leads to eventual death from a cancer or death from the side effects of cancer medications and treatments, and the damage it causes to your body. The fact that we know there is no cure, or for him the most we can hope for is inactive Multiple Myeloma results.

Where will we get the courage and strength to keep trying to keep going when we feel like giving up because the treatment doesn't seem to be working as fast as we like or wish it would?

When we have seen death just around the corner, or so it seems. I guess I'm just depressed and worried at this moment, by our whole turn of events in our lives, and for our family.

Yet the worse thing I still deal with is tense times within the family. I call that the "cancer of living life!" Right now, I don't see a cure for family because right now I am taking care of Sonny and just trying and praying for everyone.

I'm still trying to work at the shop to help our daughter in law Jill, in the office. At home I take care of the house, meals, groceries, laundry, and all of Sonny's care, needs, everyday living, and appointments.

BEFORE THIS LIFE
We once had a different life BEFORE CANCER

> BEFORE the pain
> BEFORE the biopsies
> BEFORE the diagnosis
> BEFORE treatments
> BEFORE chemo IV treatments
> BEFORE all the in-home medications
> BEFORE multiple doctor appointments
> BEFORE life looked so dim
> BEFORE others had to do things for us
> BEFORE this life sentence

He wasn't always sick and our daily life was normal, well normal for us. Which meant work was our priority. Work was our normal. Work was our before.

Today May 2 2014

We are on the twice weekly chemo train again, starting today. Let's hope it works as fast as the first round with no infection this time. All together Sonny has lost over sixty pounds. I have had to get him completely new wardrobe, from jeans, to under wear. His body is just hanging skin on bones. He has dark circles under his eyes and they are set back in his head and he has lost so much weight his ribs show just like those malnourished photos you see from third world countries in tv ads.

Thursday May 15

All seems to be going well. Sonny gets out side every day, he has been mowing lawn but very slowly. Yesterday the boys from the shop put an air ride seat on his lawn mower so he doesn't have to take the full impact of the bad bumps and take a chance of breaking more disc in his back, and becoming paralyzed. Sonny's friend Roy stops by for a visit and to see if Sonny needs help with anything. Visits are good for Sonny, it proves people still care, that's important for his morel.

Sometimes he seems a little depressed, he won't always talk about what is on his mind, but once in a while when he does, he is very insightful and knows what he wants.

Sometimes he says he just doesn't want to live like this. At times he makes me feel really hated by him, he has no appreciation for all I do. He shows no love for me, no time for me. He wants no affection or attention. Just the same I tell him daily he is loved. I guess I too would feel resentful of those who have their health if I was in his place.

We found out last week that his cousin (on his mother's side) Skip, had the same kind of cancer. He lived 6 months after the diagnosis. We never knew what Skip died of until now.

Paula, his widow, came to see us when she found out that Sonny had the same kind of cancer. Skips cancer was far more advanced than Sonny's, though Sonny's was already end stage when he was diagnosed. After Paula's visit Sonny has been very quiet and more depressed. I'm sure he is thinking about Skips death, his own mortality and a lot of other things he won't talk about right now.

May 24 Saturday

Memorial weekend and we are camping for the first time this year. This is something he thought he would never do again. Today his four-week IV antibiotic was finished, and I was able to remove the IV for the last time. He is very glad to be rid of it. Now he hopes to stay free of the infections.

Wednesday May 28 Tonight we went to our grandsons Gavin and Evans

T-ball game. By the time it was over and we got back in the car, Sonny was quite emotional swallowing the sobs coming from his heart ache. He felt so ashamed of himself because he had a hard time getting out of the lawn chair. Libby had to help him, and people were rudely staring at him.

He said "I use to be able to lift two hundred pounds, no problem at all, and now I can't lift my own body weight, and people just stare" he was very angry and choked up with emotion.

I was pissed too, not at Sonny but at the insensitive people in our little village who somehow think whispering about someone is more justified than actually talking to the man who helped many of them over the years.

He feels he's lost a lot of dignity and respect from others. They look at him with pity.

I tried to tell him by this time next year he will be strong again that the doctor said he would get back to feeling better again, but Sonny was hearing none of that tonight.

I was so angry at our adult community members for staring, how rude!

I know he cries at night some times, and nothing I can say or do comforts him. He gets very depressed, then angry. He won't let me close to him, physically or emotionally. I thought for sure that going camping last weekend would have cheered him up. Prove to him that he can still do enjoyable things.

He has emotional good days and bad days and some days he experiences both in the same day!

July 2014

I haven't written in a few months, that means everything is feeling and being a little closer to normal. Summer is here and we are very busy.

I mow around the house and Sonny mows the lawn around the pond thanks to the boys and his new air ride floating lawn mower seat. It certainly makes him feel more productive and happier.

Sometimes I wonder if he's happy to mow or just happy to not have to spend time with me. Haha!

Actually, he has always loved mowing, he calls it his thinking time.

The weekend of the fourth we went camping with Scott and Lorrie in Prattsburg, at Budd Valley Campground. It was a fairly nice summer weekend. With the exception of a funeral, I had to go to for my sister Darlene's fiancé, Flynn. He died suddenly on Tuesday the second of July from a malignant stroke. Very sad and unexpected.

Sonny could not go because emotionally he could not handle a funeral and physically because of the effects of the chemo, and the long drive to Pennsylvania. I picked up my mom and took her with me.

Most of our married life I have gone to a lot of events alone. He was always to busy working to attend family things or events.

He had a really bad emotionally depressed, and angry Saturday evening. There was a DJ at the camp ground and they played very good dance music. Music we always liked to dance to from our younger days. Dancing is one thing Sonny and I did well together even when we couldn't stand each other. Sonny was upset because dancing is something, he thinks he will not be able to do again.

We went for a long walk around the campground to clear his mind and not listen to the music or watch others dancing and having fun. He even reached out and held my hand for the first time in a very long time.

It was the worst I've ever seen him. I try to be supportive of what he can do and not dwell on what he can't do. I stay positive and build him up. Today is the first time he told me if it wasn't for me and all I do to help him, even when he knows he treats me bad, he would have ended his life a long time ago. Today he expressed appreciation for all I do. I had never heard that from him before. It was good to hear that he noticed my care. He even hugged me. He hasn't done that in so long I cant tell you the last time he did.

July 10 2014 Back to our normal, whatever normal is now days. Sitting at Strong Hospital cancer treatment infusion center just waiting for an injection of chemo IV's, and a handful of pills to go into his body, a "chemo cocktail" they call it. "Intentional poison inconvenience" is what Sonny calls it!

Many times, we think of what we are going through and start to feel bad and feel why us, then we see many others here who are worse off than we are. That of course doesn't make it right, nor does it give us the answers, but in some crazy way makes what we are going through a little more bearable. Sonny always says "there is always someone worse off than us."

July 11, 2014, the Ritter reunion weekend has started. Pot luck supper, and bon fire tonight. We had many doubts this past winter that Sonny would even be here to attend it. Thank God he is. Everyone is glad to see him even as frail as he is.

There are a few family members who are no longer here who were here last year and the many years before that. My sister's fiancé Flynn just died 10 days ago, my Aunt Sue died over the winter and Uncle Jim, her husband a few months before she did. There will be a few empty seats this year.

On a positive note, there will also be new babies to hold and celebrate.

July 12 family reunion picnic, good food, noisy kids, games, family, fun and fellowship.

Two hours after we cleaned up and were back home, the phone rang. It was my cousin Bonnie, she told me Uncle Bob was dead in his hotel room in Bath.

He died of respiratory failure, he had lung cancer and COPD.

I'm so sorry this happened here, but on the other hand he just spent his last hours at his family reunion with his siblings. He lived in Ohio.

Tuesday 4p.m. Memorial service at Campers Haven community room I officiated. I really don't mind officiating funerals, its what I do. But when it's for family it's very emotional, and not the easiest thing to do, but an honor for me to serve others just the same.

RIP Uncle Bob you will be missed.

July 25

We saw Dr Ifthi and it was good news. His cancer count is down to 2619 and he will have chemo threw the month of August. We will be seeing the stem cell transplant team sometime in the next couple of weeks. Things are finally taking a turn for the better. It feels like we can safely breath again.

Even the smallest bit of encouragement throughout this whole ordeal has been helpful and has kept us afloat when we both felt like giving up.

HOPE IS A POWERFUL THING, IT KIND OF SOFTENS THE DISCOURAGEMENTS. THEN TO HAVE GODS GRACE ON TOP OF HOPE IS THE TOPPING ON THE SUNDAE OF LIFE

Cancer Reveals

Going through cancer will reveal many things to you. One of those is the fact that you can never go back. The old life no matter how challenging, or good, or bad it was. You find yourself wanting and wishing for your old life but it's not reachable it doesn't exist. It's now only a memory, be it good or bad, you now have a new normal. When cancer is not making you angry and fearful, cancer also can give you new sight. Cancer makes you see the important things of life such as forgiveness, family, and friends.

Another thing is you have to learn to face fear, you really have no choice.

Fear of the inevitable and especially the unknown. Sometimes calming not only your own fear with self-talk, but the fear now placed on your family.

It is my mothering instinct to make everything better, to make everyone else's fear disappear or at the very least, be at ease. I will carry their fear. All while being well aware of my own fears that lay heavy on my mind, and in my heart. A personal fear only I can handle.

It's like pacing back and forth in a room with no window. A room that is to small and the scenery never changes, with nothing new to look at. Fear is two of my four walls, and the unknown the other two walls, all covered by the roof, that consist of a covering of smiles to hide under, that I put in place so no one knows or sees my fear.

As morbid as this may sound, my biggest fear is not that Sonny will no longer be with us, but the fact that he may suffer or be in pain. He has been through so much and his body has been invaded by some pretty strong poisonous medications. I would really hate for him to suffer in his death. He has even said he wants his death to be sudden and quick, he wants to close his eyes and not wake up. From all we have been told and researched it will be just that.

The things you never thought you'd ever have to talk about as husband and wife. Like how you will die, or what the one left behind should do. This should not be a subject until we are old, very old, but here we are talking about such things.

I look at all we have left of our BC (before cancer) life, and the only thing I can come up with is our kids, our extended families, and friends we have made over the years. Nothing else really matters, not our home, our money, our property, our camper, our interest, our vehicles, not one possession matters.

Cancer is like that new laser eye surgery but for your heart and soul. It causes you to see things, the same things you have always seen, but with a different understanding, and clearer lens on life. While at the same time you are being blinded by reality of the unknown.

No one really ever has anything more than the present, the here and now. I find that before there was cancer in our lives we never ever questioned "if" "we would see the grandkids grow up, graduate, get married, have children, we just always assumed we would."

Love Is Stronger Than Fear
Even When You Can't See It

Cancer so many times takes us down to our final moments then lets us come back stronger than ever to take a look at our life and see things in a whole other perspective. It's like a building being rebuilt after being knocked down, over and over again and again. A constant cycle of starting over. And questioning how many "maybe this times" are we going to get?

Many times, it gives us a false sense of security. The doctors must be wrong, he's doing good, he looks good, he feels good, he's going to beat this when no one else has. This is Sonny Obrochta they don't know who they are dealing with!

I know as in past medical issues and scares if he comes out of this cancer free, which according to statistics he won't, but if he does, I just know he will not change. He will not treat me any different or love me anymore. It's just our history, our existence, our life. Work and he himself will be his priority.

Cancer can make you feel old very quickly, even if you're not the one who has it. It's because you associate dying with being old. Being younger and stronger is what we all dream of, but we can never go back to what and who we were. We are not 30 anymore, and never will be again.

One thing we noticed is, very old people have a sense of humor so that is what we would like to do too. Keep a sense of humor if we ever get the chance to grow old.

I look at our grandchildren, it seems they are always laughing and having fun no matter what is going on around them. I love to see them laugh. Cancer makes you look at things differently even the simple things like laughter.

We should be like kids and laugh all day long. Feel the joy and energy of a good silly belly laugh. It's good and cleansing for the soul

I started this journal of our venture December 2013. It is now **August 2014**. I now think I should name this part of the journal entry:

"Life Is Not Just Difficult,
But Really Friken Hard!"

We live in a world not only damaged and torn apart by nature and all she delivers, but by diseases of many shapes and forms some man made and caused, and some genetic.

I have learned not all difficulties are of nature or disease but many life difficulties are of people's meanness, unforgiveness, and inability to accept even their own family as they are.

To live so much inside their selves that they have no room for family. I see this in both of our extended families. I have to say it breaks my heart.

I know it's not just our extended families, but all families and that is sad. Life isn't all hunky dory as they say!

BEGINING SCT
(stem cell transplant) PROCESS
AUTOLOGOUS (self-stem cells)

Aug 7 2014 Today we met with Dr Jane Liesveld and her assistant Meg. Very approachable, kind, knowledgeable, serious, and compassionate team who will see us through this stem cell transplant.

It has turned out to be a better process than we were originally told about, or maybe we assumed. The actual harvesting of the stem cells will be done as an outpatient. He is happy it won't be a hospital stay.

Four days before the stem cell harvest, he will be given a daily shot of Neulasta a blood cell building medicine. Then on the fourth day he will be hooked up to an apheresis machine similar to one of dialysis for the actual harvest of stem cells.

This machine will remove the blood from one arterial port in his neck/ chest then separate the stem cells from the blood then what is left of his blood will return to his body threw another port. This process takes about five to eight hours.

After millions of stem cells are removed the harvesting process is over and we go home. The stem cells then go to the lab and are cleaned, cancer cells are isolated and destroyed. Once that process is complete the stem cells are frozen in two million increment volume bags, labled, and stored frozen until time for the actual transplant.

In two weeks, he goes back to the hospital to be admitted. He will get a very strong dose of chemo that will kill any cancer left in his body.

We were told this is the chemo will make him very sick. He will have many side effects from this chemo that could include; total loss of hair, mouth ulcers, vomiting, and extreme fatigue, he is not looking forward to that. He could also be one of the very rare few who have minimal to no side effects.

On the second day he will receive his stem cells back into his body. We were told for the first week he will be very fatigued and sleep most of the time while his body accepts the cells and starts to recover from the chemo.

Within three to four weeks, he will be able to go home. He will be very tired and mostly sleep and have no energy. Within two months should be on his way to better health and just maintain the cancer by blood test and chemo pills at home to keep it at bay. No more IV chemo. Time will tell.

This cancer ride is like being on a roller coaster in the dark. It's never straight, smooth, and easy grade. You can never see what is ahead. When we first found out about his treatments and the success of the treatments, we were sure this would be easy but within months we were thrown into reality and the brakes of uncertainty came on.

Everything that happens makes it seem impossible to recover from.

We are however more fortunate than some going through cancer and its treatments. We are fortunate to have the finances to travel an hour and a half every week, sometimes twice a week, and to eat out when we are done, if he's up to it.

We are also fortunate to have insurance that so far has not ever denied any treatment, medications or hospital stay. The only expense to us has been the co pays.

We are fortunate to have children and many friends who will at a moment's notice helps us with the care of our dog and or anything we need around the house, and even more fortunate that we have not had to ask for much help. Just luckily so far, that we haven't needed a whole lot done. For that we are grateful to God our provider, keeper, and our savior.

I don't play the lottery, but I have decided that the perfect lottery winning better than millions of dollars, would be to hear the words "there is no cancer, you are in remission."

That would be better than any amount of lottery money ever. But with this kind of cancer he will never hear these words. We may as well be totally deaf!

No cancer lottery winner here, just tease words like; your blood numbers look better, you appear to be on the right track, and everything seems to be going well!

Words, only words, little steps, some results, but never **CANCER FREE**

I'd settle for being dirt poor and broke living under a bridge in a tent if Sonny could be cancer free.

We are waiting, ever and always waiting. In doctor waiting rooms, laboratory's, pharmacy's, hematologist, infusion centers, and treatment rooms. Waiting since last fall, which turned to winter, which turned to spring, and then to summer.

Waiting at every day, every hour, every moment, every turn of the calendar page. Wait for our lottery to be called. Our lottery is called remission.

A lottery we can't buy tickets for and even if we could buy a ticket, there will never be a winning ticket drawn for Sonny.

Forever Waiting

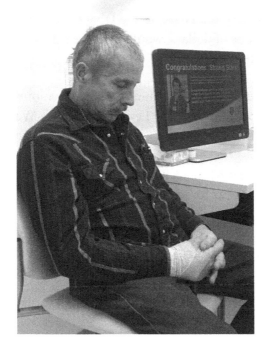

Sunday Aug. 10 2014

Today is a celebration put on by our children in celebration of our retirement.

For those who rode the path of growing our business no matter how bad it got and who also supported us in every mile stone no matter how small Sonny and I are forever grateful.

The party turned out well, I'm not sure just how many people came, there were hundreds. We enjoyed seeing everyone. To us though it was bitter sweet. It was like giving into what everyone else wanted for us. To retire it feels like we needed to drop out of sight, get out of the way, move on, never to work again. When work is all we have ever known. If only we could have retired under our terms and not cancers terms!

Left to right Scott, Libby, Eric, myself, Sonny, Douglas

Aug 18 We had a nice cook out get together at Sonny's sisters for their moms' birthday. It was a hot day but everyone had fun and good food.

Left to right Myself, Sonny, his mom Mary, his sister Barb and husband Steve, Sister Lori and her husband Tim

September 29, this past week we lost a friend who had been battling lung cancer which metastasized. A very nice man who was only 72. He was our neighbor. He was just here in our home visiting with us last month.

He leaves behind a huge family of children, grandchildren, great grandchildren, and a step family also.

We didn't go to calling hours, Sonny just can't do those things. Not because he isn't physically able to but mentally, he just can't.

Our friend Roy stopped by to see how Sonny was doing and to take him out to eat.

We call Roy our woodchuck friend, always popping up.

He helps with things that makes Sonny's life easier. We really appreciate when he just pops in.

Funny thing about Roy and Sonny, or Dick and Sonny. They love to share their stories of life experiences, work and their childhood, over and over, and neither of them ever seems to mind or remember they heard it all before. They laugh as if they are hearing it for the first time. All I do is roll my eyes, smile, and shake my head!

On October 9 we will be seeing Dr. Liesveld the stem cell transplant doctor. Who will start the process of putting everything in place so he can have stem cell transplant.

Last week we got a call and were told Sonny's cousin on his dads' side of the family was just diagnosed with MM the same cancer as Sonny. We hope to be able to help them through the beginning process and ease their minds. We will see them this week. He is same age as Sonny, Mike will also be going to the Wilmot Cancer center.

We visited with Mike and his wife Ginny on Sunday October 5 for a couple of hours. I think we did ease some of their fears. Seeing Mike in that much pain brought back a lot of memories of where Sonny was just ten months ago. Mike will have his first visit to the cancer center on October 8. We are curious to hear about it.

That makes two family members besides Sonny who have Multiple Myeloma. Though it's not genetic. A cousin on his moms' side of the family (Skip) and now one on his dads' side of the family (Mike).

Today October 9 we will see the transplant doctor and start the process of getting prepared for stem cell harvest and replant. We can't wait, everyone is so encouraging about the success of SCT.

We saw Dr. Liesveld Thursday. Sonny has to go through a lot of testing to be cleared for transplant. He needs clearance from: the dentist, the cardiologist, a pulmonary doctor, a complete body scan, and a psychiatric evaluation, plus numerous blood test and new medications.

Right now everything is being submitted to the insurance company. That process will take about two weeks. After that is completed then the other appointments can be made.

I talked to Ginny on Saturday Mike has been in the Corning Hospital since they got back from his first visit to the cancer center in Rochester on Wednesday. His doctor called him after they got home and told him go straight to the closest emergency room. He needed some blood filtering to remove and abundance of calcium from his blood.

That happens when the Multiple Myeloma is advanced to the point where it basically dissolves the bones from the inside, the marrow and plasma. Then those tiny particles get into your blood system causing a high calcium deposit.

Mike and Ginny are seeing a Dr. Akwa. From our understanding he is also a Myeloma specialist. Their news for future SCT did not sound as hopeful. Ginny told me they have already been told that he is not a good candidate for stem cell transplant at this time. There is always prayer and hope.

Ginny told us; Mike has a few other health issues going on.

He has high calcium count in his blood, which means the myeloma is deteriorating his bones. He has arthritis, he has already had knee replacement in one knee, and he has been on a breathing c-pap machine for some time now. He is losing a lot of weight. Which is typical of most cancers and he is in a lot of bone pain which is typical of Multiple Myeloma.

My heart aches for what he and his wife and children are going through. We will be there for each other always.

This Friday we will see the oncologist again. We should find out how much longer Sonny will have to stay on the IV chemo and bone strengthening medications given at the infusion center.

Between Sonny and I at the very first diagnosis, we were in a kick cancers ass mode after the being scared mode. We felt love, care, compassion, and determination to get each other through this. It didn't last long before it turned to anger Anger at the diagnosis, anger at God and anger with each other.

Neither one of us could do anything right by the other. We were on edge and on each other's nerves all the time. I think this was because we were dealing with the diagnosis each on our own and not together.

Also, the biggest thing we were dealing with in the beginning was, we are a fix it couple.

We don't talk about what needs to be done, we just dig in and do it.

Multiple Myeloma on the other hand, **"WE CAN NOT FIX IT"**

Here we are eleven months later, and we have settled into a routine. Not acceptance, but a routine of appointments, prayers, hope, and waiting.

My good friend Lilian said something profound to me this morning.

She said "I am praying for you and your family, and I want you all to know if you were the only family on earth Jesus still would have given his life for you"

Today October 17 we meet with Dr. Ifthi, he stopped the chemo IV's because it is no longer effective. He told us the stem cell team will go ahead and start the procedure of SCT.

After the stem cell harvest Sonny will get a chemo called Revlimid. It will be a pill he takes at home for three weeks then one week off. After that he will be put in the hospital in isolation and have the stem cell transplanted back in him. It will be about three to six weeks before he comes back home, depending how he tolerates the Stem Cell Transplant.

Friday October 24, 2014 we are here at Strong, nearing the end of this phase of our journey, and on to another new beginning, or at least we are hoping.

Today he started on the Neupogen, a shot to increase the stem cell production within the bone marrow. He gets his first shot here at the cancer center, if all goes well with no reaction to the Neupogen, on Saturday and Sunday we do the shots at home then Monday back at the hospital for the final shot.

Today we saw the hospital psychologists to determine if he was mentally stable enough to go through the SCT. Sonny also had a pulmonary test, and an EKG. All of these tests were so he can be cleared to have the stem cell transplant. As far as we know he passed them all.

October 27 Monday We are at Strong 7a.m. for blood work and hopefully the last shot of Neupogen. Then off to Science Park Imagery for the artery PICC lines to be put in for the stem cell harvest. This will take about two hours. We will have breakfast, then wait around the city until we get a phone call on the blood work weather or not we can go home or if we have to stay until 8p.m. for another shot of Neupogen.

As they say, time will tell. That is how it's gone the last ten months, time will tell, and hurry up and wait, and wait some more. Then I guess at this chapter in our lives all we have is time.

Thing is we are both doers we hate waiting and clock watching!

I feel really bad for Sonny he has been through so much since last October and a lot of it very painful. It's a wonder he still has his mind. Sometimes his thinking is very foggy and his memory not so good. It bothers him to have no recollection when things happen. I help him as much as I can without giving it a single thought. I shrug it off and try to act like it's perfectly normal reaction when I help him with things he should know and remember but he doesn't.

The IV PICC lines in his chest are in and we are waiting to see if we can go home. We got the phone call at 4:30p.m. saying he has to have the Mozobil shot. Mozobil helps the bone marrow to release stem cells into your blood.

Only thing is he can't have it until 8p.m. Then we have to wait thirty minutes after the shot until we can leave the hospital. They need to make sure he won't have a reaction to the medication. It's been a very long day, and we have to be back here at 8:30a.m. for the actual stem cell harvest.

October 28 2014 We got home last night around 10p.m. I was very tired but could not sleep. I hate nights like that. Just to wound up with worry.

Back at Wilmot Cancer center this morning at 8a.m. It was a very restless, short night.

He is hooked up to the apheresis machine to harvest his stem cells. This process will take about six hours. We will have to wait two to three hours before we can leave because we have to wait to hear from the lab if they got enough usable stem cells. If not, the we go back to the sixth floor for another shot of Mozobil and back here tomorrow morning for another harvest of stem cells.

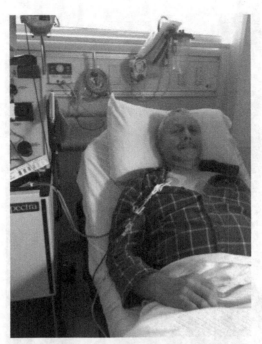

The apheresis machine looks similar to dialyses machine.

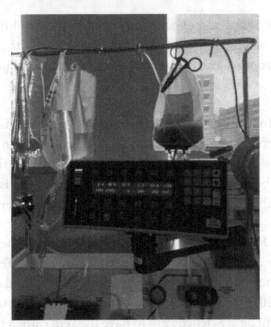

Stem cells gathering in the collection bag at
the top of the apheresis machine

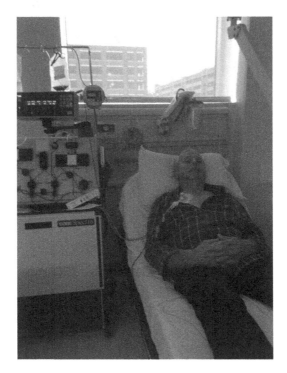

Waiting is very hard and exhausting. Even harder on him because as the cells were being harvested, he could not get out of the bed, even to go to the bathroom. Once the harvest is started it cannot be interrupted or halted.

When he got done today the nurse that was taking care of him, processed the stem cell collection bag with his labels of information to be sent to the lab. She asked us if we wanted to lay our hands on them and she blessed them before she sent them out. A very nice Christian gesture. We felt good about that, and were choked up with good emotions.

Wednesday October 29 8a.m. we are back at the apheresis unit at Strong. Sonny is once again hooked up to the machine. Yesterday went well but they only got 5.6 million stem cells and they need eight million so today he will only be hooked to the machine for three to four hours. At 2p.m. we will be at Science Park to have the vein catheters, PICC lines removed. Then home hopefully not have to come back until November 7th when we see his oncologist again.

Sonny is very tired and very sore. He had the PICC lines removed and all went well, but it is a painful process. They called this evening and enough stem cells were collected. We get about a week and a half break.

Poor Mike, we just found out he broke his arm and that will delay the start of his treatment. He is in a lot of pain. It sure doesn't sound like a good start for him. Seems he is headed for a much longer time of it than Sonny, because of the delay in treatments. I do hope and pray they can help him like they did Sonny. I hope this is just an inconvenient hurdle that Mike has and will soon be on his way to better blood numbers and successful treatments.

Friday November 7 we saw Dr Ifthi today and he was happy with the stem cell collection. Because Sonny was off chemo for three weeks his blood cancer protein number was growing. Which was expected.

He will now start the new chemo medication called Revlimid. He will take it at home and go to the cancer center twice a week for the Valcade shot, bone strengthening medication and the steroid pills. Even though we are not happy with going up twice a week it will only be threw the end of the year. Then on to the transplant.

This gives us a chance to get all the holidays over with and the new grandbaby will be here. Winter will be in full swing.

December 5

Sonny and Roy went out for breakfast for Roy's birthday. They have done this for a couple of years now for each other's birthday.

Not just on special days, but quite often every other Sunday when Sonny is up to it.

They do ask me to go too, but I'd rather not. I have heard the old stories of their youth and working years so much I could tell them better than they can. Haha

Besides that, I like my breakfast food hot and find when I go out for breakfast the hot food is only minimally warm at best!

Sonny has been on the new chemo therapy for about a month now, one month equals one round. What a big drop in the cancer IGG numbers, that is good the lower the IGG number then we know the chemo is working. Over 1400 points lower in one round. He is now down to IGG of 1600. Everyone is pleased. It looks like transplant will take place sometime in the next two months. We are once again very hopeful and breathing a little easier.

December 13 2014

We have come full circle of a year since he was diagnosed with cancer. There were a few times through this past year I really had my doubts he would pull through. Though I never said any different out loud, and **"I never did say so to Sonny."** I never ever want to be anything but positive and keep my faith. This journey has certainly tested my faith at times.

I don't have any idea what this next year is going to bring. We are all in it for the long haul. Even if we were the perfect picture of health, even then we would not know our day to day existence. No one really knows what tomorrow will bring.

December 22 2014 A very good appointment with Dr Ifthi. Sonny's cancer IGG number is now close to 1000 and he will not have to see Dr Ifthi for two months. We will see Dr Liesveld on January 8 2015 to find out the date for the transplant. Our 43rd wedding anniversary

Christmas 2014

2014

Our beautiful innocent grandkids. Be still my heart and time.

This year's Christmas is much happier and more promising than last years. Yet Sonny seems depressed, and if he is, he won't say or he won't talk about it. I think it may be because he will be in the hospital for at least three weeks, maybe longer. He has a lot on his mind. I want to hug it all away but he won't let me close.

The transplant team of doctors told us, at first, he will be very sick from the high dose of chemo he will be given. That is nothing to look forward to. I can only imagine it would be very depressing just to think of that possibility. The results of having the cancer and pain under control is very real and so much closer. Thing is under control is the best we can hope for, so we will take it.

I don't know what God has planned for us as a couple, or for Sonny as an individual. I can't help but know it will be a great testimony that only Sonny can share straight from his experience and from his heart. This ride of no one's choice called Multiple Myeloma.

Today December 29 2014 Today is Sonny's very last chemo at the infusion center. We are very excited about this event. We only hope it gets better from here on out, time will tell.

We celebrated with dinner at The Texas Steak House in Rochester. The food was amazing, the atmosphere comfortable and we are both happy and hopeful. It was very nice. I think it's the first relaxing meal we have had in over a year.

2015

January 8, 2015

Today is our fourty-third wedding anniversary. We saw Dr Liesveld to get set up for the stem cell transplant. She told us about all the procedures and side effects of the transplant and the heavy dose off chemo that Sonny will get. Sonny had to sign a stack of consent forms.

It's crazy the red tape and hoops to go threw for a medical procedure that will give you a better life even for a short time.

But, the doctors, the hospital and the insurance company all want to have their "butts covered". What about the patient? Well, they put them in an open back gown, butt exposed, nothing covered! Haha

Today he had to have a chest X-ray and an EKG. He will go back the day before he is admitted and have an IV port put in and get the big dose of chemo. The day after that he will be admitted and his healthy stem cells will be put back into him. We will get a phone call from the doctor to tell us when those dates are. She said to expect the call sometime within the next two weeks.

We found out one interesting fact today. At about three months post-transplant he will have to get all his childhood immunizations all over again. This is because the chemo he is going to get is so strong it totally destroys all of his immunity. What little he has left.

It looks like Sonny and Jax, our newest grandson will be getting immunized at the same time.

Mary D. our SCT care coordinator called Friday the 9th at 8:30p.m. She gave us the following schedule.

Tuesday January 13th 11:00a.m. be at IPOP (in patient out patient) floor for the pre admission work up and 1p.m. to get the IV port put in.

Wednesday January 14th be at IPOP at 10:30a.m. for the IV of high dose chemo.

Thursday January 15th he will be admitted to the hospital for the actual transplant. Healthy stem cells readmitted to his body.

This means if everything goes as good as it has already, he will be home by the middle to end of February.

Tuesday January 13 We met with one of the transplant doctors who will be on the transplant floor next week to care for Sonny. Her name is Dr. Milner, nice lady, and so very tiny, no bigger than a third grader. She said she can't believe how well he is doing. She believes he will breeze right through the transplant.

Then he had to be weighed, measured, and vitals taken. All double checked by two nurses at the same time. They also did his pre admission blood work up. Then he was off to radiation and had a two-line IV catheter PICC put in. Everything went so smooth and easy.

Wednesday January 14th A very windy, cold day -16 at our house.

We arrived at the hospital at 9:45a.m. Our luck is holding out, we got a parking spot just three cars down from the lobby entrance.

On to the 6th floor IPOP unit for the Melphalan, high dose chemo and another break. We got to the elevators and the door was open, we walked in pushed the button for the sixth floor and in one swift swoop we were there. No stopping on another floor, straight up, another perfect sign.

When we got to IPOP they took him right in and here it is twelve noon the chemo is already done. He is getting IV fluid flush and can go home around 1p.m.

We can't believe just how good and easy everything is going. Things are looking up!

Thursday January 15 10:30a.m. He had a really good night and slept really well. No reaction to the chemo, no mouth blisters, no sickness, no grogginess. He had no reaction at all. Thank you, Jesus.

We are here on the sixth floor of the Wilmot Cancer center, room six. He is all settled in and hooked up to an IV of fluids to protect his kidneys before the transplant. Transplant will take place at 1p.m. today. The reentry of stem cells will take about an hour.

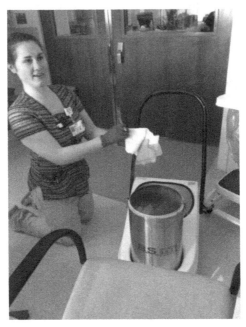

Stem cells coming from the deep freeze storage. Ready
to be re-admitted to Sonny's body via IV lines

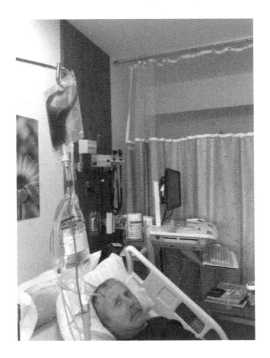

2:30p.m. The transplant is complete. Everything is so good. All the side effects they told us to expect never happened. He was hooked to the monitors and all vitals stayed normal. No fluctuation at all. He has no nausea, no vomiting, no fainting, no bad odor or smell coming from his body, or no bad taste.

This is an amazing process. I am sure of it as I am sure of myself God is definitely in control and with Sonny. Sonny is blessed.

I left around 3:30p.m. and got home at five. It was a quiet night at home, and I was glad because I am very tired. Not a physical tired but an emotional tired, gratefully tired. Like we can both breathe a little easier now.

Maddie and I slept pretty well, without Sonny's snoring, haha, and knowing he's in the very best of care possible. Feeling thankful at this chance for a longer and better quality of life with Multiple Myeloma.

Friday January16 Maddie went for her grooming appointment today. I talked to Sonny on the phone he is doing very well. No side effects yet. I hope it stays that way for him. He said he walked the tread mill a few times today. He likes going to the exercise room. It has a great view of the city. Three of the outside walls are glass.

Mike is on the mend and back at the cancer center today. He and Ken S. stopped to visit with Sonny after Mikes chemo treatment.

Libby skyped him, he had a less lonely day. He said his meals were good and all the nurses are wonderful.

Saturday January 17 2015

I got up at 3:45a.m. to let the dog out and I stayed up. I made coffee and read my daily Bible chapters. I had gone a few days without reading it so I was behind. This is my fifth year of reading the Bible threw in a year. Today I will have baby Jax while Libby takes Kendal to cheerleading competition in Hornell.

Today is "day plus two" which means his transplant day plus two days. That is how they count his progress and where he is with this treatment.

Thursday was his transplant day and now two days later, day plus two.

I talked to him this morning and he had a good night. He sounds good and says he feels great.

We have two wood pellet burning stoves. I loaded up pellet bags in the back of the Kubota RTV side by side last night so I could bring them into the house first thing this morning. Well, when I went to the garage to bring them in this morning most of them were on the floor. The dump box on the Kubota had tipped up during the night and dumped the bags on the floor. I neglected to lock the dump mechanism lever last night.

Now that was hard. Picking the forty-pound bags up off the floor and placing them back up on the Kubota. My neck and shoulders are really feeling it. I should have known better. I thought I was saving myself some time and work. I hate to call our kids, Roy, or other neighbors to come to bring in pellets. They have their own homes and families to take care of. Oh well, lesson learned. I will rest tonight!

I am remembering at the beginning of our journey. I was so angry I was so mad at God for what he was putting us through. There was one scripture that kept haunting me.

1st Thessalonians 5:18 *"in all things give thanks."* Wherever I turned that scripture was on my mind. At the time I didn't know why but I'd wake up with this on my mind. I go to sleep with that verse on my mind. It literally haunted me all day long, every day.

I found it hard enough to read my Bible, to pray, let alone try to be thankful. How are we supposed to be thankful for the cancer sentence that Sonny has been given? How can anyone ever be thankful for a life sentence of any illness?

I did pray but to me it sounded like senseless words. I prayed more out of habit instead of gratitude, yet the scripture still haunts me.

Eventually life with cancer settled into a daily routine, a new normal if you will. I got back into my daily scripture reading. I forced myself to be grateful, to find the good in everyday, even if it was for one little thing.

I forced myself to thank God on a daily basis. Even if it were just one thing even if it were only in my words, because often I did not feel it in my heart.

I didn't see it then but I can look back and see it now things did start to turn around for the good and look more hopeful. I also could not see what my problem was then but looking back I can see what my problem was now. I was dealing with a lapse in faith and trust in God, and telling God how I wanted things to go instead of letting Gods word be my guide.

What I was doing was looking into the future trying to figure out what was going to happen. Actually, trying to manipulate in my mind the future of what I wanted for Sonny and not what was happening.

At that time, I could see in my own mind that it didn't look like Sonny would have a future. I never wanted to be accepting of that. Not ever. That's what was making me so angry with God. The unfairness of cancers lack of choice of victims. Cancer doesn't choose a victim, it just happens. What then could we really find to be grateful for?

Once I resolved to stop planning the future to hand it over to God. Really hand it over. To look at one day at a time and be truly grateful for what goodness and hope that was given to us at any particular moment.

It was then that a light came on. A little bit less complicated and a little bit easier to tolerate.

Once I became grateful for all the little opportunities, for all the little improvements, grateful for each and every day and every moment that we had right now life did become happier even with cancer to take care of. I pray my attitude of gratitude will stay with me no matter what comes up next.

Sunday January 18 2015

Sunny and forty-six degrees. I took Mom and Libby up to the hospital with me today to see Sonny. For all appearances he looks like he is doing super. He looks like he doesn't even need to be on the hospital. He is walking on the tread mill four times a day for ten minutes each time. He is eating good meals, he is reading his books, he does puzzles and word search books. For all outward appearances he looks like he's on vacation.

I feel bad that he or any one has to go through this whole ordeal with any type of cancer. He was once a vital and strong take charge, do anything person. Now he is reduced to having to forever be under medical care, advise, treatment, and appointments as long as he lives.

He has lost some mental clarity and I'm not exactly sure why. I mean he forgets things so easily. He used to be very sharp in his memory and recall. Not so much lately. Maybe it's all the toxic chemicals that are raging in his body from the treatments. At times he has a very faraway look in his eyes, like I don't know where he's at or what he's thinking.

I pray for him daily. I think God has been good to him to bring him this far after all that has been done to him. I think God is not done with Sonny. I feel God has bigger and better things for Sonny to do.

Possibly be a testimony to others, even to his own sons. He is on many prayer chains all over the country. We appreciate each and every prayer. Especially when I find it hard to pray it's good to know others are holding us up.

Behind my daily good face forward, at times is a heart full of fear for what Sonny is going through. The selfishness in me is thinking how could I ever go on without him. I pray I don't have to. Even after turning everything fully over to God at times my mind speaks louder than my heart feels.

It's an awful thing that we have endured this last year. But here we are.

We have seen a lot of worse cases we could be in, and that breaks my heart to see disfigured people at the cancer center who are visibly just existing. Yet they persevere, something keeps them going.

Beneath my smile is a lot of stress and worry. On the outside for all appearances, I stay strong for others and our kids. I'm the mom, moms take care of others it's what we do.

Thursday January 22 2015 Sonny's blood numbers have bottomed out.

He literally has no immune system at all as I write. Zero, white blood cells, and the doctors say this is what is supposed to happen, it was not unexpected. They can only go up from here.

He feels very tired, and no energy. Starting tonight he will get shots of Neupogen this will help his cells to regrow rapidly in his bone marrow and his blood numbers should start to bounce back up.

For now, he stays in his room, he is isolated and very fearful of getting an infection. He was going to the gym four times a day, now he just paces his room for ten minutes at a time instead of risking going out. He is trying to stay active and in motion even if it's just a few minutes at a time.

The nurses, doctors, and all staff are just fabulous at Wilmot Cancer Center transplant floor. He is getting great care and I think that makes a big difference in anyone's overall health. To trust in your care staff is a very big thing.

Friday January 23

I took Sonny's mom with me today. Sonny is doing fabulous, the doctors cannot believe it, they say he is a model patient. Still his only side effect of the transplant is fatigue, no sickness, no loss of appetite, no pain.

He has gotten a lot of cards from all over the country, friends, family, customers, and many community members. He is a loved and well thought of man. I believe all the prayers and knowing others have not forgotten him are what has helped him the most.

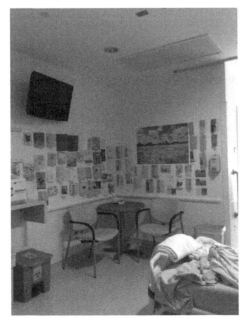

Cards of support, prayers, and thoughts, in
his room at the cancer center.

Saturday January 24

Today Sonny's blood platelets are so low he has to wear a helmet when he gets out of bed because of a chance of brain bleed if he so much as bumps his head. I hope his blood numbers recover quickly.

Sunday January 25 Not a good day, blood platelets are very low down from four white blood cells to zero.

Sonny is very tired, no energy, feeling nauseous, and running a fever of 102.

Today he was given many IVs, calcium, magnesium, potassium, antibiotics, and platelets. All was going well until he had an allergic reaction to the platelets. He developed a deep chesty cough and trouble breathing. They gave him Benadryl and continued with the IVs. He recovered quickly once the Benadryl took a hold. I understand this is a normal side effect and is expected in most patients. Still, it's very scary to go through inability to breathe.

Monday January 26 He is doing well, so much better than yesterday. His blood count and other numbers are on their way up, things look good. He is feeling wonderful, not so fatigued and hopeful. All in one day. Amazing! Praise the Lord!

Tuesday January 27 Snow Snow Snow Overnight we got about eight inches altogether. It is very pretty though.

11:30a.m. Sonny just called; he is being discharged. I'm going to bring him home. Thank you, Jesus, I am so happy.

Wednesday January 28 Sonny is doing really good. Glad to be home. Eating and sleeping with no problems. Pacing the sun room back and forth ten minutes at a time to keep up movement, circulation, oxygen, and exercise. Taking a few cat naps throughout the day. He feels really well. The hospital called today just to check on him and see how he was getting along. I thought that was a nice gesture.

Thursday January 29

I went to the shop to help Doug this morning. Then I came home and had to go to the grocery store. Sonny rode along but stayed in the car due to his lack of immune system. We filled the car with gas and went through the car wash. Came home had lunch and then he went out with his Kubota and plowed the snow from the barn doors to the road. Today seemed normal and that felt good to both of us, very good. These things may seem normal or mundane to most people but to us it's a blessing.

Friday January 30,

Today we had a nice visit with Don Mc. one of our customers we have had for years. He is quite elderly in his 80's and he lives in Hammondsport N.Y.

Matter of fact he went to school with my mom. He's a really great man. Good kind and very concerned and thoughtful.

Sonny's hair is falling out in bunches due to the high doses of chemo he had. Sue our hair dresser is coming near the end of the day around 5p.m. and brining her clippers to shave the rest of his hair off. I will take pictures! He is actually looking forward to being bald. They tell us it will start to grow back within a month.

What a difference a year can make. Where we are now compared to a year ago and all he has been through. I remember being so confused having so many questions and doubts. The awful pain Sonny was going through, and not being able to help him.

I remember distinctly Dr Ifthi saying to Sonny "give me a year I guarantee you will feel better." If Sonny not gotten so sick in March and April, a year mark would have been absolutely right.

Sonny defiantly walked the valley of the shadow of death. Did he fear the evil cancer? Yes, he did. He feared because he is human. He knows the Lord, and he said he knew where he would end up in eternity, but that he was scared for those of us he would leave behind.

He told me today that it was knowing that I believed he was going to be ok and the strong support of all our children, family, and friends, that kept him strong when he could not be strong for himself.

Today we go see the transplant doctor, Dr. Liesveld, and his oncologist Dr. Ifthi for follow up post-transplant appointments. We hope to hear that we don't have to go so often now.

This morning's devotional scripture readings were appropriate for us both, all about strength for the day.

> **Deuteronomy 31:6 Be strong and courageous. Do not fear or be dreadful, for it is the Lord your God who is with you. He will not leave you or forsake you**
>
> **Isaiah 41:10 Fear not for I am with you. I am your God I will strengthen you and help you**
>
> **Philippians 4:13 I can do all things through Him who strengthens me**
>
> **Exodus 15:2. The Lord is my strength and my song. He has become my salvation. He is my God and I will praise Him always.**

What a great start to the day!

February 5

Sonny had his follow up with Dr Liesveld today. Very thankful for answered prayers, Sonny's white blood cells went from 2.3 to 3.3 in one week, and his blood platelets went from 21,000 to 80,000 in one week. This is very good because it means the transplant is working. We are once again very encouraged and grateful for modern medicine.

Our case worker PA Mary Dibly, said she is amazed at Sonny's progress that they have never seen anyone go through transplant as easily and progress as fast as he is. She said they see men half his age that go through this procedure and not fare near as well.

They just have never seen such progress and gain like Sonny has made.

She told us everyone is just in aww of him. He has clearly been a text book case for exceptional progress throughout the whole transplant procure. He has had many doctors and student's enquirer with him and about him for papers and journals they are writing on stem cell transplants with MM. After all Strong is a University Hospital.

During his stay on the transplant floor of the hospital he was visited several times by classes of students who were studying stem cell transplants. They were interested inhis experience and progress.

Tuesday February 10 Sonny has a touch of the stomach bug, very weak, vomiting, and diarrhea, but no fever. He is very tired and is sleeping a lot.

Wednesday February 11 Sonny is a little better but he doesn't feel like eating and he is very exhausted and no energy, but he is able to keep ginger ale down.

Thursday February 12, I have the stomach bug now I am very sick also. Sonny is doing much better.

Friday February 13 I am still very sick, fever, vomiting, diarrhea, the whole nine yards! First time I've been sick in over two years. I hope this isn't the beginning of how the rest of winter is going to go!

Saturday February 14 I am a little better my stomach and ribs are very sore and I'm very achy but no fever today.

February 17 I'm having a hard time getting over this stomach thing. Turned out to be more than a twenty four hour bug! Seems no matter what I eat it sits heavy in my stomach and makes it hurt. Terrible headache on and off every day. I'm sure it's has to do with not being able to eat, and being dehydrated.

Monday, March 30 the beginning of Easter Holy Week 2015.

Sonny is much better than he was last year at this time. Last year he was very dire and pretty much not aware of anything.

March 31 I am so very sick for the second time in as many months. Last month the stomach bug. Now full-blown flu. Head ache, ear aches, fever, sore throat, head congestion, chills. Every part of my body is on fire or hurts. Could be just run down from being the care giver. Who knows.

Libby gave me the rest of her Tamiflu because she had the respiratory flu a few weeks ago but didn't take all her medicine, no big surprise. In her case, she got over it in just a few days. Probably because of her youth.

I took the rest of her medicine I had enough for three days. It was enough to knock the worse of it out of me. No lectures please about sharing medicine!

April 5 2015

Today is Easter Sunday. It may not be as warm and sunny as last year's Easter. The ground is covered in snow and still coming down, but on a good note Sonny is in a much better frame of mind.

I'm not sure if we will have an egg hunt outside today or not. We'll see by this afternoon what the weather is doing.

As for me I really don't feel up to a house full of company. Oh, I love having family in for the holidays but this year I have no energy. I am still a little achy and very tired in spite of sleeping pretty good the last two nights. The flu really took a lot out of me.

Thursday April 9 today was Sonny's last appointment with the stem cell doctor. Dr. Leisveld. She said all is well his blood test all look good.

We go back to oncologist Dr. Ifthi in two weeks and then we will find out just how far he is into any kind of remission from the stem cell transplant.

Saturday April 11 I wish I could get over this cough it's going on two weeks now. My ribs are very sore from the violent coughing spells I get. I haven't had this kind of cough in years I think I probably need an inhaler. I don't know when I'll have time to go to the doctor. As usual even before Sonny's cancer, he comes first. I will wait it out and hope it goes away.

Saturday April 18, 2015

Sonny had a very bad night last night. A lot of pain in his arms and shoulders. He also has a lot of pain in his knees. He only gets relief by getting up and walking around. Tonight, he started doubling up on his morphine and see if that helps him. Another thing he seems bothered by any cold draft; he can't stand the cold.

He will see Dr. Ifhti this week, we will find out what is going on. My fear is that the cancer is active in his bones. But I have not said so out loud. Once again, I have "not said so to Sonny."

My cough is a little better. I did get an appointment with Dr. Parker, and am on an antibiotic and an inhaler now. I'm also taking Alka Seltzer chest and cough medicine. It's going on three weeks now. I still feel so exhausted and have no energy. But really, what do I have to complain about? Nothing, absolutely nothing compared to Sonny and so many others much worse off than me!

Thursday April 23 Today we see Dr. Ifthi I sure hope its good news we can live with.

Sonny is so bummed out with pain that he is getting depressed. He doesn't say what's on his mind. When I ask him, he always says nothing.

Things are so much better than we thought. We were really fearing the worse because of the pain he has been having.

We saw Dr. Iffti and he told us Sonny was in "**partial remission.**" It's not perfect but we will hold on to the promise of a better future.

Amen and praise the Lord.

December 2013 when he was first diagnosed his blood para protein number was 5.5 it was final stage Multiple Myeloma.

Today his para protein number is .6 and complete remission is zero. He is so close. He was told he will never see zero because that is the kind of cancer this is. There is no complete remission, only "inactivity", which means always present but not always active.

Dr. Ifthi ordered up a quick release morphine along with his every day long-acting morphine for his pain. I know Sonny doesn't want to take anymore medication, but I hope he will take it to relieve his pain. The doctor thought it was arthritis pain that Sonny is having.

Now for the next two weeks we will be busy with other testing. He has to have a bone marrow biopsy, a very painful procedure, a PET scan, an MRI, a full body structure X-ray, a 24-hour urine and big blood draw test and cultures. Dr. Ifti needs these test to compare to the same ones that were done in December 2013. It will give the doctors a better overall picture of Sonny's cancer data.

From now on we will only have to go to the cancer center once a month. As long as his weekly blood work stays good. The blood test he can have done at our local lab in Dansville. He will be on a low dose chemo pill, 25mg. Revlimid at home that he will take every day.

The reason he needs a weekly blood test is to keep track of his immune system. Especially the white blood cells, since chemo also affects and destroys them.

He is a hard person to read some times. I think he is happy about the results! He doesn't say much about it but I can tell he is thinking.

I was told by Sheri, Dr. Ifthi's nurse, that once cancer patients reach some form of remission or inactivity in the cancer and they do not have to see the doctor every week, cancer patients will experience a letdown, or a loss of security that they feel within the doctor's office and staff. The security of being seen every week, and being under the doctor's care.

I was also told there is a survivor's guilt that cancer patients deal with too. From being at the cancer treatment center for months and then now not having to go because you don't need to, and knowing others are still going because they are not better.

I guess it's a lot of emotions and it can be mentally challenging and confusing. To be happy, sad, angry, and elated, at the same time. It's a lot to deal with in one's mind.

In the last 18 months we have lost two friends and one family member who had cancer and lost their battle. At the times of their deaths Sonny could not, would not go to their funerals it was just too close for him.

He is now a cancer survivor! We don't know why some people survive cancer and some don't.

Sonny is a fighter, but that is not to say the others didn't fight it as well. We hate to see or hear of anyone who didn't make it.

Once again, he asked me to officiate his funeral. I really don't think I would be able to do that.

I said to him, what would I say? What do I tell them?

This is what he wrote:

****

What do you tell them?

Tell them that I never had so much knowledge about life til Dec. 2013

That it was then that I finally realized what was most important to me.

It was only then that I completely cared about what is really important.

And that is my family and my life

Up until that point I was all work. Work had been my whole life what I loved to do

The most important lesson I had to learn was that I had to not only forgive all that was against me and then the hardest parts, forget the hurt and pain and moving on

Now my priorities have changed and I know it's much to late for me but when you tell them this "give them all that Mom look and they will listen"

Make my funeral funny make people laugh.

I want you to tell them stories of our 42 years together, but only the good parts haha

Make sure they know I am in heaven how do I know this?

I know because of you, the one who never gave up on me the one who told me so many times that Jesus loved me no matter how much a sinner we are and because

of you I will never forget the feeling I had when I finally learned about and accepted The Lord

So yea I know I will be in heaven and I know I get to see my Dad again and Pastor Armstrong and all my other relatives.

I guess lately my favorite scripture would be the one about those that wait upon The Lord because I have become a person who has to wait and wait always waiting and it's a nice little song too

Also, I like the one about bind us together it always makes me think of family.

My favorite life story is the day we were married followed by the day we brought all four of our kid's home days I will never forget.

My regrets are that I wasn't more about family than I was I regret I didn't spend time with you and our new babies when you came home. I regret I didn't help you more.

When he gave me the paper on what to say at his funeral, he also gave me the following. Pertaining to me

To you my wife. I heard a song once about a man who was singing about what his wife was to him. You are to me a lot of what the words in the song said.

I have not been a good and respectful man but I saw a lot you did but I took it all for granted and you deserve respect you didn't get

Wives come in all shapes and colors blonde brown red and black

A wife is pure class and beauty, at least mine is.

She is wise beyond me always has been.

She is as tough as an army Sargent and as soft as babys skin

She has been a beauty in my eyes since before we even dated problem is I never told her very much just how pretty she is.
To me she aged with perfection beautiful skin and a body that is easy on my old eyes.

If I were able to speak here at my funeral I'd play tribute to her she is great to me.
Her hands and arms are strong and a little wrinkled because of work that never seemed to get completely done
Her jet-black hair is now white as snow and is so beautiful
She has disappointment and tiredness in her eyes and most of it caused by me

She is the solid rock that our family leans on she is the glue that holds us together.
Most days of our marriage from day one has been an uphill climb and she was always there by my side no matter what
I was often weak and many times so discouraged but she was my strength always there with encouragement and a smile she never gave up on any of us

She was my lady who when she put on a dress looked like an angel to me
I often lost control and lost my faith so many times but there she was she carried us both through those times
I just want to say Lord when she gets to your gate you know what she's worth
Give her that mansion because she has been through hell with me here on earth
As the song goes. "Give her my share of heaven if I've earned any here on earth"
She deserves so much more than I ever gave her

I never knew he felt this way about me.

Monday May 4 2015

What an awful day. I went to the shop at 6:15a.m. as I always do. I make the coffee, run a stock order, print it and go upstairs and check it off. Today coming down the stairs, I missed the bottom step, fell onto my knees and went head first into the steel post of the alignment rack. My head hurt so bad and I heard my neck crack from the impact.

I rolled over on the cold hard cement floor onto my back. I remember ripping off my glasses and throwing them. I thought they were broken and they cut my head. I laid there for a short time got my bearings and my head to clear, but I didn't dare get up. I called out to the guys in the shop that I needed some help. I could feel my hair getting wet with blood, but I had no idea how bad it was.

Doug, Andy, and Rick came over. They all looked at me and said "oh my God." One of them grabbed a bunch of clean cotton grease rags and put them on my head, Andy called 911, and Rick called Sonny.

Sonny was still at home. He was in the bed room getting dressed, he did not hear the phone. Rick went to the house to get him. Sonny immediately came to the shop. I could see a shocked look on his face when he saw me laying on the floor and blood coming from my forehead.

I asked the guys for ice, and there was none. There was however a bag of frozen broccoli in the freezer. They broke it up so the bag was flexible, wrapped it in clean paper towels to apply to my head.

After waiting for almost an hour for the ambulance Sonny drove the car up to the shop door, put the front seat of the car in a reclining position and had the boys help load me into the car. Sonny took me to Dansville hospital.

The ambulance never did show up.

I don't remember to much after that. until I became aware that I was in a hospital bed talking to a nurse not knowing how I got there. They put a big neck collar on me and sent me for a CT scan. The scan came back that there was no broken neck, and no brain bleed, but I did have a broken nose. My forehead took 15 stitches, and I'm sure it will leave a nasty scar.

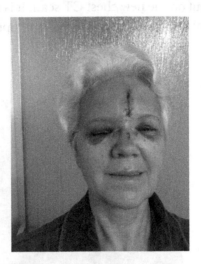

May 5 My doctor's office called today they want to see me. I need further CT scan unrelated to my injury. They saw some suspicion shadows in the upper part of both lungs. The upper lungs were visible in the scan. Today I have to go for a complete chest CT scan. We will get the results on Friday when I go get my stitches out.

Sonny is so scared for me, he cried and choked back sobs, he said he doesn't want me to go through what he has been enduring. When he hears "shadows" or "something suspicious" understandably his mind goes straight to a cancer diagnosis.

I think the "shadow" is just because I am getting over a bad case of respiratory flu from three weeks ago.

I think is related to that or my allergy season. Which I get bothered with every spring and fall. Dr. Jessica told me she heard wheezing when she listened to my lungs.

I am thinking positive thoughts that they will find nothing today in the scan. I trust the Lord to reveal a clean lung CT. If not, it will just be another hurdle to add to my uphill battle.

May 14 all is good. My face is healing quite well the bruising and swelling is fading a little, and the stitches came out on Friday. There was nothing to be worried about on the new chest CT scan. It is just thickening upper lung tissue. Probably caused by all my years of upper respiratory issues from allergies.

May 25 2015

Sonny is having quite a lot of pain in his arms at night, from his wrist to his shoulders. I think it may be joint pain due to arthritis. All he has to do is get out of bed for a change of position and the pain subsides.

Another thing is he is so stubborn about taking pain medicine. If he would take it regularly, he could stay on top of the pain, but no, he tries to tough it out.

May 27 2015

Our first month visit since Sonny was put on a maintenance chemo of Revlimid 15mg. Dr Ifthi was very pleased with Sonny's progress. His cancer blood number is low, and the bone marrow test came back as a small amount of myeloma, but non active. All is very well, we can breathe again.

May 29 on our first vacation since early 2013. We are going to North Carolina to visit our friends Dick and Dale H. Then on to see Bob and Shelia W. also in North Carolina.

Around 2:00p.m. we were driving through Virginia and a tire blew out on the camper. Sonny got it changed and were on our way in less than an hour. The blow out caused some damage to the camper; wires tore out and damaged side panel on the camper slide out. Sonny got it fixed up temporarily and will fix it completely when we get home.

We left home at 4a.m. and arrived at our destination camp ground at 4p.m.

Over all it was a good trip. It was nice to visit with our friends and step out of our comfort zone and away from the cancer routine for a few days.

July 2015 Over all Sonny seems to be doing pretty good for all he has been through. His pain is on and off, he is on maintenance chemo and only has to go to the oncologist every six weeks now instead of every month. However, he does have to go to infusion every month to get his bone strengthening IV of Zometa and big blood draw for monthly blood test.

The chemo he is on now at home is Revlimid. Also known as Lenalidomide. It is used as a maintenance drug after stem cell transplant. An expensive and powerful drug. Every month it has to be renewed and approved by the insurance company. A twenty one day supply cost over $15000.00.

Every month he also has to take a phone survey and talk to the pharmacist before it gets sent to him. In the survey he has to promise not to have unprotected sex, not to donate blood or sperm. Do not share the medication with anyone. Agree that he has the knowledge that this will cause extreme birth defects and must agree to two different forms of birth control should you choose to have sex. Even in males who have had a vasectomy. You have to agree to the knowledge that this medication can cause low white blood cells and platelets. You have to agree to the knowledge that this medication can cause blood clots which can cause death and or heart failure, fibrillation, and heart attacks. You have to agree to monthly blood test.

When you talk to the pharmacist they go over this same list from the survey and add that: you must not ever open the capsules, you must not handle them with your bare hands. If you do you must immediately wash your hands with soap and hot water. If you miss a dose do not take two at a time. They go over all the side effects, rash, diarrhea, constipation, fever, itching, swelling of hands arms and legs, headaches, muscles spasms, shaking or trembling, joint aches and pains, sleep problems insomnia, shortness of breath, nose bleeds, as well as agreeing to the risk of it causing liver failure and new and different cancers.

Then and only then will they send you the Revlimid.

This is something we had to hear and agree to every month. As if we never heard it before.

I suppose its all a liability issue, after all no one ever reads the side effect sheets that come with prescriptions anyhow. If we did, we'd all be to scared to take it!

He goes to the shop just about every day. He just likes to stay busy. It drives him crazy to just sit in the house and to think about the terminal diagnosis. To know all the treatments he has had just buy him a little bit more time, never knowing when the cancer numbers will start to go back in the wrong direction.

He loves it when his cousin Dick stops by, or other men who want to chat and get advice on how to repair something they might be having an issue with. It helps him to know he hasn't been forgotten and better yet he hasn't forgotten his self-taught education.

Wednesday July 28 2015

Today Sonny started getting his childhood immunizations. He got measles, mumps, and rubella, polio, DPT (diphtheria, tetanus, and pertussis) meningitis, hepatitis. He had some reaction afterwards but it was mild; dizziness, upset stomach, achy muscles and bones and profuse sweating. That lasted a few days. By Saturday it was pretty much gone.

Tuesday August 4

As I write this Sonny is at Dr. Parkers office because he has a bad pain in his lower back under his ribs. It has been there for a couple of weeks now but he has been tolerating it. I have no idea what it might be. I could not even guess, I wouldn't dare, after all the cancer pain was under control. Not eradicated completely, but under control.

He is very afraid of what he might find out today, he didn't want me to go. He says it's the same pain he had when he was originally diagnosed and a tumor was found. Also, he has lost over eight pounds in less than a week. I hope and pray Dr. Parker can find answers for Sonny so he can have peace instead of worry, and also get relief from the pain.

Well sort of good news. They sent him for X-rays but they found nothing wrong. No broken ribs, no pneumonia, no tumor, nothing at all. He does have bone pain and it's real. Now we wait until the fourteenth when he sees his oncologist to find out if the cancer in the bones is active again.

Multiple Myeloma is a very painful cancer. Every pain you get you immediately think the cancer is getting worse.

Sonny's Aunt Sue had a nice get together for his moms' birthday and this year and we were invited.

Left to right Sonny, myself, Barb, Steve, Tim,
Lori, and Mary sitting in the chair.

October 4......It's been a while since I wrote in our journal. Things are going surprisingly well.

As I write we are in Indiana at my cousin's place. We came out on the first of October and are going home tomorrow. We haven't gone out much with the camper this past summer because we are tied down to all the grass we have to mow and summer is such a busy time for family. Maybe this winter we will go south for a few weeks. We'll see everything depends on Sonny's health, and our finances.

Sonny had an oncologist appointment before we came out to Indiana. He got the rest of his immunizations and did better this time with no reactions. He also got his flu shot. He doesn't go back to see Dr. Ifthi until November. He still has to have the bone strengthening IV Zometa every month until February or March.

His blood numbers are still good and he is still in a state of partial remission they call it which is as good as it gets with Multiple Myeloma. With this cancer when it is present but non active, that is considered partial remission.

December 12, 2015

It has been two years since we were told Sonny had a mass/tumor on his spine. The mass was resolved after radiation treatment and weekly IV chemo. We have been through many discouragements and many positive times. To say it has been a roller coaster ride in and out of dark tunnels only to keep seeing the light dimly lit but not always finding it bright enough to see our way out would be one way to put it.

We have been through situations that have torn us apart. Situations that made us question what and why we were called to do this. Looking back on the last two years I can't say that any of the situations were good for either of us. Definitely not the life we chose. Not the life anyone would choose.

Looking back at the hard health situations, we have handled, we both have been so mad at God and life for this cancer. There are times we were and still are so angry about it. We had to decide to stay where we were, mad at God and mad at the world, mad at the unfairness of a healthy life turned upside down, mad at our forced medical retirement, or we could get mad enough to not stay in the situation. We could learn to live our new normal and move forward. To live our life together, and not live "our cancer".

We had to accept the fact that God did not cause our situation, as much as we wanted to blame Him. We knew also, neither is God ever leaving us. He will be with us where ever this fate takes us. Someone once said "to get to where God wants us to be, we have to trust Him and rest in His word and promises". That is a very hard pill of life to swallow.

At the time of this writing, he seems to be doing well. The cancer is under control with the daily dose of chemo. He has only three more Zometa IV treatments, and is on a six-week rotation of seeing the oncologist. All of his blood work comes back really good and there are no other issues at this time except for the cancer.

He does go to the shop a few days a week.

What can I say it's in his blood he loves the work, the grease, the mechanical or fabricating challenges and the customers. Plus, he has a lot of knowledge to offer up to the younger mechanics. He's not one to stay home.

I just wish he would help his other sons once in a while. I guess it's just easier because we live right next door.

I go in Monday, Tuesday, and Wednesday mornings for two hours then I come home. I'm slowly backing out of the working world also. After all we are retired.

Christmas 2015

It was December 24, 2013 that he was diagnosed with the cancer. We have come a long way and met a lot of great people along the way. If it had not been for our faith in God, our family, good friends, and great doctors he says he would have never lived this long.

His prognosis in 2013 was eighteen months to three years without stem cell transplant, and up to fifteen years with the transplant.

A blessed and hopeful Christmas this year

Clockwise starting at 6 oclock Kylie, Jax, Trinity, Evan, Aidan, Gavin, Trevor, Ariana, Kendal

The People We Meet

I love the people we met at the cancer center, the doctors, nurses, the cleaning staff, and other patients.

Just today a young woman came into the oncology waiting room on the sixth floor. She was very obese and in a wheel chair. I imagine her legs could not hold her weight without pain. She went right to the complimentary snack basket on the end table. She grabbed a few packages of cookies and put them in her coat pockets.

She looked at me and I looked at her, we both smiled. Then she wheeled her chair over by me. I was working on knitting a scarf on my hand loom. That is always a conversation starter. Knitting seems to makes me approachable, I guess, because it happens all the time.

We began to talk first about the knitting, she was very interested in hearing all about it. Our conversation turned to the mild weather for December, our families, then to computers and other random life things, and of course cancer. Everyone's reason for being where we were!

We talked for about twenty minutes before she got called in for her appointment. I found out she had cancer four times and survived. Ovarian cancer three times and uterine cancer once. She is now in remission. This is all typical of conversations with strangers, who become friends at the cancer center. Many times, we don't even know each other's names, yet we are not strangers.

The thing is when she left to go back to her appointment, she said to me, "I just knew when I saw you, I could talk to you, you seemed like and angel sitting there with your halo of white curls and then I saw the cross on your necklace and I knew I was right".

She made my heart feel warm and so much love for her. All I know is her name is Nancy.

May God always bless Nancy. A passing moment of shared humanity and a connection that was real.

We met so many people up here at the cancer center, we don't know them and they don't know us, yet we do know them!

Hebrews 13:2

Do not neglect to show hospitality to strangers. For by doing so some people have entertained angels without knowing it.

I must admit there were a few times over the last two years that I thought Sonny was not going to make it. Here he is getting ready to have the last Zometa IV.

We don't know what will happen in the coming year, but then none of us really do, cancer or not. Only God knows. After all he wrote our life, from the beginning to the end and everything in between.

> **Ecclesiastes 3:11-13**
>
> **He has made everything beautiful in its time. He also has put eternity in their hearts, except for the fact that no one can find out the work that God does from the beginning to the end.**

March 4 2016

Today was his last Zometta IV treatment. He is very happy about that and at the same time kind of bitter sweet. Glad to not have to go to the cancer center every month, but somehow there is security in coming every month.

We really will miss all the great staff of people in the infusion center who were always very kind to Sonny and I during his treatments.

When he was in the treatment room he always came first, his comfort, their concern about him as a person with a life outside of cancer. Not just his health, but his interest and how his life is going. They become family that you never knew you needed, and wish you never did.

Now he only has to go every two months to the oncologist. Things are definitely looking brighter and encouraging.

July 2016

It has been months since I last wrote. Sonny is doing well, hanging in there as they say. For all appearance sake he looks like he is doing well.

He is working full time at a big dairy farm in North Cohocton, the farm of John Schumacher. He works in the shop keeping the farm equipment repaired, and drives truck during the harvest of the field crops.

He really loves the farm work, but he wants nothing to do with the cows. He does not like the cows, never has even on his dad's farm when he was a kid.

His attitude about cows is "the only good cow is between two hamburger buns".

He had the last of his immunization shots, called booster shots. He is glad to be done with that. This time they did not make him sick but his arms are bruised.

This summer has been a very dry summer so there hasn't been much lawn to mow it's all burned up. Usually, he looks forward to mowing throughout the summer.

We have only had the camper out twice this summer, once he went to Scotts during the air show weekend and camped, I didn't go because, I was in WDC with our granddaughter Kylie, and her class at that time so Sonny and the dog went camping without me.

Then late summer we went to Sampson St. park on Memorial weekend. Well, Sonny did alone again, he and the dog.

I had two weddings to officiate that weekend and I never got there until Sunday. We came home Monday and the camper has been parked ever since. We do have reservations at Lake George in September for a week. After that the camper will be put up for the winter.

September 2016

The weather is starting to become a little more tolerable. We still have to have the AC on due to the high humidity that has hung around all summer.

Sonny is still working every day at Schumacher's farm and loving it. It not only has been an asset to the farm but good for Sonny to feel useful as well.

I took most of the grand kids to the farm on a field trip. The only ones not with me were the two oldest ones, they had other plans. All in all it turned out to be a good time and a lot of fun.

I watch several of my grandchildren on and off all summer while their parents work, they are now back in school.

As much as I love them, I am truly grateful for school! They are exhausting and they think grandma is a toy. My own fault really, because ever since they were born, I played with them on their level. On the floor, with building blocks, cars and trucks, chalk drawings on the driveway, bikes and scooters outside, fishing, basketball, nature walks around the pond, swing sets and sand boxes, their toys, stories to read, crayons and color books, play dough, puzzles, and games and as they got older cooking in the kitchen. I will still get them now and then after school when their parents have something going on, and school vacation days.

Health wise there are a few things going on in Sonny's life. He had his three months check up with Dr Parker our family physician for his A1C and his diabetes. There was good news there. He is no longer considered diabetic. His A1C has been below normal for the last nine months, so the doctor took him off his diabetic meds. Dr. Parker has no answer for it, no reason why, it just happened. Could very well be a side effect from the SCT.

As for the cancer, last week he had his two-month checkup and his blood numbers are staying the same which means the cancer is there but non active. The full body Xray he had in July shows increasing lesions in his bones. At this point they don't know if they are old or new, so in October he will have a PET scan that will give a more accurate reading when they compare it to the one from a year ago. When we get the results from that his treatment might change. Until then it is what it is and we will continue our life as normal as possible.

October 18 2016

Sonny has had his CAT and PET scan October 11. We won't get the results for a few weeks when he goes back to the oncologist, unless there is something that needs immediate attention. Then the doctor will be calling us. Until then we will go on with life as normal as possible and just enjoy the beautiful fall colors and weather. Which for this time of year has been about 20 degrees warmer than normal. Matter of fact Sonny is still riding his bike. Today we are supposed to see temperatures in the eightys.

Our life has changed a lot in the last three years. Some for the good and some that is very hard to understand or accept. Every day is a new beginning, a second chance, into infinity we hope, to get things right.

In my heart I know just the same, somethings will never really change. Like they say "the more things change the more they remain the same"

I have been strong and independent through all of this, not just the cancer but my marriage, my family, my work and home. I have been accepting though not always understanding of all that is and was important to everyone but myself. I have always been a peace keeper, the one who moves over and steps aside so others can do what they want, get what they want. I am a cargiver, I do for others it is my heart. Why, well because I believe in until death do us part.

Life went on, children, homes, and business. We have invested time and money in our lives and each other. Always trying to work on us never giving up. To go our separate ways was never an option. Please don't get me wrong there were happy times, very happy times, no matter how tough things got when it comes right down to it, we really do love each other.

All marriages or living together couples have good and bad times and choose to stick it out, fight for or work on what they have. Like I said in the beginning of this journal. This is a hard, honest account of the reality of our journey.

We have changed over the years. There has been a lot of water under the bridge as they say. I have changed and so has he. This journal is not the place to air such issues and grievances, this journal is about the cancer trip! Just the same if this ever turns in to a book, readers need to know we are human, we had a life before cancer. We are not perfect, we are accepting, we compromise, we both have said things we shouldn't have; we apologize, we forgive and we try to do better. A terminal illness puts a strain on life and how you live.

Christmas 2016

Clock wise starting at 6 oclock Trevor, Evan, Jax,
Gavin, Aidan, Kylie, Trinity, Ariana, Kendal

2017

March 2017 Not a good start to our new year. Sonny had had pneumonia since January. He has been on three rounds of antibiotics and is now on a low dose prednisone. The prednisone has helped the most and he is definitely feeling much better. He would like to stay on it but we don't think either doctor will allow it.

He wanted me to order prednisone on line so he can take it all the time. I researched it.

My goodness the medications you can order on line without a prescription is amazing.

Risky in self-diagnosis though. No lectures please until you have been where we are.

I did order it and he will take it for the next month then ween off it. His choice, though I know the doctor would not approve and won't be happy if they find out, and I told Sonny so.

I was very sick myself on February 12 and ended up in urgent care. It was not sudden, I tried to treat myself because I thought all I had was a sinus issue or a bad cold. It ended up being the respiratory flu. I hurt all over, a horrible cough, fever of 102.6 which lasted three days, I can truly say I have never been so sick with a cold virus, ever!

It is now March 7 and I still cough but everything else is better. I know I'm not contagious, yet I have found that nothing I take gets rid of the cough. It is relentless!

We are planning a trip to Florida on March 24th to see his sister and a few of my Aunts who live down there. We are both hoping that the warm weather and sun will make all the difference in our health!

Summer 2017

It has been mostly an uneventful summer.

We are both working, Sonny at Schumacher's farm, and me at the Twin Kiss ice cream store. We both love our jobs. Just the same our families worry about us.

We took our moms to the farm one Saturday afternoon then out for dinner.

Both our moms were raised on small dairy farms. Very small compared to farms now days. Sonny's family owned and operated a small dairy until his dad passed away and his mom then retired the cows and farm life.

Sonny and his mom

Mary, Sonnys mom   Mae, my mom

July 6,7,8,9 we were at my cousin Brian and Brenda's in Indiana for this year's Ritter family reunion. It was a nice time, but went by way to fast as it always does.

Somewhere during the week of July 24 Sonny started to have difficulty breathing. He thought it was one of two things, allergies to mowing lawn and cut grass, or pneumonia again.

Monday July 31 His breathing was very bad so he drove himself to the ER from work at the farm to find out what was going on and possibly get some antibiotics. He never let me know he was going until he was seen by the ER doctor, then he called me.

Turned out it was congestive heart failure. Which does not really mean the heart is failing but means he has fluid around the heart which makes the heart have to work harder. It happens to a lot of older folks. We just don't know why it's happening to him or why he is retaining fluid.

The ER sent him home with some fluid pills and an appointment with Dr. Parker the next day.

Dr Parker then in return made him an appointment with Dr. Varoon Sonny's cardiologist for Wednesday Aug 2.

By then he had been on the water pill for three days and has had some relief on his breathing.

At Dr Varoon's he was given an EKG and two more appointments for Dr Varoon's office in Geneseo one for an echo cardiograph and one for a stress test. Which could not be done at Dr. Varoons office in Dansville. Then when those test results are in, he will follow up with Dr Varoon.

Right now, it's a wait and see kind of thing.

They did tell us that the chemo he is on affects the heart and can cause heart disease. We did not know that was a side effect. Seems we learn something new at every turn.

We have not told the kids yet, because we don't want to get the lecture about how he should not be working. Working is our life, it's what he likes to do. We are not sure our kids understand that.

Neither Sonny or I want to resign to sitting around the house all day every day, we have energy and face it work is and has been both of our lives since we were kids.

Sonny went to Geneseo today for an Echocardiogram, must be it was somewhat ok, or safe enough for him to go home, because they didn't keep him. I say that because the doctor in Rochester said if he has the test and they let him go home then that's a good sign.

September 2017

A few things going on.

Sonny has a new oncologist, Dr. Passero. A younger man but he seems very through and nice. Biggest plus is he is American! Dr. Ifthi is semi-retired, and not seeing patients. We will miss him and Sheri.

Dr. Passero cut Sonny's chemo back to 21 days on and a week off. We are hoping that his will keep him from getting sick to his stomach every month.

Every month he has a few days of vomiting, and or diarrhea, usually the fourth week of chemo. They think it's because his system was getting too toxic with so much chemo.

Chemo has a positive effect on killing the cancer cells. In Sonny's case it is given to keep the cancer from growing, a maintenance dose. The down fall is it also can have an adverse effect on other body parts.

September 7 2017

Yesterday my dad passed away. He was 84 years old. He laid down to take a nap, because he was having stomach pain. This was nothing unusual at his age, the nap that is. He also had an abdominal aneurysm for over twenty years. He never had it repaired he just lived with it under doctor's watch and care. My dad did not like doctors and hospitals.

Dad was a very kind and thoughtful man. He loved his children and all children matter of fact. He was very good with all of them from infant to teens.

He and my mom were married thirty-eight years before he left her from to many years of her abuse. Not physical abuse, but verbal and emotional abuse. At times I think she actually hated my dad.

I will officiate my dad's funeral/memorial service. Not an easy task but an honorable one.

Sunday, September 11 Sonny thought he got bit by a spider. There was a small red mark on the small of his back, just above the cheek of his right-side butt. It was very itchy.

By the end of the day, it was painful and he thought maybe he scraped or bumped the spot on something but didn't remember what it was.

By Monday evening his right hip and butt was covered with little red blisters. He soaked in a hot bath with Epsom salts and it did help relieve the external pain and itching, but not the internal pain.

By Tuesday morning the pain was pretty severe.

He went to Doctor Parker, and was told it was shingles and is in the worse spot to get shingles.

They increased his Lyrica to double what he was taking and put him on Acyclovir as well to help shorten the duration of the disease, plus extra morphine for now to help with the pain.

The pain is pretty bad, he said it's like nothing he ever felt before. It's an internal pain that goes deep beyond the blisters you can see. We have no idea how long the pain will last. He does take a lot of Epsom salts bath soaks to get relief from the itching. We learned the pain with shingles is nerve pain that's why they put him on extra Lyrica.

October 4, 2017 It has been all most a month with shingles. The blisters are gone and he is covered in large burgundy colored scars on every spot there was shingles blisters. The scars themselves are now very itchy.

The pain is now isolated deep in his muscles. The pain is happening less and less, and ice packs help to numb the pain. He uses calamine lotion for the itchiness, and he has to stay on the Acyclovir for a very long time, possibly a year or shingles could come back.

First weekend in October We took my mom and her sisters to Kentucky to tour the life size Ark exhibit. It was impressive and a very nice time except for my mom's attitude, very pouty, unsociable, and not happy at all. My mom's attitude is nothing new and at times is very hard to deal with.

...was...uncomfortable when driving long distances whatever because of the resident shingles flare.

When entering the Arc there is a video room that shows the building of the Ark very impressive. Sonny and I had a good time and would like to go back some day.

Sonny was a bit uncomfortable when driving long distances at a time, because of the residual shingles affect.

I did a lot of the driving so Sonny could lay down in the camper so he's not sitting so much and causing his body heat and irritate the shingles pain. I don't mind driving the fifth wheel camper but I cannot back it up to park it.

Shortly after we got back from Indiana, we decided we would look for a Motorhome. That would be easier for me to drive and I could back it up and park it with no problem. We found a beautiful used 2013 Winnebago with less than 10,000 miles on it. We traded in the 5th wheel.

December 4 2017

He has been having a bad week, unable to sleep without sweating up a puddle. He has moments of confusion, more weight loss, always thirsty, and though he drinks a lot of water and pees a lot he can never empty his bladder and has bladder leaks without control.

His fasting over night blood sugar reading is in the 400's, very high and not good. He went to the doctor to see what was going on. Doctor Parker said everything was due to his diabetes flaring up again. The doctor put him back on Metformin 850mg twice a day. His A1C was at 9.3 It has never ever been that high.

Sonny and I think it is due to the steroids he has been taking. Without doctors prescription.

He couldn't tell the doctor about them because he orders them from a mail order pharmacy. Not under doctor's advice but under Sonny's insistence because they help with his pain.

Dec. 10 Sonny has been on the Metformin since the fifth and is doing much better. He still test high, still over 200 but coming down, and he is feeling more like his old self again. High blood sugar can sure make one feel strange.

December 20

Sonny is feeling pretty good in the last week. Blood sugar is getting under control and all body functions are or seem to be back to normal. He is very happy about that. I have been getting ready for Christmas. The weather hasn't been all that bad for December.

Another year has passed since the diagnosis and over all things are good, one day at a time.

There are so many things he used to just do without even one thought, things he wanted to do, things he had to do so he did, but not now!

He can't just jump out of bed and get moving, get on with the day. First of all, soon as he goes to move to sit up to get out of bed, he has immediate bone pain. First he sits on the side of the bed, when pain in his bones subside, he then gets up on his feet, shuffles to where ever it is he is heading.

If it's to the bathroom, well that too takes a little longer, movements to sit or the desire and action to stand are all pending on his pain level.

Then to get dressed takes a while too. Be sure and choose socks that are easy to get on, because the back has so much pain in his spine to bend over and put on his socks. He gets cold easier than he used to, so does he put on layers and therefore be able to take off a shirt if he gets to warm, or does he dress like everyone else.

Will his hands work to even button the buttons on his shirt, or tie his shoes? Where he used to be dressed, coffee in hand and out the door in twenty minutes or less, sometimes now takes about and hour to hour and half, and leaves him exhausted.

Most normal people can start their day with all the energy they need without even giving it a second thought, they just move, get things done, all their possibilities completed in a single days' time. They don't worry that what they are about to do, will affect how they feel later.

Sonnys whole day's decisions all depend on what move he makes at the moment always having to think ahead how what he does at the moment will affect the rest of his day.

The hardest thing he has had to learn or should I say accept, is to slow down, to realize he can't do everything in a day or two days or even in a weeks' time. You see he has always been a man who goes a hundred miles per hour from sun up to sun down. Then would get up the next day and do it all over again. Nothing stopped him.

Some days are worse than others, but I have to say this, his determination is endless no matter how he is feeling on any particular day, he always tries to give every day his best effort.

He has resigned to the fact that he can't do what he used to. He can do some things but most take a whole lot longer or even if at all, and that is hard for him, because he has been the go-to guy for everyone. He knows how to build or fix anything anyone has ever needed.

If Sonny or anyone can think it, Sonny can build it.

Just to plan his day he always has to strategize, and factor in what he wants to accomplish with how he feels. It's a whole new life style. The life style difference of being healthy or being sick. The kind of sickness or disease no one sees when they look at him, but he feels with every breath!

Christmas 2017 was another great day, and another year under his belt. Four years now since the cancer diagnosis. We are coping very well and deal with any issues that come up. Feeling invincible.

Clock wise from 7:00 Jax, Evan, Gavin, Aidan,
Trinity, Kendal, Ariana, Trevor, and Kylie

February 4 2018

Today is Libby and Trinity's birthday. Our daughter in law Vanessa is having cake and ice cream for them. On the way to their house, Sonny and I stopped to pick up his mom. She doesn't drive any more. We also had to stop and pick up our two youngest grandchildren, Kendal and Jax at their other grandmas.

I went into their grandmas house to get them. I knocked on the door, and Karen answered it. As I stepped inside, their rottweiler dog lunged at me and bit me on the thigh of my right leg. It hurt like hell. We don't know why she bit me. I was no threat I only stepped inside the door after Karen opened it.

I dropped my jeans right then and there to look at my leg. There was a hole in my leg from the dog's teeth. All I could think about was there is my toddler grandson, his face the same height as the dog's mouth. What if it had been his face and not my leg?

They helped me get the kids out to the car and we left.

I never told Sonny what happened until we were on our way because I know he would have gone in and killed the dog or worse.

The next day Karen and Jay reported the dog bite to the department of health. By law they had to. The county health department contacted me and told me to go to the doctors to get it looked at and documented. The dog has had all its shots but I was not its first time it has bit someone, just the first one that had been legally reported. The dog had to be quarantined and then put down in ten days.

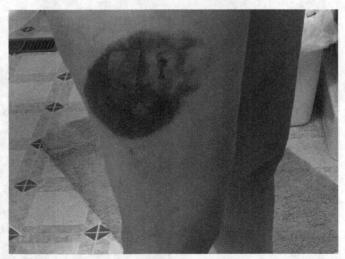

It bleed for some time and left a huge bruise on my thigh muscle

Last week in February 2018

We packed the motorhome and hit the road for a three-week vacation to Texas. We traveled to see Sonny's cousin Joe and his wife in San Antonio. Then we went to see our old friends Jack and Sherill and their family.

It was a great time; the weather was perfect. On the way back to NY we stopped in Nashville Tennessee for three days.

While we were in Texas, NY had a big snow and ice storm. People in our area lost power for many days. Our place included. But it didn't really matter no one was home. Turns out it did matter because when the electric came back on our freezer motor burned out from the power surge. When we got back three weeks later everything in the freezer was spoiled and very stinky!

June 2018

It's been almost six months since I wrote, which means our life has been uneventful and normal. Well whatever normal is now days. Just no major health issues and he is doing well.

We had the huge pine tree in our front yard taken down. It towered over sixty feet tall and the roots were exposed above ground, huge branches fell weekly. We were afraid one of these days it was going to topple right on the house.

Sometime a couple months ago Sonny's right upper shoulder started hurting more than just the normal arthritis. They both bother him but the right more than the left. It was interfering with his sleep so he mentioned it to Dr Passero in May, and doctor ordered an MRI of both shoulders.

June 25 Sonny went to Noyes in Dansville with the order for the MRI. When he got there, he found out that our health insurance company, only authorized one shoulder to be done with MRI. He had to choose which one, he chose his right because that is the worse painful one out of the two.

A week later Dr. Passero called him and told him he has a deep tear in his shoulder muscles and is referring him to an orthopedic. His appointment with an orthopedic is on July 20th.

July 11 Sonny had to go see the oncologist. We thought it was just a routine for his pre orthopedic visit, so he can get approved for shoulder repair. Turned out he wanted to see us because Sonny's blood proteins numbers are going up.

This means the cancer that was present but non active, is once again becoming active. He has to go back to blood work and being seen by the oncologist every month now, vs every other month.

Along with a bunch of follow up testing, full body X-rays, PET scans, bone marrow biopsy, to see if anything in his bones have changed since the last test, he had a year ago.

Right now, we are on hold until yesterday test results are in.

I understand doctors being precautious, but really, we feel this time they blew this test all up in our face. They got us all worked up, upset, and worried. Later what we found out exactly what the increase in proteins means, and we feel it was uncalled for.

In actual reality the protein increase was .1, point one increase in proteins!

REALLY .1? Sonny is so pissed. When he found out the protein increase number was only .1 Get real, let us know when there is something to really worry about!

July 20 2018

Today we went to an orthopedic specialist surgeon Dr Volasian. In Rochester. He told us Sonny has two out of four shoulder muscles on his right shoulder that are torn and detached from the shoulder joint. He told us it can be repaired but to be prepared for a long hard recovery.

Sonny has to have clearance from all his doctor's. Dr Parker his primary care dr. His oncologist and his cardiologist. Then he will be scheduled for the surgery.

The orthopedic said it can be done by laparoscopy, in and out the same day surgery. As long as he can reach and repair the muscle in the front of the shoulder.

There will be at least six months recovery to full use of his arm, excuse me!

They don't know my husband's determination and drive.

They say the pain is cruel and like nothing you'll ever know.

He has to get it done. He can't keep living with the pain he has from the way it is.

I suspect that this is all part of the reason he has had shoulder pain for the last twelve to eighteen months!

July 2018 Another great family reunion

Sonny has achieved clearances from all his doctors.

He is scheduled for right shoulder arthroscope surgery

Rotator cuff repair

Shoulder arthroscopic with debridement

Bicep tenodesis

This will be done in Rochester at the surgical outpatient center on Sawgrass Road

On Wednesday August 15, in and out same day surgery.

August 2018

We have replaced our couch in the living room with a double recliner so that he can use a left-handed recliner for comfortable sleeping while he recovers, since it's the right shoulder and he won't be able to use it to put a recliner in the sleep position. Therefore, he needed a left-handed recliner. The doctor said he needs to sleep in the recliner for several weeks

Wednesday August 15 2018

6a.m. we are at the UR medical and surgical center on Sawgrass Drive Rochester for Sonny's shoulder surgery.

All pre op done by 7:30a.m. A hundred questions asked over and over, by registration personnel, by the nurses, by the surgical team and same answers given to everyone. IV started, his shoulder marked, nerve block administered.

They gave him Tylenol and slight sedation to relax him before they take him to OR.

Surgery took almost two hours. All went well. The surgeon said there was massive damage and tears to the muscles and he was able to repair it all. We are thankful for that.

We were back home by 1:30p.m.

He has no pain today because of the nerve block which is set to start wearing off after fourteen to sixteen hours, which means by midnight he might start to have pain.

Over all he is doing very good and has his positive attitude back.

We are thinking ahead to when his shoulder doesn't hurt.

September 28 2018

He has been doing quite well in the shoulder recovery. Going to physical therapy twice a week. That usually leaves him in pain for a few hours after wards, but he's getting good movement, much better than we ever expected.

Our friend Roy has been helping him a lot. Taking care of the pellets, and end of summer season mowing.

He is out of the sling now and only wears it occasionally when he sleeps, so he doesn't try to put his arm over his head.

Basically, his only restriction is not to lift anything yet. He's not supposed to lift for three months.

A lot has happened in the last month. I traded my Chrysler Town & Country in for a 2019 KIA, all-wheel drive, leather heated and AC seats, GPS, and a lot of other perks. I love it. I think it's the most comfortable car I have ever owned. A bit smaller than the SUV's I have owned in the past, two row seating instead of three.

Two weeks after I got my car Sonny sold his big dual wheel dodge pickup truck and goose neck trailer and downsized to a 2018 Ford Sport pick up. His truck also has all the comforts of luxury driving. It's a very nice pick up. Both our new vehicles are the same color burgundy. We have always loved red vehicles.

Matter of fact Sonny once had a bright red 1960 souped up Ford Galaxy convertible with a black rag top. He loved that car. He got into so much trouble with it. Scared the crap out of me, how fast it went!

The cancer is becoming a little active again and showing in his blood numbers with an ever so slight increase. He is back going to the oncologist every month. They are monitoring him closely.

Dr. Passero said he can change Sonny's treatment and add a boost to his chemo. That would mean monthly trips to the infusion center. Sonny isn't sure he wants to do that. He just doesn't want to be drugged up, the shots in the stomach are very painful, and he hates taking so many steroids that go with him getting the IV's.

Steroids are part of the chemo cocktail they want to put him on. Steroids really mess up his diabetes and his neuropathy, but at the same time help control the pain. He just doesn't want to go through any of it any more. He just wants to wait and see. Ultimately the doctors leave his treatment choice up to him. They give us all the information and its always up to Sonny whether or not he goes on with what they are suggesting.

October 2018

We took my mom and her sisters on their annual sister vacation. This year to Mansfield Ohio to visit with their sister-in-law Cheryl and to go through the Bible Walk Museum and Church.

It was very nice and quite interesting. It is also the church where their brother Bob preached. For the most part all went well except, again my mom with the poor me, childish, wait on me attitude.

I will not do it again; I am done taking mom on vacation so sick and tired of all the pout and no happiness from her. Everyone has to cater to her, trying to make sure she is happy. It's a constant battle. If she's not happy, which is most of the time, she makes it miserable for everyone else!

Sonny seemed to be coming down with a cold and was quite run down by the time we got back from Indiana and Ohio on Thursday.

By Monday he was having a hard time breathing and coughing up bloody mucus. He is very run down. He thinks it's pneumonia again.

He did not want to go to the doctor because he had an appointment coming up on Wednesday so he stuck it out with cold and congestion medication and humidifier.

Turns out he had pneumonia and was put on antibiotics and again the steroids. He took three days off from work.

It took until Saturday for him to even start to feel a little better, and things are getting better for his breathing too, he is just left with an awful cough.

November 20 2018

Sonny is still coughing quite a bit and I think he needs another round of antibiotics and steroids. He's been coughing for a month now. He rattles when he breaths, and when he sleeps, he sounds like an old-fashioned coffee percolator.

We have both lost a lot of sleep in the last month. Him from coughing and me from either his noises and or his pacing around the house.

I do everything I can think of to make him comfortable but it doesn't work.

He goes to work almost every day except the weekends. He comes home exhausted every day, he really needs to stay home until he gets some strength and energy back.

He gets home from the farm and has energy to eat supper and that's it.

One thing, his appetite is good so he has that much going for him.

Sometimes he doesn't even have energy to take a shower. He does very little around the house until weekends. Then just what he has to, to get by. Such as clean the pellet stoves, and or clean his truck. He calls Roy quite often to help him with projects around the house. Roy doesn't mind. Usually when those two plan a job it always starts with food and goes from there! Hahaha

When I look back over the last five years, I see a man who is half of what he used to be. I see a man who at times looks defeated and has no hope and other times is determined to beat every health issue that comes up.

He used to always believe in himself and that he was going to beat this, but now more often than not all he talks about is dying. I try to encourage him and turn his thoughts to our future, but I see defeat in his eyes and his manors.

Many times, he says he's sick n tired of being sick n tired. He hates taking the medicines. He always said, he never wanted to be the person who takes a dozen pills a day. He says he just wants to go to sleep and not wake up. He doesn't want to linger in pain and a long-drawn-out painful death.

November 21 2018

Today was his regular oncologist appointment, but with sickness. He has had a chronic cough for a month now. He was treated last month with ZPack antibiotics, and steroids. That seemed to help for a few days but then the cough came back just as relentless as before, if not worse.

Dr. Passero sent him for a chest X-ray and sent him home with two antibiotics, amoxicillin and doxycycline, and an inhaler because the doctor is sure it is pneumonia.

His blood numbers are a bit of concern. Dr Passero is concerned about the white blood count being so low, and the total proteins number is very low. Sonny has to wait one more month to see if he can get over this pneumonia. Because the pneumonia can cause lower white blood count as well as the chemo.

Right now, only time will tell. Eat right, build his immune system, and get over the cough.

December 2018

Still coughing Dr Passero ordered a CAT scan before the next office visit.

December 19 We are back to Wilmont Cancer Center for routine visit. Blood numbers look good, much better, but persistent lung issues with chronic cough are a concern.

I suggested a treatment for lung fungus, but the doctor didn't seem to think that fungus was possible. The doctor once again put him on another round of antibiotics and steroids and referred him to a pulmonary specialist to see what is going on with this cough and reoccurring pneumonia since October.

He cannot get into the pulmonologist until April 29, 2019. Ridiculous!

I e-mailed Dr Passero and asked for an antiviral medication to see if that would help if it is fungus.

Dr Passero said no that Sonny had to wait until he saw the pulmonologist in April.

In the mean time since October Sonny has gone through multiple bottles of NyQuil.......Robitussin......Halls cough drops........sinus medication.......cold and flu medications........essential oils....... vaporizer.........diffusers...........Vick's vapo rub.......Blackberry Brandy...... whisky.......... all to try to help the relentless coughing.

He does not sleep well he is up about every one to two hours pacing, coughing, sleeping in the recliner. Yet he has to wait until April to see a pulmonary doctor!

This does not seem right to have to wait that long when his condition is chronic and has been ongoing for months!

He seemed to be pretty good over Christmas, except for the relentless cough. Another year behind us. We are blessed.

Clock wise from 6 o'clock Ariana, Trinity, Kendal,
Aidan, Trevor, Evan, Gavin, Jax, and Kylie

January 2019

Happy New Year

Sonny still has a relentless miserable chronic cough. I feel bad that he can't get any relief. His ribs are so sore from coughing so much.

At this point I really don't know what to do for him. He has an appointment with his primary care Dr. Parker in two weeks. I can only hope that Dr Parker will listen and hopefully prescribe an antiviral to see if it is a lung fungus and if an antiviral will help alleviate the cough.

Why won't the doctors address my concern about a lung fungus?

To Sonny and I it makes sense due to him working in such an environment as the farm shop and equipment with all the fungus and mold spores in the air on a daily basis. No one will address our concerns.

February 13 2019

Today Dr. Parker referred him to Dr Sakar in Dansville a ENT, (ear, nose, and throat doctor)

Dr Sakar did a scope through his nose and into his throat and did not find anything wrong. He felt it was involuntary cough spasms, due to having the cough for so long. He prescribed a cough suppressant pill that has codeine. The very first night it worked, the cough and night time gurgling has stopped too.

Ahhhh blessed quiet sleep for both of us.

Sonny woke up well rested and feeling much better, we both did. Thank you, doctor, Sakar.

March 3 2019

The prescription for the cough pills worked until they ran out, and the doctor will not give him refills.

He's back to coughing again. The time of no coughing and relief for him, only lasted two weeks. I feel so bad for Sonny. He should not have to go through this on top of everything else.

Sonny is not breathing very well. He is short of breath especially when he does any kind of work or even walking upstairs. He thinks he has pneumonia again, but he is home medicating he does not want to go to another specialist or doctor. They won't work with him or listen to us. He is taking mail order Zithromax, and prednisone 10mg, over the counter Mucinex, using a steam vaporizer with Vick's vapor rub in it, and sleeping upright in the recliner.

I guess we will give it a couple of days on this regimen and see how he feels.

March 17

He is off the antibiotics and steroids. His blood sugar is back too normal. He has an on again off again cough, and phlegm always percolates in his throat when he lays down. He sleeps with his mouth open. He spends most nights sleeping in the recliner. It's the only way he can breathe and we both can get sleep.

March 21 2019

In the last week he has been losing his balance and being very clumsy. Not really sure what that is all about. His blood pressure is good and so are his glucose levels. Possible short on oxygen due to all this congestion.

He has a rather large hernia in the lower middle of his abdomen. The chronic cough he has had only has exacerbated the hernia. At times it is quite painful for him, but he doesn't want to go to the doctor. He says he will either live with it or die with it. He is really hating going to doctor appointments. He hates that all doctors want to do is throw another pill at whatever the symptoms are.

March 31

Sonny is Sick with the stomach flu. Vomiting, feverish, and achy all over. He is only keeping ice chips and ginger ale down. He has coughing and a lot of congestion. He is self medicating again taking Pepto bismal and even that comes back up. I hope I don't get it.

Monday April 1

He is still sick with the stomach flu and stayed home from work and slept all day. He is still dealing with a bad cough but is now able to keep a little food and ginger ale down.

Tuesday April 2

He decided to go to work but came home at noon because of difficulty breathing. He has prednisone 40mg. in the medicine cabinet and he wanted to take it to see if it would help.

He's back to taking Zithromax and prednisone one in the morning and one at night

It's from an on-line pharmacy and expensive but it's what he wanted and it helps him. I cannot deny him the relief he gets from this when no doctors will help him.

Wednesday April 3

He really isn't much better, coughing, hard time breathing. Not sure what is going on.

After he was in bed about a half hour tonight, he said to me

"You know how some people complained of ringing in their ears? I hear music. Do you have the radio on in the sunroom? I said no, and at this time none of the TVs were on either.

I was reading, he said do you hear it too?" He told me he can hear the music perfectly clear. He does not have his hearing aids in his ears.

I told him "no" he said "I wish you could it is the most beautiful music I have ever heard........I can't even tell you what kind it is, not country, not rock n roll, just beautiful, peaceful, calming, and I'm not much into music but it's comforting to listen to."

Then he went to sleep.

Thursday April 4

He said he's feeling much better this morning, his cough doesn't seem quite as bad, but his breathing is a bit labored. He said he might call the doctor today. He did go to work, he probably shouldn't have, I'm not sure if he will stay all day.

I have to take Sonny's mom, Mary, to her doctor appointment and for her blood work. She doesn't drive anymore because her dementia is getting worse. I'm sure she knows how to drive but she may not remember how to get back home, or even where she is going.

Thursday April 4, 2019 2pm

I got a call from Sonny; he was at Dr Parker's in Cohocton. He called the doctor office from his job at the farm because he was having difficulty breathing and they told him to come right in.

Dr Parker did an EKG and told him he had congested heart failure and his heart was in afib. Now there is another diagnosis we never heard of. He needed to go to the hospital ER and be checked because the hospital has more equipment than the doctor office does.

Dr Parker wanted to call an ambulance to come to the office to pick Sonny up, but Sonny said no and called me to bring hm some clean clothes and pick him up at the doctor's office. I took him to the hospital.

We got to the ER around 2:45p.m. They did another EKG, heart ultra sound, and chest x-ray. He was having a hard time breathing, he was wheezing, and coughing. The ER doctor gave him a nebulizer breathing treatment of albuterol, but it did not help much.

They put oxygen nasal tube on him set at 2L. Then gave him a double dose of albuterol in the nebulizer plus an IV steroid to open up his lungs.

Around 4:30p.m. the ER doctor explained that his biggest worry is his afib. He told us an irregular heart beat can cause a stroke. They thought it was best to admit him overnight so he could be on the heart monitor and continue the breathing treatments and the IV's.

Sonny was not very happy about having to stay and is hoping they let him come home tomorrow.

Sonny was resting well and was breathing better. I left the hospital around 7:15p.m. to come home before dark, and take care of the animals and the stoves. I hate driving in the dark.

When I got home and walked in the door, Arlene was here. Of course, not in person but in spirit, she's been dead for years. I could smell her, the way her house always smelled when I would walk in. Kind of musty, with a mixture of food odors. My house smelled like that. Am I turning into that old lady smell?

Arlene was an elderly neighborhood widow lady that my family and I would take care of at her home, until she passed away in 2007.

Friday April 5

I arrived at the hospital around 10:00a.m. Sonny was a little bit improved, and breathing better.

They have him on albuterol nebulizer every four hours, IV antibiotics, IV steroids, IV heart rhythm medication called Diliazem, and Eliquis blood thinner.

They are very concerned about the afib, but did agree to let him go home at his insistence.

He was discharged and We came home around 3p.m.
I got him settled in at home and then went to get his prescriptions
He is taking Diltiazem 30mg every six hours for afib
Prednisone 5mg steroids on eight-day taper
Amoxicillin 850mg for seven days
Eliquis blood thinner 5mg three times a day
Mucinex DM twice a day
Albuterol nebulizer treatments every four hours as needed

Sunday April 7

He has terrible congestion and cough with a lot of choking phlegm

He is very uncomfortable trying to sleep. He cannot lay down flat it constricts his breathing so he sleeps in his recliner.

Very bad coughing spells, night sweats, and discomfort. I hate seeing him like that. As hard as I try and want to do more, there is nothing I can do to help him.

Monday April 8

This week is full of doctor appointments due to his being hospitalized last week.

Tuesday April 9 2019

Finally, a good day for Sonny, the medications seem to finally be taking hold and working in his favor. He's feeling very good. Today he took his mom to her doctor appointment in Corning to get her skin cancer mapped for radiation treatments starting next week.

He picked up his sister Lori at her job in Corning and they all went together, then went out to lunch.

It was a good day for all of them. I'm glad they had that time together. It meant a lot to Sonny.

It's very rare for his family to include him or us in anything.

It's not because we haven't tried. We have invited them to holiday and family dinners and gatherings, but most of the time they always have plans already in place. That's ok, we understand that.

Wednesday April 10

Today we went to Rochester for his monthly oncology appointment.

Dr Passero was very concerned about Sonny's congestive heart failure and afib and wants him to follow up with his cardiologist.

As we already found out chemo can affect the heart.

On the other hand, we got some good news the cancer and blood numbers were all in the normal range. So many friken ups and downs with this cancer and the treatments. It messes with your mind and body, as well!

Thursday April 11

Back in Rochester this morning to see Dr Varon, his cardiologist.

They did an EKG and it still shows his heart in afib

Sonny told the doctor he did not want to take the blood thinner and heart pill any more due to side effects of dizziness, and foggy thinking.

Dr Varon changed his prescription to:

Metoprolol 50mg once a day for afib
Digoxin .25mg once a day for heart rhythm
Fulmoside diuretic to help get fluid out of his lungs

I picked up his new change in prescriptions, but Sonny refuses to take the heart medication and the blood thinner due to side effects. He has on his own, gone back to taking just aspirin 81mg once a day against medical advice. He says it's his body, his choice not mine, or the doctors.

He said he's getting so sick of doctors shoving this pill and that pill at him and constantly going to appointments. He questions taking so many medications altogether and them working against each other in his system. He does have a point.

Dr. Varon ordered up a bunch of blood work, an echocardiogram, and chest X-ray. He will have a recheck appointment next Thursday.

The echocardiogram showed some concern with possibility of heart infection. They said the valve looked sludgy. Off to the lab he went for immediate blood draws for infection cultures. Cultures take much longer for results than blood test, and can take days to over a week to show results.

He is very tired and glad to finally be home and back in his recliner.

We aren't sure how long it will take for the infection culture to return. Hopefully within the next three to five days we will hear something.

Friday April 12 2019

Today he has an appointment with Dr Parker. A follow up from last Thursday when Dr Parker sent him to the ER.

Something very strange and good happened to Sonny, in the middle of the night last night.

He woke me up around 1:45a.m. and said he just had to tell me what was going on. He said he woke up because he felt different. Suddenly he felt very peaceful, he had no trouble breathing, and was very happy. I mean very happy.

He had no congestion, he felt rested, but most of all very happy and was just laughing out loud.

He woke me up and wanted me to know he felt good, very good. His breathing is not labored, he has no phlegm or rattle when he breaths.

I cannot explain it, other than for some reason he is much favored by God and it feels like a divine intervention. Even if it were for a short time. I'm glad he has this peace and comfort.

Time will tell. We will see how the day goes.

Today was a good day, he was actually human, he was nice to me, happy, and feeling healthy. He even took his motorcycle out for a long ride.

Saturday April 13

Oh, the difference twelve hours can make
I have been up most of the night because of Sonny
He was very noisy, bad phlegm, coughing, gurgling, talking loudly in his sleep, moaning, humming, singing, pacing the house, sweating profusely. I don't know what is going on. I couldn't even dare guess. Just half a day ago he was feeling very good and doing well.
Such a roller coaster ride, up, down, up, down!

It's 5a.m. He has only been up an hour, he is very confused. He moans, he sings songs that make no sense, he tried to test his blood sugar and put the test strip in the devise upside down, he didn't know how to use the needle pen to get blood for the test strip, I had to show him.

Then he wanted coffee. I had already made the coffee. He went to the kitchen got his cup and put the creamer in the empty cup and added a couple scoops of fresh coffee grounds, stirring it together, came into the living room and darn near choked on it before I realized what he had done. I took his cup cleaned it and made him a cup of coffee. He is very confused. Possibly chemo brain again.

Today he was nasty and mean to me. He asked me for hot dogs, I told him it would take a few minutes to thaw them then I'll cook him a couple.

He told me "that is to long, "go get fucked, on second thought go fuck yourself cause no one else would fuck your ugly ass" and then said "I don't even know why I loved you in the first place, I should have never married you" he was very mean! He put both fist in my face and said I could take you out in a heartbeat" then he laughed.

He is clearly out of his mind. I don't know why he gets like this, like his brain doesn't even function.

I have to keep reminding myself "its chemo brain, its chemo brain, he would not say those things if he were in his right mind" That still does not erase the fact that words like that hurt me to the core!

Then he wanted to use his nebulizer and he opened the top and put a cough drop in it and turned it on. I asked him what the hell he was doing he said he just needed some fresh air. I took the cough drop out and put the albuterol in and gave it to him he used it for a few minutes then tried to make our little dog use it, and he laughed and laughed.

The news was on tv, and a story came on about a recall on baby seats because children were getting injured, and he said to me, "that could have been me, I wonder why I didn't die" He gets out of his chair and goes to the bedroom and checks all over the bed to see if it was the same brand as the baby seat.

I told him he was crazy; he doesn't sleep in a baby seat. He told me go back to the living room that I was the fucked up crazy one.

The moaning and humming sounds are driving me nuts. Maybe I'm just tired from hardly any sleep!

Yet, yesterday was such a good day and held so much promise.

I have to take my mom shopping later this morning. I'm wondering if I should even leave him alone. I have no idea what he will do if I'm not here.

He is acting like he did a few years back when the doctors said he was experiencing chemo brain. Come to think of it, that was around April and Easter time too.

He fixed his own breakfast because he decided he didn't want hot dogs after all, he had a bowl of cereal and took his pills. While eating he was on his I-pad tablet and came across an old massy Ferguson tractor someone is selling on the market place. He was trying to figure out how to contact the man.

I told him just send a message and the person will get back to him later, it's too early for most people.

He said "it's six in the morning the ass hole should be out of bed by now."

After he ate his breakfast, I told him to go get dressed, he argued with me that he was dressed, I said "no you're not you just have under wear and a t shirt on." He goes to the bed room to get his pants, he comes out with his belt around his t shirt and no jeans on, just underwear.

I told him he forgot something, he asked what? I said your pants, he said well we can't have sex if I put my pants on. I told him "we haven't had sex in six years, nothing has changed, go get your jeans on."

He went out in the back room and put his work jeans. He was out there quite a while and didn't come back in so I went out and checked on him. I found him scooting around in an old office chair on wheels, that belonged to my dad. Back and forth repetitively in front of the storage shelves. When I asked him "what are you doing, he said just having a little fun."

I came back in the kitchen and next thing I know the Kubota RTV is running and parked in the drive way. I went out and asked him "where he was going?" He said "oh just for a ride."

At this moment 6:45a.m. and he is out riding around somewhere.

I'm not sure where he is or what he is doing. Because of his state of mind, I get out of my nightgown and dressed in case he needs rescued from who knows what situation he may have gotten into.

I decided I better go see if I could find him, due to his confusion. I get in my car and drove down around the pond and shop property. I could not see him anywhere. I drove two miles up to the village and could not find him. By the time I got back to 70A he had hooked the yard roller onto the RTV and was rolling the big ditch in front of the shop. I have no idea where he had been.

8:30a.m. He still has not come back home, or so I thought. I went out once again to check on him because I knew he was out with the roller.

I went outside to find him and see if I could hear or see the Kubota somewhere. I could not. I checked the garage and the barn he was not there. Then I spotted the Kubota RTV parked in the equipment lot.

I went down there to see if he was ok. I found him his head against the window, sound asleep inside the Kubota. I just let him sleep.

Somewhere around 9a.m. he unhooked the roller and parked the Kubota in the garage and came in the house.

By then he was thinking a bit more clearly, like himself. He said to me, "I'm so fucked up, I have no idea what I'm doing" then he changed his shirts because he was all sweaty again. Now he's in the sun room in the recliner talking to the cat and dog. Currently at this moment he is in his right lucid mind.

I took my mom shopping like I promised her I would. It was a very worrisome four hours until I got back.

Turned out while I was gone Libby had called her dad with some questions about picking out windows they needed. He apparently was in his right mind and went to Hornell to meet Libby and Derick to look at windows for their gym. Libby ended up riding back with him because he kept falling to sleep leaning against things in Lowes. He also had moments of not very clear thinking while they were shopping.

After they got back from Hornell, he had a fixed himself a sandwich lunch and slept the rest of the day until supper was ready at six. He seemed pretty clear headed, and more like himself after his nap and he ate a good supper.

Over all it was a normal nice warm afternoon and evening. He seemed clear minded enough so he got on his motorcycle and went for a ride.

He came home, he was in a good mood, he did his nebulizer breathing treatment, then fell asleep in his chair.

His hands shake and tremor a lot. He has gone through this with the tremors for about three years now, it's our understanding that the chemo has caused nerve damage in his body, he just can't steady them. At times this really bothers him, especially if he's trying to do any kind of precise work where a steady hand and fine motor coordination is needed.

Sunday April 14 2019

Up at 4a.m. same as any other day.

He is doing well today, seems almost normal.

Just like a switch, from yesterday not able to function, to being seemingly normal self today.

I don't get it. I really don't understand this part of the cancer or should I say the treatment. We don't believe the cancer causes all this confusion but that it has everything to do with the treatment, toxic chemicals and poison. We just never know day to day anymore.

The thing is when the confusion and agitation hits him and then his system returns to normal, he never remembers how he was acting and talking during the confusion. That time is just lost to him, and he is totally dumbfounded, remorseful, and very sorry when I tell him all he did during those times.

He always feels bad about mistreating me and others when he gets like that.

We just don't understand. It's an awful fact that chemo can control the cancer but also destroy other body parts such as your brain and heart!

Tuesday April 16

We had to go to Batavia to Dr Varons his cardiologist today for vitals check and EKG. We stopped at Noyes Hospital in Dansville for a chest x ray and pre work ups before the TEE on Thursday.

Thursday April 18 2019

We had to be at Rochester General Hospital for a heart procedure called TEE this morning.

Where they put a tiny camera down his throat and look at his heart from the inside to see what is going on and if they can see a reason why it's always in afib. The plan from there to shock his heart to try to get it back in normal rhythm.

We get there and get checked in and settled into a pre op room. The procedure was supposed to be at 8a.m. We found out after the preadmission questioning, that they wouldn't do the procedure because he stopped taking his blood thinner.

Thing is Dr Varon said he didn't need to take it, that he could go back to taking his aspirin.

Turns out we were given the wrong pre op orders. In this case he should have stayed on the blood thinners until after the procedure.

They had to give him an Eliquis blood thinner and wait four hours for it to take affect before they can do the procedure.

They finally took him in a 12:15p.m.

Around 1:30p.m when Sonny was still in the procedure room, the OR doctor came out to get me from the waiting room. He took me to a conference room to talk to me. My first though was, this can't be good if he couldn't tell me in the waiting room.

He told me the TEE showed both the aortic and mitral heart valves are enlarged and leaking. They shocked his heart four times with the defibrillator to try to fix the afib. It didn't work his heart is still in afib.

We got home around 6p.m. We were both exhausted. Neither of us got much sleep Wednesday night and then to be at the hospital all day was very tiring.

If you have never had to just sit around a wait, you wouldn't believe how tiring it can be to always be waiting. You might be just sitting, reading, watching the waiting room tv, but your mind is doing cardio training at a hundred miles an hour.

He has an appointment Thursday April 25 with Dr. Varon in Dansville. He will go over all the findings of today and make some medication changes and decisions.

Sunday April 21, 2019 Easter at our house with all our kids and grandkids. It was a beautiful sunny day.

Wednesday April 24

Sonny has been on Eliquis, a blood thinner two times a day
Metoprolol ER Succinate a heart regulation pill one time a day

He has been taking these since last Thursday and has had a lot of moments of confusion and inability to follow conversations. Easily confused, and a lot of brain fog.

He has vomited almost every day. We think it may be the medication change that is causing the stomach upset.

He is having a lot of cramping in his hands. His fingers cramp up so bad he can't use his hands. Holding ice packs in his hands is the only relief he gets

I'm not sure what is going on there.

We thought maybe it's like the leg muscle cramps so he started drinking more water and added gator aid. The cramping has become less painful. Maybe it is a low sodium issue from the vomiting, sweating, and loosing body fluids.

April 29

Early start today 6a.m.

We are on our way to Strong in Rochester for a heart catherization, to look for blockage.

Dr. Fred Ling did the procedure. I have to say we were not really educated on what was going to take place.

They put in an IV in his left arm, for medication. They put in an IV port in the right arm for blood draws.

Turns out they went through three arteries two in his right arm, and one in his right groin. All of that was done ahead of the procedure. If they find blockage, they will put in stents right then and there.

Even after all these years of doctors, specialist, and appointments, we still can't keep up with all the information thrown at us. Many times, I feel so uneducated but at the same time know I have learned more than I ever wanted to know about cancer, chemo, medication and its side effects!

1:30p.m.

I just talked to the surgeon he has no blockage in any of the arteries.

His heart pressures are good and the doctors are pleased.

They did confirm what his cardiologist already suspected. The pig aortic valve replacement from 2010 is deteriorating and the mitral valve is leaking and separating. All of that in turn allows blood to pool in his heart and not get pumped out like normal, and that pooling blood has caused his heart to enlarge.

He is in recovery from the catheterization. After recovery we were told to wait here in the conference room to talk to one of the heart team doctors to find out what the possibility of surgery is, his options, and the risk are of replacing the valves in the near future.

They said there is a big risk of infection due to the cancer treatments and no immune system because of the chemo. We waited for a couple of hours in the conference room, and no one from the cardiac team ever showed up! Total lack of communication on the part of the staff.

Turns out we never saw anyone from the heart team because we already have an appointment on May 8 with Dr Knight, Sonny's cardiac surgeon.

They let us sit there in the conference room all that time. It wasn't until I went to the unit nurses' station and asked a staff member when the cardiac team member was going to be there, that we had been waiting two hours already. Then I was told we didn't need to wait any longer, we could go home!

Sonny was not happy at all. He hates waiting, even more than I do!

Dr. Knight was the one who replaced his heart valve, aortic tube, and removed the aneurysm in 2010.

It's been a hard couple of weeks.

Wednesday April 24 Sonny's mom was admitted to Noyes hospital in Dansville NY. She had to be admitted because her blood pressure was falling fast, she could not sit up, hold her head up, walk, or stand. She was in very bad shape.

Turns out she had a UTI and the infection was invading her whole body through her blood system, including her brain.

She was put on IV antibiotics and responded very well as far as the infection goes.

As she started getting better her dementia made its self even more present.

Evenings and nights were especially bad for her. A condition of elderly dementia patients called sundowners.

Sundowners syndrome is basically like a baby who gets days and nights mixed up. With Mary there was a side of angriness, and combativeness.

They turn into a type of person you don't recognize. Very sad.

Sonny's sister Barb flew in from Florida on Wednesday to help Lori with their mom.

I do what I can to help when I can, but at the same time I am taking care of Sonny and he is my priority. Barb is planning on staying until Friday then she will go back to Florida.

Mary has been diagnosed of Dementia/Alzheimer's with meanness. Though not all of us have seen the side of meanness. At times she directs it to Lori. I know if Mary was able to think clearly there is no way she would ever say anything bad to or against Lori. Very sad to hear this.

For now, she remembers who we all are, and our children, but is confused on the great grandkids, that in time is bound to change. Most time she has a hard time following a conversation. She can talk clear headed when remembering the past. Her early child hood, her parents and siblings, her early married life and running the farm with Paul. But many things about the present upset her and confuse her.

Today April 30th Mary is being moved to Taylor Health care in Bath for rehab.

Personally, I don't think she will ever come home, or at least not alone.

The doctor said she cannot go home unless she has around the clock care. Unfortunately, her insurance won't pay for that, they only approved two hours a day.

Stupid health insurance writers! Simple pencil pushers who sit behind a desk and call the shots about our health!

She is not at all happy about going to Taylor, she thought she was going home. All she has asked for since she got admitted to Noyes was that she wants to go home. She doesn't understand the safety issues and concerns if she goes home alone. From her inability to safely shower and dress herself, to preparing meals safely to taking her daily medications. It's not that no one wants her home, it's just a safety issue.

I understand her want to be home; we all just want to be home. She wanted to die at home in her own bed. Seems that is the request of most all elderly people.

May 8 2019

Today we have to go to Strong to see Sonny's cardiac surgeon to find out how and what they will be doing to repair his heart valves.

Then he has an oncologist appointment afterwards.

I think we will be there most of the day, we are preparing for that.

We saw Dr. Knight and one of his interns.

We were told Sonny's heart is strong but that the aortic valve is leaking badly due to tissue deterioration. The mitral valve is leaking also but not as bad as the aortic valve. His heart is enlarged, and the aortic artery tissue is deteriorating also. All of it needs replaced.

This time they want to put in mechanical valves, and pig tissue aortic artery. He will have to have an open-heart procedure again. This time the recovery might take a bit longer and be more difficult because at this time he is not as physically strong as he was nine years ago.

We won't know when he will have it done until the surgery scheduling secretary calls us later this week.

Sonny is feeling positive and a bit apprehensive at the same time. My feeling is, in the long run he will be ok but that it will take a little longer this time than it did in 2010.

If he doesn't get the surgery, he won't live another year, if he gets it done, he can die on the operating table of complications.

Not much of a guaranteed life choice. We will go with faith that once again he will be healed and well.

He said he's tired, tired of living a medical life that has no guarantees. Tired of taking so much medication, tired of the demanding doctor appointments. He said he'd give anything, everything he owns to have his health back. It's all so heart breaking to see him go through all of this.

Dr. Knights office called today his surgery is scheduled for June 10, 2019. He has month to change his mind or go through with it.

May 9 Sonny's birthday.

Uneventful quiet night. He got home around 2:30p.m. from the farm.

His knee hurts pretty bad and is bruised and swollen a bit.

He fell off the scrap metal truck on Monday the sixth of May, right onto cement floor, hit his face and knee. We will keep an eye on it, because at this point, I can't convince him to go to the doctor or the ER to get it checked out. He is fearful they will admit him in the hospital.

Monday May 13

Sonny has been falling asleep in a blink of an eye. He can sleep all night, with the exception of going to the bathroom a couple of times, and can still fall back to sleep very quickly. He is eating good again, and getting good sleep.

Today he got home from the farm around 2:30p.m. same as every day now. Thing is, I did not know he was home. He never came in the house until around 4p.m. He said he got home parked the truck in the barn and rested his head against the window and instantly fell asleep, he never took off his seat belt or turned off the truck. What woke him was the need to go to the bathroom, then he realized the truck was still running.

He came in went to the bathroom, took a shower, changed into his pajamas and a clean T shirt, sat in his chair and went back to sleep. I woke him at 5:30p.m. for supper.

At supper he was a little confused about what day it was. He was talking about the farm as to what was accomplished yesterday on the new wash bay. I reminded him that yesterday was Mother's Day and no one worked on it then. He insisted yesterday was Monday and he went to work.

I corrected him and reminded him that yesterday was Sunday, that it rained all day and we took our moms out to breakfast. He still insisted it was Monday and told me to stop fucking with his mind. I got his tablet and showed him the date on the home page, then he just said "my mind is so fucked up I can't even think".

After supper he took his evening medications and went to sleep.

I guess sometimes I should just let him think what he's thinking without correcting him. I just don't know how to handle these things!

Tuesday May 14

He seemed to sleep well last night. I only heard him up a couple of times. His knee is still bothering him and I want him to go get it checked out but he said it's just bruised it will take time to get better. He fell on it a week ago, if it was just a bruise it would feel better by now.

He got up at 4a.m. same as always, got dressed for work, fixed a cup of coffee and sat down to watch the news but went right back to sleep. He didn't even drink his coffee. I woke him up at five and asked him if he was staying home today, he said no. He got up and ate breakfast. I packed his lunch, and he went out into the mud room to get his work shoes on.

Next thing I know he came back in and said he would go to work later that he was going to go take a nap. He didn't even get undressed, he crawled under the covers in his work clothes and went right to sleep.

He woke up around 9:30a.m. and was doing much better. He went to the farm and came home around 3:30p.m.

He napped very little before supper and not at all after supper. I'm not sure what's going on, because he hasn't stayed awake after work in months. Today turned out to be a good day for him. We both love days like this, very encouraging.

Wednesday May 15

He slept well last night, was wide awake this morning feeling pretty good, and went to the farm.

Friday May 17

Sonny went to doctor Parker on his own because he can't stand the pain in his knee. Dr. Sent him for X ray and is setting up an appointment for an orthopedic to look at it.

He argued with me that it happened over a month ago. I told him it was two weeks ago last Monday. He basically called me a liar. I showed him the entry in this journal, then he believed me.

Thank goodness I have kept up on this medical journal. The dates and treatments records have come in handy more than once.

Saturday May 25

We decided to go away for the weekend, so we packed up the motorhome. A change of scenery, might make him feel better.

We are in Cuba NY at Maple Lane RV campground.

We have been here since Thursday. We decided to take a long Memorial weekend away. It's a very quiet camp ground. Not much happening and not a lot of campers.

It's actually very boring, as the kids would say, no activity at all. At times that's ok. We both need the rest and escape from everyday life at home. If we could only escape to recovered health.

Thing is no matter how far we go or where we travel, we can't escape the reality of life's health complications and issues.

Sonny cannot walk even fifty feet without having to stop to catch his breath, and because his knee hurts. I know it's because of his heart not pumping blood to the lungs like it's supposed to plus whatever damage he has done to his knee doesn't help his situation either.

We are hoping the heart surgery will improve his breathing or it could also make things worse and a lot will change in his life. Including not being able to work. That would be devastating for him.

The first night camping was a bad night for him, he was up a lot, could not sleep due to inability to breath well, even with the nebulizer treatments. We brought the nebulizer with us so he wouldn't miss treatments.

The second night he could sleep a little better. He never left the camper, and refused me to go on walks, he would not even let me take Maddie out. He insisted she could do her business in the grass, in front of the camper on her leash. He said there was no need for her to be walked.

I could not go any farther than the dumpster to take the kitchen garbage out. He didn't want me out of his sight, he is very clingy, like he is experiencing separation anxiety.

I insisted and took Maddie out for a walk once. I got about six camp sites away, I heard him call my name, he was walking towards me and Maddie. I waited for him to catch up and he was very short of breath when he got to us.

I had asked him before I left the camper if he wanted to go with Maddie and I, he said no, his knee hurt to much.

Next thing I know he's trying to walk. He wants me to come back to the camper, he told me "I didn't need to go anywhere."

I'm not sure where this control, anxiety, or insecurity is coming from. It's just not like him.

Even he got bored from sitting in the camper. We went to the cheese factory and store in Cuba NY one day and Walmart the next day. That was the extent of our walking, because then he could lean on the store cart! I hate sitting around and normally he does too.

His behavior isn't making sense to me. I understand the knee pain, so I never expected him to do a lot of walking. I actually thought this camping trip would give him the opportunity to rest his knee and not have to be walking so much, like he does at the farm.

There was a fish fry tonight at the RV park. It was put on by one of those portable catering food vendors. Sonny had fish fry, cabbage salad, and fries

I had shrimp and fries, it was all very good and freshly made.

Saturday, I got up at 4:15a.m. and made coffee. I had been lying awake or just dosing since 1:30a.m. because of his consistent coughing and pacing back and forth in the camper. He naps a lot during the day and then can't sleep at night.

This morning his feet are swollen to twice their size, his breathing is rattling and difficult. I think he is running a fever and he seems to have retained a lot of fluid. He cannot get warm and is very shaky, but at the moment he does not want to go to the hospital to get checked out, he wants to wait it out. He says we might as well go home today.

He is fully dressed in winter sweat pants, socks, a tee shirt and a heavy flannel shirt, with a heat pad on his back and a quilt over him, the furnace is running, set on seventy-six.

He had half a cup of coffee, and then puked it all up into the waste basket by his chair. Last night's dinner as well as his coffee. Maybe a touch of another stomach bug.

Not sure yet if we are going home today or not. He has to be able to stay awake for an hour drive home because he drove the motorhome and I drove the car, otherwise I'd drive the motor home back home!

He took some Pepto bismol and drank a ginger ale.

Guess we will see how the day goes. 7:45a.m. He went back to lay on the bed to sleep, but he couldn't breathe laying down so within twenty minutes he came back out in the living room and is sleeping in the recliner

When he came out in the living room and made me shut my movie off and get out of the recliner. He actually said "turn that fuckin noise off and who the hell said you could sit in my recliner"

He sat in the recliner and fell asleep for a few minutes. He got up drank a lot of orange juice and said "get packed up we're going home" just like that we were packing up.

We left Cuba around 9:05a.m. I followed behind him, we were not even on the road ten minutes and he pulled into a rest area on the highway, to go to the bathroom and to see if tv worked.

Really you want to check the tv in a road side rest area!

We got back on the road. I am following right behind him. He did ok driving the motorhome, no issues from what I could see. We got to our exit in Howard and he pulled over in the Howard fire department parking lot. Just seven miles from our home, he needed to use the bathroom again, I wonder if he has another UTI?

10:15a.m. we are home

Thank you, Jesus. We are safe and everything is good!

As we were getting ready to open up and unpack the motorhome, I realized I made a huge mistake when I closed up the motor home at camp. I did not pick up the throw rug in front of the kitchen counters, now it's jammed and packed under the biggest slide on the motor home. He tried to use a pry bar to help me free up the jammed rug. In doing so he broke a couple cupboard base boards.

I really screwed up this time and he is so pissed! In my defense I packed up rather quickly.

He went in the house, sat in the recliner and crashed, fast asleep. I emptied out the camper, put things away and started laundry.

I'm glad we're home. I think it will be a very long time if, we ever go anywhere again with the motorhome. He's not really too fond of traveling anyhow. He does it to appease me and because others think he should. Truth is he'd rather be working.

Sunday May 26

He is feeling a little better this morning. He and I worked on my screw up in the motor home. It took over two hours but we got it unjammed. Our effort and end results did some more damage to the base boards and the cupboard. Lesson learned, no more throw rugs in front of any slides.

In the time it took us to clear the jammed rug, he became very confused, and had no idea what he was doing. I finished up putting everything back together that we took apart, and repair cupboard base boards to the best of my knowledge.

I have such pain in my abdomen from pulling on that rug, I sure as hell hope I did not damage or undo anything from my prolapse surgery!

He wandered around the yard outside of the house. He went to the barn and came back with some tools, a plastic dish of small bolts, screws, and nuts. When I asked him what it was for, he said to fix my flower pot and the bird house boxes.

Thing is they don't need fixed. When I told him, they didn't need anything he was pissed at me, told me I need to "fuck off get the hell out of his way." He took off walking around the house again, so I just let him wonder, but kept an eye out for him.

He came in the house and took a short nap in his recliner. When he woke up, he ordered me to get him a glass of cold water "right now," When I handed it to him, he went through the motion like he was going to throw it at me and laughed and said "I'll wait til the water is gone, and empty glass will hurt more!"

What an ass, I am so sick of being treated like that, all I do for him and care for him and he treats me like I'm a nobody!

I have to remind myself that it not really him. Even so it doesn't make the words sting any less.

He drank the water and I proceeded to my house cleaning and mopped the kitchen. Next thing I know he's sitting in the living room, carrying on a conversation and no one is here. Then he started singing songs with words and tunes he made up as he went along. Nothing he said made sense.

Early this afternoon, Derick, our son in law stopped by to drop off our lawn mower he borrowed. I see Sonny outside talking to him. I'm not sure if he was making sense to Derick or not. I'm in the house taking care of things.

Next thing I know Derick is gone and the motorhome is running. I know the leveling jacks are down and the slides are out.

I ran out of the house to the driveway, thinking Sonny was going to take off with it. I opened the driver side door, asked him what is he doing, he said going to town.

I said "Sonny you're not going anywhere." The jacks are down and the slides are out.

He said he'd put the jacks up and the slides in. I told him he couldn't do it from the driver's seat. He argued that he could that he needed to push this button, the button he was pushing was the head lights. I told him "please shut it off we aren't going anywhere until after lunch"

I told him lunch was ready. He was pissed but he did shut it off and I took the keys out of the motorhome. I went in the house to put lunch on the table.

He did not follow me into the house. I went out to see what he was doing. He said he decided he would go to the farm to get his tractor after we eat lunch. That right now he was going out to the barn to get his truck and hooked on to his trailer so he can go get the tractor and roller. I agreed but asked him to wait until after lunch, and went back into the house to finish getting lunch around.

He never came back in the house he had taken off!

Oh my goodness! Life is getting so friken crazy!

Doug called me and said "Dad called him and he lost the tractor off the trailer on Knight Settlement Road I need to go find Dad.

Doug is in a panic because he is a few hours away in Lavonia at Trevor's baseball game and can't go to his Dad to see what he is talking about and what kind of help he needs.

I got in my car and drove to Knight Settlement Road and found him about three miles up, alongside the road siting in his truck. I parked my car and he got out and told me he lost the tractor on Loucks Pond road, the tractor had gone down over a ravine. I asked him why he was on Knight Settlement if he lost it on Loucks Pond road, he said he doesn't know. My heart is breaking for him and at the same time I just want to scold him for scaring me and taking off.

Scott our oldest son showed up a few minutes after I got to Sonny. Doug called him too so he could help me. Sonny told Scott the same story. I was standing there shaking my head no as Sonny was telling Scott the same story about losing the tractor off the trailer.

Sonny got pissed and said "what the fuck are you shaking your head for."

I said "because you did not lose the tractor, you never even went and got it. It's still at Schumacher's."

Scott told him to go home and park his truck, and he would take him up to Schumacher's with Sonny's truck and trailer to help him get his tractor.

Scott was behind me when we all left the Knight Settlement road side. I was behind Sonny He was driving so fast I could not even see his tail lights going down Knight Settlement Road. The road is too curvy to be going as fast as he was. Then when he turned on to State Rt.415 N and headed home he was going at least 90 mph on the road. I could not catch him or keep up with him and I was doing close to 80mph before I backed off.

So much friken craziness. I don't know what to do and I don't understand. He could have killed someone or even himself at those speeds. What the heck was I even doing driving those speeds? I just wanted to make sure he got home. Reality is even if he didn't go home, how could I ever find him or stop him.

We all made it home safely thank God. Scott got in the driver seat of Sonny's truck, without any argument or resistance from Sonny. He took him to Schumacher's to get the tractor.

They got back about an hour and a half later and Sonny's thinking was a lot clearer.

He was aware of what he had done, he felt bad about being so confused and said it was very scary to be out of his mind and not be able to control his thoughts or actions.

It's the first time he actually was aware of his actions and could remember his behaviors as not normal, but at the same time he couldn't even control his own actions or thoughts.

He was just very tired when all was said and done, he came in the house, sat in his recliner, turned tv on, got a dish of ice cream and then took a nap.

The rest of the day he was fine. He even took the motorcycle out and went to Lowe's to get a hinge to fix the cupboard in the motor home that he broke trying to fix my screw up with the slide and the rug.

Doug was at the shop working outside and called me when he saw his Dad take off on the bike. He wasn't to happy about it because of the frame of mind Sonny was in earlier today. I could not stop Sonny, I wouldn't stop him. He has to live his life and I know he was thinking clearly when he left.

Doug must have called Libby because next thing I know she called and was telling me I shouldn't let him go out on the bike in the shape he was in. She wouldn't let me get in a word that he was doing better and thinking clearer.

Then she and Derick went right over to Lowe's with the full intentions of taking Sonny's bike and making Sonny ride home with them. I told her that would just piss her dad off. She has no idea how mean he gets when I ask him not to do something, he has set his mind on doing! I will no longer stop him. I learned over the years it's not worth it! He needs to be allowed to make his own decisions. He is still a man and I still need to respect his decisions and his thoughts. I really can't stop him. My objections mean nothing to a man whose mind is made up and determination stronger than a brick wall!

We can't stand the fact that we are 66 years old we should be able to do what we want when we want. We can't imagine what our life will be like when we are really old!

We understand their concern is out of love and safety, but we hate it, like they have to know our every move. Guess this is what teenagers fell like.

I understand for his own safety and the safety of others on the road I should have stopped him. But how, someone tell me how!

Monday May 27

Last night everything seemed normal. I went to bed to watch tv and he went to sleep.

About 2a.m. he got up to go to the bathroom. He went back to bed and the humming and talking started. He became very loud so I got up and recorded him so he could listen to it in the morning, because he never remembers doing that stuff.

He got up again around 3:15a.m. and went to the bathroom all the while humming and talking to himself. I finally got up and made coffee it was only 3:30a.m. I was sitting in the living room and I heard him opening dresser drawers. I figured he was getting dressed.

He was making a lot of noise in the bedroom but never turned on a light. Then there was a crashing sound of things falling. I went in to see what happened, turns out he was trying to figure out how to put his socks on without tuning on a light. Somehow, he knocked everything off his bed side table and broke the lamp.

I found him sitting on the bed, naked, trying to put on socks. Three pairs of socks no less. He took them off and put his underwear on and put all the socks in the clothes hamper. He refused to let me help him.

The bed was wet, he must have peed in his sleep. Because of the water pill he takes he loses control of his bladder. I know it's embarrassing for him so I just clean up and don't mention it.

I am after all the care giver.

He has to pee a lot, every hour or less. He will talk to the doctor about that at next week's appointment. I think it's a combination of the fluid pill and maybe a UTI.

He came to the living room and asked me for a sip of coffee? That was a strange way of asking. I told him coffee wasn't ready, but it will be shortly so he got himself a glass of water.

All the while he does this insistent constant humming it drives me crazy, and he isn't even aware of doing it.

He then got on his tablet and for some reason was on an internet safari search and was looking at houses to buy. He couldn't figure out how to get out of that screen or how to buy a house.

He started talking about going to get Schumacher's man lift and how he was going to load it on the trailer to take to Libby's gym. I told him he did not have to do that today, that they weren't ready for it.

Again, he went back to his tablet and asked me how to get out of that house hunting screen.

I got him on to his Facebook page. He came across our son Scott's post about the RC air show that was coming up.

He asked me if Scott was going to be able to land his plane up there this year? I asked "what are you talking about?" He said Scott hasn't been able to land up there because the run way is to short for his big plane, he thought he'd be ok this year since they added length to the run way. Thing is Scotts plane is a small one-man plane and the runway is plenty big enough.

It's now only 4:30a.m we are having our coffee and watching the news.

He is still endlessly humming!

Ugggggggggg, so damn annoying! I hate to lose my patients with him. I know those behaviors are not his fault. Often, I just bite my tongue, and take deep breaths, knowing that he has no control over chemo brain. But his chemo brain has given me Caregivers Brain! Not sure if that's a real thing or not, but my brain is sometimes fried from caring for him, and trying to figure things out.

I think it's going to be a very long day. I dread even running into any of my kids today. I am so physically and emotionally stressed, and exhausted, taking care of him and keeping him safe. I know the kids love their dad and are just concerned for him. They also feel helpless and I know they mean well. Thing is none of us can fix this!

No one has any idea what it's like.

I am taking care of my husband the best way I know how, trying to keep his dignity, and treat him the way I would want someone to take care of me. Keeping him and I safe. Yup "Caregivers Brain" I made it up, the phrase/title and I own it!

Sonny knows I am doing a good job even when he has the brain and logical thinking upsets. He knows I will always take care of him. A few years back we talked about making choices for each other if we ever become incapacitated. I am his health care proxy and he is mine. We know what each other wants and expects.

5:25a.m.

We are watching the news, his humming is driving me crazy, he doesn't even know he's doing it, over and over again and again.

He heard a news story about student debt and he told me

"We have no way around it we are going to have to get it paid whether we like it or not" I asked what are you talking about? he said "the dam democratic debt we can't get out of it we have to come up with the money."

Sometimes in his frame of mind he takes the news very personally.

I don't know what to do, I don't know who to contact, his oncologist, his primary, or his cardiologist? Do I just go against his wishes not to ever go to the hospital and take him to the hospital anyhow?

Right now he is napping in his recliner, guess I'll see how the rest of the day goes.

6:10a.m.

He just woke up and I had to tell him to go get cleaned up.

He wet himself and did not even know it.

He has had incontinence for a few days now, I think because of the diuretic.

I noticed his lips are bright purple. Not sure what that's about, and it worries me. He said he's fine to stop bugging him.

He said "who the hell do you think you are to say that to me?"

I said "I'm your wife, please go get cleaned up."

I was shampooing his recliner and I heard him struggle with something plastic. I went into the bathroom to see if he needed help. He was trying to get a new razor blade out of the package. I told him his razor already had a blade in it and I handed him the shave cream.

He puts the shave cream on the razor and was going to brush his teeth.

I yelled because I wanted to stop him quickly "you can't do that it's not tooth paste" he pointed at the can of shave cream and said "its shave cream that's what I'm supposed use."

I had to explain to him to put it on his face not his razor, and do not brush your teeth with it.

He got it right and shaved and brushed his teeth all while being naked standing at the sink.

He finally got dressed and when he came out of the bedroom he had on his jeans, socks, and sneakers, and three tee shirts. I told him it was going to be very warm today to take two of the shirts off. Surprisingly he did without an argument.

He wondered what time it was, when I told him 6:25 he asked "is that night time or morning?" I told him morning he said "oh wow guess I missed a day or two." Yes Sonny, sadly you missed a day or two. For a moment he had some mental clarity.

He put his winter coat and beanie hat on and said "let's go to Burger King for breakfast"

I told him I wasn't hungry, and didn't feel like going out. I had been up since very early and I was already exhausted. He was pissed about that; he hung his coat and hat back up.

Then he called Roy to go to breakfast, but there wasn't any answer.

I offered to fix him some eggs and he told me he really didn't like eggs and never did.

Which is not true he does like eggs. I asked him if he knew what he wanted. He saw a cantaloupe on the counter he picked it up and was tossing it from hand to hand. I told him knock it off before he drops it. Then he proceeded to try to twist it open and handed it to me saying he couldn't get the top off. I cut it open and cut some up for him, and he ate that for breakfast.

After he ate, he seemed a bit better and thinking clearly. He said he was going out in the barn to clean the wood shop and wanted his phone. He cannot find it anywhere. We checked dirty clothes hamper, the motor home, the motorcycle, his truck, all his jackets, every inch of the house and all the vehicles we cannot find it.

I called Lowe's to see if anyone turned his phone in from yesterday when he was there, they said no. I called his phone several times while we were searching around the house to see if we could hear it ring but we didn't. We really don't have any idea what he did with it.

Later in the day when I went to the baking cupboard to get sugar, I found his phone. It was wrapped up in his winter beanie hat on the baking supply shelf. He does not remember doing that, but he must have.

7:45a.m. he may be coming back to his right mind, for a few minutes anyhow.

8a.m. He is out mowing the grass area around the pond. The grass is very wet but he's mowing anyhow. It's what he knows! There's is nothing I can do about it. I really can't keep him inside like a child.

Sometimes I think he does love me and I do love him. We have been married 47 years. We are not each other's children! I have taken care of him through a serious heart surgery and five plus years of cancer. I think I do pretty good for all the nastiness he has put me through!

We went to the Memorial Day parade in Avoca. He was very unsteady, with shaky hand tremors and at times quite confused. I'm not sure if it's a sugar low, or chemo brain. He really doesn't know what causes this mental confusion either. It breaks my heart to not be able to help him or fix him. It's just not right. He really is a good man.

I took him right home after the parade and he had a nap.

I know Libby was upset because there was nothing I could do about him. I was trying to keep her dad's dignity and treat him like he was a man not a child.

He had to change his clothes three times today because he peed right through everything. He doesn't even know it, I had to tell him each time. Something is causing this incontinence. We need to bring this up to the doctor next week.

3:30p.m.

We are in the ER at Noyes Hospital. I know I know against his wishes, I just had to. Something is very wrong.

I brought him here because after he napped this afternoon, he said he was going to the barn to clean the wood shop again After a while I went out to check on him, because of the frame of mind he has been in today. He was stark ass naked walking around the barn looking for the bathroom so he could take a shower.

I yelled at him to get his clothes on and get in the house. He didn't even know he wasn't in the house. I'm not sure what's going on in his mind, he hasn't had IV chemo for quite some time, his chemo is in pill. I guess any kind of chemo can cause chemo brain. Maybe a side effect of new heart medications, or something else is going on.

I probably shouldn't have yelled at him. I keep thinking he should know better. I'm just glad he was in the barn and not out in the yard!

When he came into the house, I told him he was going to the ER. I wanted him to be checked out, and he knew enough to refuse to go.

I waited a few minutes, knowing in his frame of mind he would forget about the ER. Then I told him a lie.

I told him he had a doctor's appointment he needed to get cleaned up, and he agreed to that. I was sure all of his behaviors were somehow related to his new heart medications and how they lower his BP.

I had to find out what was going on with him. I went against his wishes never to go to the hospital. But I'd hate myself if anything ever happened to him that could have been prevented.

I have kept a lot of his behaviors from the kids. I never intended to. I always told them I'd be honest with them. If they ever find out I can only hope they would be understanding. On the other hand, I know they will be very mad, not mad about what he's going through but upset because I never told them.

Until someone is in this situation themselves, no one knows how they are to handle it. I know I don't have the answers. If I did this cancer would be gone forever.

I had to handle these situations myself in order to keep the respect I have for my husband and his dignity in himself and the man I know he is/was. That part of his wishes I had to keep.

I'm doing the best I can for everyone, but Sonny is my priority. We don't want the kids to interrupt their lives and families.

I don't know how I found the strength to get him to the car and then into the hospital.

When we got to the hospital, he didn't want to go in. I reminded him he had to see the doctor in here for his appointment. Then he agreed to go in.

When we got into the ER and were checking in. They ask you why you are here, Sonny told them "there is something wrong with me, I have an emergency, I don't know what I'm doing and I always piss my pants!" In some sense he knew it was for his own good.

I told them briefly about his condition, the cancer, and what has been happening the last few days. They got him right into a room and into a bed to be checked out.

Right now, they are running a lot of test on him. A lot of nurses and doctors are in and out of his room.

X-ray......urine.......blood....ect.

They suspect a UTI that has gotten into his blood (sepsis) and affecting his brain. That can cause the incontinence, and confusion he has had the last few days they see it often in older people. Funny how a UTI can do that!

When we got here a little after 3:00p.m.
BP 162/67
Oxygen 86
Temp. 101.8

I'm just sitting here just watching the machines and all the activity with the nurses and doctors coming and going. There is nothing I can do but silently pray that they can help him.

4:05p.m.
BP 126/57
Oxygen 95
Temp. 103.6

Chest X-ray shows some fluid in his lungs, possible pneumonia again.

His temperature is going up as I sit here, definitely some kind of infection going on.

4:20p.m.
133/61
97 oxygen
104.8 temperature

4:30p.m. They gave him 800 mg of Tylenol for his fever
Started an IV antibiotic called
Piperacillin and Tazobactam

When that runs through the IV, they are going to give him another
called Bancomyancin

This combination will help haunt any kind of bacteria and or virus that
he may have.

4:45p.m.
125/55
95
104 temperature

Beep Beep Beep Damn those machines!

He had wet the bed twice since we have been here. He had no idea or
any control over his bladder.

They put adult diaper on him. I cried quiet tears, and choked back the
sobs, because of the loss of his dignity.

I know if he was in his right mind he would protest and fought very
loudly. Right now he is pretty much out of it and sleeping.

5:10p.m.
BP 104/51
Oxygen 95
Temp. 101.9

5:20p.m.
BP 95/53
Oxygen 94

5:35p.m.
BP 107/53
Oxygen 88

5:55p.m.
BP 92/54
Oxygen 87

6:10p.m.
BP 91/53
Oxygen 87

BP and oxygen dropping over the last hour

6:25p.m.
BP 104/56
Oxygen 92
Temperature 100.2

His stats have been changing so fast up down, up down. It's so eerie to watch the machines and no one has any answers yet, for sure.

Beep Beep Beep Stupid machines I hate that sound!

6:30p.m. They decided to admit him in ICU at Noyes because all regular rooms are full

His fever has broken and he is starting to have moments of clarity about what is going on and where he is. The clarity doesn't last long but it's there at times. I know Sonny is in there somewhere.

The nurses urged me to go home. I went home about 8p.m. to take care of the animals and get some sleep. He is resting well and in good hands.

Tuesday May 28

4:20a.m. I'm awake and having coffee. The house is quiet, no tv, no Sonny humming or singing.

Oddly I miss that! Strange I know, especially after complaining about it! As ill as he is, we are still us, we are still a couple, we are still Sonny and Shirley. We always will be no matter what.

It's doesn't much matter about the silence, when he is here, he never carries on much conversation anymore. Guess after this many years there's nothing left to talk about. Haha

I slept pretty good until about 2a.m. then it was toss and turn until 4a.m. when I finally got up.

No call from the hospital last night that's good so must be he is still stable.

I have to take care of my mom this morning to help her get her car back on the road. I know she shouldn't be driving; her license is revoked but at this point I can't be running down there all the time, and my siblings can't help either.

I have to take care of Sonny's appointments. I don't have time or energy to argue with my mom on why she cannot drive.

First and foremost, Sonny is my priority above anyone else. That's the way it is, and that's the way it's going to be.

11:45a.m. I am finally at the hospital and he is sitting in a chair doing much better.

His BP is still low 98/54. There is no fever and more coherent than he has been in the last few days. He's very aware of what's going on, and his "Sonny humor" is back.

He is not mad at me for bringing him in. He was totally in shock when I told him of his behaviors yesterday. He didn't remember any of it.

He said to me

"I don't think anyone around here knows who is the president or what year it is, everyone keeps coming in to ask me, what's up with that?"

I laughed, and I told him they had to keep asking you to see where you are mentally.

He was up most of the day sitting in the chair. By 4p.m. he wanted to lay down he was cold, and was running a fever of 101. They gave him Tylenol and within an hour the fever broke and was normal.

I left around 6p.m. to take care of the cat and dog, and things around the house.

Wednesday May 29

BP 126/54

Oxygen 98

He had a bad night did not get much sleep. Very uncomfortable, and a very bad headache. I think it may be some of the medications, or dehydration. Though he is on IVs.

He never gets headaches so this was something new for him.

His blood cultures came back with three different kinds of bacteria so they upped the antibiotics he is now on

Piperacillin
Tazobactam
Bancomiacin
Vancomycin

There is never a break of antibiotics he is always hooked up, one right after the other. The infections are aggressive and the doctors are concerned they may affect his heart valves once again.

They did a chest X-ray and the pneumonia is clearing up, that is a good sign the antibiotics are working already.

The hospitalist doctor said it will be a day or two before they can actually name the bacteria's they are dealing with. They separated them and are now re-growing them in the lab to identify.

He will be getting out of ICU today and going to a regular room.

He is getting grumpy and wants to go home, so I know he's feeling better!

1:30p.m.

The nurse just came in and added another antibiotic

Pure old-fashioned Penicillin

She said the doctor just changed the orders.

3:45p.m.

A technician from cardiologist Dr. Iqbal office came in to do an echocardiogram.

His office is the only one in the area that has a portable machine. At least that's what we were told. It doesn't make sense to be in a hospital and they call someone from a cardiologist office to run the echo with a portable machine. They hope the echo will tell them if the infection is in his heart

The technician said she saw some debris on the valve but the cardiologist will have to diagnose the full results for sure.

He is in a bit of pain in his knee and bones. They have not given him any of his medication that he takes at home. He has not had morphine since Monday. His back is hurting and his knees are hurting. His neuropathy is acting up because he is not getting his Lyrica

The only thing he is getting is Eliquis his blood thinner.

Of course, he gets antibiotics through an IV, that's it for medication.

I left at five today. I am exhausted all this running around between my mom and Sonny.

I came home and got a letter off to his oncologist about the pain he is having and about the hospital discontinuing his morphine.

I hope he has an answer for me, or at the very least calls Noyes Hospital to help Sonny get the medication he needs for the pain.

Thursday May 30 2019

What a day

I got to the hospital around 9a.m. hopping to be there when the charge doctor came in so I could find out about why he isn't getting his regular prescribed chemo and pain medications.

Turns out it's because the pain medicines lower his blood pressure and his blood pressure was declining when he was admitted so they stopped his regular medications.

Why the heck don't they tell you these things?

He originally had an appointment today with the orthopedic Dr Okeefe to find out what damage he did to his knee earlier this month when he fell. I had to cancel it because of him being in the hospital.

When I called them to cancel, instead of canceling it the orthopedic office sent Dr. Capecci, from the same orthopedic office to see him in his hospital room. He gave Sonny an injection of cortisone. He administered it very fast and forceful. From what I remember I really don't think that was a good idea. Years ago, when Sonny had cortisone shots, they administered it very slowly and precisely. Sonny said this time it hurt like hell!

The hospital director Dr Amiran came in to see us. He explained that Sonny would be getting transferred to Strong because his cardiac surgeon and cardiology team wanted him up there so they could keep an eye on the heart valve sludge and infection and replace the valve as soon as they felt was safe.

He already had a date of June 10 for the heart valve replacement surgery, so maybe by him already being at Strong he could get it done sooner and be back home recovering sooner too.

His mom's cardiologist came in to see him today, Dr. Iqbal. He wanted to meet Sonny because he has his mom for a patient. They both have a heart in Afib and her doctor wanted to talk to Sonny. It was one of his technicians that came to Sonny's room yesterday to do the echo on Sonny's heart

He is a very nice Indian man. He talked to us about the heart valve replacement that Sonny will be having. He explained to us that a tissue valve would serve Sonny better.

They can be replaced years down the road, vs the mechanical valve. If the mechanical valve failed, they cannot be replaced also with a mechanical valve he would have to be on blood thinner the rest of his life. Sonny said he definitely doesn't want that. He's on enough medication as it is.

Dr Iqbal told us that one of the four bacteria that have invaded Sonny's body is listeria. It is rare, can be deadly, and not good. Most likely from raw vegetables, found in the ground and attaches to whatever food is grown there. He told us if we would have waited two more days before bringing Sonny to the ER he would have succumbed to this infection. Wow, very scary!

A huge light of the past few days came on in my head. There is the answer of where the deadly infection came from.

Last Friday when we were camping at Maple Lane RV in Cuba, NY we had fish fry.

Sonny had fish, cabbage salad, French fries and a dinner roll.

Within twelve hours he was sick and vomiting.

We packed up and came home Saturday morning.

Sunday, he seemed to be doing good when he woke up, but later in the day is when he was starting to get the shaky hands tremors and mental confusion.

It was the listeria and other bacteria invading his brain through the blood system. What we thought was an ordinary stomach bug, or stomach issues from his heart medication, was really a type of rare food poisoning caused by the bacteria called listeria.

4:30p.m. He is on his way to Strong by ambulance. He was not happy about that, he wanted me to take him. The hospital informed us that he was still their patient, under their care and because he was the ambulance to Rochester wouldn't cost us anything.

He did not want me to follow the ambulance up to Strong so late in the day, then have to drive back after dark. I will go up to Rochester first thing tomorrow morning.

Friday May 31

I arrived at the hospital around 9a.m. I wanted to be there to hear what the doctors have to say when they come in for morning rounds.

Sonny told me he arrived at Strong cardiac floor early last evening. Testing went on for hours all through the night.

Echocardiogram, blood test, EKG, urine, x-rays, ect.

He is hooked up to a portable heart monitor and is able to be up walking around not hooked to a wall unit like at Noyes, where he had to stay in bed or the chair beside the bed.

He is very tired today because of having a busy night of testing and very little sleep.

His knee is doing much better pain wise since he is able to get up and walk.

Today they are going to do an angiogram to check on the "infection/ sludge/vegetation" inside his heart on the valve surface and to compare the damage to the aortic valve since April when they did the first one, with intention of replacing the valve.

He has not had anything to eat and he is miserable. He can't eat until after the procedure.

He was put on Cumiden blood thinner here at Strong. They took away the Eliquis. Seems every time we turn around a different doctor prescribes different medication. Remove this, give him that!

He is in a private room with his own bath and shower. He doesn't have to share a room, because of his immune system, or lack thereof, and his risk of getting more infections from others.

A scientist from infectious diseases department stopped by and was interviewing him for over an hour. She wanted his whole history from birth to now. Some of it from his youth was hard to remember.

Then when she leaves, she said she'd be back in a while with her supervisor.

Gosh I hope we don't have to answer all those questions again!

It's times like this that I'm glad I have kept this journal and take it with me to all of his appointments and procedures. I can look back and know what was done when and where, at least the last few years. Before this journal we have to rely on our memory.

Today they added another antibiotic called gentamycin.

Supposedly he is on any and all antibiotics that will kill every bacteria known to man.

Next thing he needs to be watched for is thrush or a yeast infection in his mouth, due to the regimen of antibiotics he has been on. They also kill the good bacteria in his body.

Saturday June 1

I'm feeling very emotional and tearful today. Just on information overload and confusion about what is happening now with his condition and treatment. Every time we turn around, he is being seen by yet another specialist and they all have their own opinions and its very mind boggling, frustrating and overwhelming.

Not to mention the sheer exhaustion of keeping up with the drive to and from Strong Memorial in Rochester, eighty-five miles each way. I wish I knew how to fix everything for him so he didn't have to go through all of this. It's heart breaking. We want one doctor who does it all!

I am feeling overwhelmed at all the information we have been told the last five days. Trying to keep it all straight and in this journal as the information is told to us. Trying to give the appropriate and correct answers to all the enquiring professionals and specialist. It's a teaching hospital and listeria infection is very rare. We are visited everyday by many students and doctors.

So many doctors, so many students, so many professionals, so many blood tests, so many results, so much new medications, so much I don't understand, yet we have to trust them and we do.

Though a better explanation of test results and why the added medication would help. Sometimes it's like listening to a foreign language and being expected to understand.

I reached out to his oncology nurse today by e mail, but I won't hear back until Monday

Sunday June 2

Kylie stayed overnight with me so she could come see her grandpa.

We got there around 10a.m. He is up and about says he's feeling pretty good. He loved seeing Ky and Oscar her service dog.

They are still doing IV's of antibiotics every hour. From what I understand when he gets to go home, he will go home with IV antibiotics for about six to eight weeks. We have done that before, but that's ok at least he'll be home.

On the way home Ky and I stopped in Geneseo and bought KFC to go. We got home around 3:30p.m.

Libby and the kids came over and Kylie boyfriend David stopped by too.

Everyone left by 5:30p.m. I shampooed the coffee mess on my living room carpet that I missed in the morning when I dumped a full cup all over me, my recliner, and the carpet!

Monday June 3

Back at Strong today 10a.m.

We are supposed to see the cardiac team to tell us when they will do the surgery to replace his heart valve. Also, he has to go to pulmonary today at 1p.m. for pre op work up for the surgery.

Tuesday June 4

I did not go up today. It's to expensive and exhausting to go every day. He told me to stay home get some rest and take care of me.

Sonny did see the cardiac surgeon. He wants him to remain on the high protein diet to gain his strength from being malnourished and dehydrated.

He still has Sonny on the schedule for Monday June 10th for heart valve replacement. He wants him to stay in the hospital on the IV antibiotics until surgery.

Over all he is feeling much better. I am happy to know that.

I'm sure he didn't miss me today. He had a lot of visitors today.

Roy went up to see him

Dan Schumacher from the farm stopped by for a visit.

Ginny and Mike Hargraves stopped in after Mikes chemo infusion treatment.

Dave Hall stopped by also.

Thursday June 6 2019

Yesterday Wednesday June 5, he was visited by hospital administrator. She was very nasty and rude.

She wanted to know why he was still there. She told him because he was feeling better that he was taking up a room un necessarily. That he can be home on the IV antibiotics and the heart monitor until it's time for his surgery.

She wanted to know why her office and administration was not told of his surgery date. I was not there but I guess she went on and on about Sonny taking up a room when he didn't need to be there.

Sonny was getting pissed at her questions and insinuations. He told her he had no idea that was up to his doctors not up to him to inform her or anyone in administration what was happening on his care.

He came to the hospital in serious condition and has greatly improved.

His cardiac surgeon and oncologist were the ones who wanted him to stay in the hospital on IV antibiotics and to be on a high protein high calorie diet to improve his overall health and strength to prepare him for heart surgery.

He had several serious infections in his system when he was admitted. Most of them have been cleared or are clearing and he needs the antibiotics to assure they don't start growing and are completely cleared from his blood system. One serious one remains in his heart and surgery to replace the infected heart valves will take care of that one too.

It really makes me angry that some pencil pusher administration can call the shots on a person's health.

He has Medicare and a very good supplemental insurance policy. They will get paid they always have! Heck he doesn't even have an unpaid balance with the hospital, all his copays have always been paid.

I know there are people who get admitted with no insurance and no intention of paying their bill. Do they get harassed to leave before the doctors say?

I have contacted both his cardiologist and oncologist by e mail this morning about what administration did. They are very good at getting back to us on any of our concerns.

We will bring it up to the attending physician this morning when he comes in.

I can't wait to hear what they have to say.

I'm sure it all has to do with the insurance companies who put time limits on hospital stays according to your condition and what their medical transcripts tell them of how long a person should be in the hospital. They in turn or in hand with hospital administration now decide.

There was a time when your doctors could keep you according to your health condition, not according to pencil pushers!

I'm just feeling bullied, and frustrated by "the system."

Thank you, Obama, for your very broken, un affordable, health care system!

I will never understand how a politician can make a call any kind of medical decisions. Shouldn't the doctors do that? Even health insurance has become political!

UPDATE: regarding the hospital administration

This morning when the doctor in charge came in Sonny explained to him what happened. Sonny asked him if he should be getting discharged. He told us if she comes back to not answer any of her questions and to refer her to the 7th floor to his cardiac care team. What she did was single Sonny out and it was wrong and unprofessional.

I came home at supper time and received a message that my cousin Sis, took her mom, my Aunt Nancy to the Bath hospital with a very high fever and mental confusion. Turns out she has a severe UTI, fever, pneumonia, and heart palpitations and low blood pressure issues. They started her on IV fluids and antibiotics and transferred her to Arnot Ogden in Elmira.

Her condition is an eerie rerun of when Sonny was admitted a few weeks ago.

Thing is, I heard this with Sonny's mom last month, my sister Theresa same diagnosis last month, then Sonny, and now aunt Nancy.

What the heck is going on with all the UTIs that they affect everyone's brains?

Thursday June 6

I will be going up today and Roy is going to ride along. He wants to see Sonny. We also have another mutual friend who is also at Strong Hospital that he wants to see.

Lenny G, the lawn mower guy, he has been in there a month he had pretty serious back surgery and now in a wheel chair with limited to no use of his legs caused by the surgery and he is in rehab and PT to learn to walk again. Roy will visit with both of them.

Sonny's BP is very low today 93/41

Not the lowest he's been but regardless it's still low.

He doesn't seem to be himself today. Very lethargic and tired, he falls asleep while talking.

Could be the low BP, or his pain medication.

There seems to be a problem with his IV ports today too. For some reason every now and then they get plugged up with blood clots. I'm not sure if this could become a concern or serious issue or not. The nurses act like it's a normal thing when someone has IV ports. I sure don't understand it.

Friday June 7

I'm not going up today. I will be watching Jax while Libby goes up to see her dad for a few hours. Kendal will ride the bus to my house after school.

Update on Aunt Nancy

This was from Sis this morning

Good morning everyone! Glad to report that things are looking up a little. Heart is looking good. Off that med. Going to ween off the O2. She's able to get out of bed now, with lots of help and support. Still very winded easily from the pneumonia and tires quite rapidly which frustrates her to no end. And she's been telling Dad to make sure he keeps up with the lawns and such. She's still got it,!!! Thank you all for your continued thought and prayers. Oh and my brother got home safely and will be popping in here soon, which will be a surprise to my mom.

I am so glad she is doing better. I will take my mom to see her Sunday. Nancy is mom's sister.

Saturday June 8

Headed to Rochester to spend the day with Sonny.

I need to stop at Walmart for a few things before I go.

Uneventful day at the hospital. He was doing well, up for walks, eating well, in a good mood, able to stay awake and carry on a conversation. Ready to get his heart fixed and get on with his life. I am so happy to see him like this. Seems like my old Sonny is back with a positive attitude and determination.

I went home around 3:30p.m.

I got home changed into work clothes cleaned and rearranged the garage so I can now park the pickup truck in the garage instead of the barn. I cleaned the back-room shelves and mopped the floors. I'm going to bed very tired but glad I'm able to get the truck in the garage. Now Sonny won't have to walk to the barn in bad weather to get the truck.

Sunday June 9

I cleaned the inside of the truck; it was filthy and smelled like the farm.

After church I took mom to see aunt Nancy at Arnot hospital in Elmira.

She is doing well and will be coming home in a day or two. Thank God for answered prayers.

I came home and did the weed whacking around the house, so I can mow this week.

Heart Valve Replacement

Monday June 10

Today Sonny will be having heart surgery to replace his failing valve.

He called me at 5:30a.m. and wanted me there soon as I could because they should be taking him into surgery by 7a.m.

I hurried as best that I could and got here at eight and he was still in his room on the fourth floor.

Then his nurse came in about 10a.m. and did vitals and hooked an IV up, and she said he won't be having surgery until around 7p.m. tonight. Which means he won't be in recovery until midnight or later.

It's going to be a very, very long day and night.

He is pissed, and so am I.

Waiting around is so exhausting and for him he is starving and so thirsty, they won't give him anything to eat and drink because of the surgery.

I could have stayed home and come up this afternoon.

Now I will be here all day and night. It's so hard to get any kind of rest in these recliners.

This is unbelievable!

His blood sugar is so low 71 and BP is 78/31

He is very shaky and light headed because his sugar is too low.

He hasn't eaten or had anything to drink since 5:30p.m. last night.

11:30a.m. The nurse gave in to his demand for something to drink and gave him apple juice and checked his sugar at 12:30p.m

and his sugar came up to 91

BP is now 101/32

Libby came up thinking he was having his surgery early this morning. I told her she didn't have to because it will be a long day but she came anyhow.

She left to go back home about 1:30p.m. since his surgery time was changed to evening.

He was taken to pre op at 3:45p.m.

In pre op they shaved his chest and groin for access to the main arteries.

Put in two other IV lines in his left arm and an artery wire line to get exact internal BP.

In the OR they will put in a line in the neck artery, and a catheter. He then will be put on the heart lung bypass machine and a breathing machine; his head will be packed in ice to prevent brain damage, and then they will start the surgery to replace the aortic valve and mitral valve.

He was very calm and not nervous at all. I prayed for Sonny and his doctors and know that no matter what God is always in charge and always with us.

They took him into the OR around 6:00p.m. the surgery will take five to six hours. Looks like it will be midnight or so before I head home tonight.

I am waiting here by myself, it's ok, I like it that way. My kids need their sleep they work hard every day. I don't want them to worry. Long as I can protect them from worry I will. It's not that I want to keep them from what is going on I just don't want them to worry.

I am very tired, very tired. I just want Sonny to be ok. I want to be home in my own bed with my little dog Maddie. Home is safe, if I'm home then I know Sonny is ok.

Poor Maddie she must be very confused

Doug has Maddie at his house, granddaughter Ariana will be taking care of her.

Libby stopped to feed Harley Fat Boy our cat.

Everything is good no worries except for the drive home, and staying awake for eighty-five miles.

9:00p.m. update

OR nurse just called me. They are getting ready to place the aortic valve, all is going well he is doing well on the bypass machine stats are good.

She said there is a lot of work to do but all is going just as planned and there are no concerns at this time.

10:30p.m.

Update

OR nurse just called me. The new aortic valve is in place, and all is functioning well.

Turns out they did not have to replace the mitral valve, once the new aortic valve was in place the mitral valve sealed its self, so that's promising and very good news.

The new aortic artery is completed also and hooked into his heart everything is working perfectly. Thank you, Jesus. Praise the Lord!

11:30p.m. He is still in surgery

The OR nurse called.

He is off the lung heart bypass machine and everything is working normally with a normal heart rhythm, lungs are functioning normally, blood pressure has returned to normal, Dr Knight is pleased with the heart function and strength.

They have some bleeding they are dealing with and when that is under control they will be closing his chest and he will be going to recovery within an hour.

June 11 12:30a.m.

The OR nurse called again, said they are giving him blood transfusions in the OR due to blood loss, but they cannot close up the chest yet due to bleeding that they can't stop.

Dr Knight will be calling me with more detail soon.

I'm glad I have my journal with me to write all this down. I'd never be able to remember the details if I didn't.

1:15a.m.

He has been in surgery for seven hours now.

I think something is very wrong, a gut feeling or premonition if you will. I am wide awake with concern and worry.

The OR nurse has kept in touch with me but I know he should have been out of surgery by now.

Are they just sugar coating the information for me, or do they not know themselves what is causing the excessive bleeding?

I am so very tired, not sure it may be just my mind working overtime on exhaustion.

I close my eyes trying to rest or sleep if I can. Sleep doesn't come these cold hard couches are not comfy at all, and rest isn't restful for me at all. My mind won't shut off. Time is moving so slow. I'm sure the surgeons and the OR staff are very tired too.

I am so glad I am here alone, not that I don't love my family I really do, but I always feel if someone's with me I need to entertain others with conversation when all I want to do is not talk to anyone!

It's just me and God in this cold cold lobby.

I trust his doctors, but the bleeding issue doesn't sound good.

I'm just waiting on the lobby phone to ring. I am the only one here at this time all others have gotten their good news and have gone home or gone to their loved one's room.

I have been moved to three different waiting areas since his surgery started. First, I was sent to the surgical family waiting room. When they closed that room at nine, I was sent to a second family waiting room, and when that closed at 11p.m. I was sent to the front lobby. All of them very uncomfortable.

I won't call the kids until I have answers myself, and it's so late. I'll let them sleep. I'll call them if the situation gets dire.

2:15a.m. June 11

Dr Knight just called me he is sending Sonny up to cardiac ICU.

He said he cannot close up the chest due to bleeding that won't stop.

He said he has done everything he can do and pulled out every trick under his hat.

He also said he was pleased with the new heart valve and the success of this operation on the heart, that he is doing well in that aspect.

The next couple of hours will make a difference if they just let him rest they feel the bleeding will stop.

For now, he is packed with surgical sponges and gauze and taped up but his chest is not closed.

When the internal bleeding gets under control then he will go back to surgery to close up his chest and ribs. That could be a day or a few days. Until then he is in a medical induced coma and on a ventilator.

2:30a.m.

I was sent up to ICU family waiting room to wait for them to bring him up to his room.

As I write I am up at ICU waiting to see him.

He needs to know I am here.

I was told I will get to see him in about half an hour.

After I see him, I'm going home and get some sleep.

When the desk nurse just came in to talk to me. I was told he will be sedated for a while in a medical coma because they don't want him moving, they need him to be as still as possible to get the bleeding under control.

She said he won't know if I'm here or not and if there is any change, they will call me and I can call them any time. I can go home or I can wait until he's is in his room and I can see him. I waited to go see him. I did not want to go home until I saw him and until he knows that I'm here.

I went into see him there were so many attentive nurses getting him hooked up to monitors and machines. There were at least six people attending to him around his bed. So many machines, wires and hoses I couldn't even begin to say what they all were.

They stepped aside and let me see him and talk to him for a few minutes. I told him I was there that I love him and we are all praying for him, and to keep on fighting. I'd be back after I got some sleep.

UPDATE GROUP TEXT I SENT TO EVERYONE PRAYING AT HOME

He went into surgery last night a little after six

They replace the aortic valve and the aortic artery coming out the top of his heart once they pumped the stagnant blood out of his heart the mitral valve seated back in place so they did not have to replace the mitral valve

once the surgery was complete on the heart they went to close him up and they couldn't they had to leave the ribs open and The incision open they packed him several times between 11:30pm and 2:00am in the morning they could not stop the bleeding they've given him several units of blood and blood clotting medication.

They moved him up to cardiac ICU and that's where he is now

There are two drain tubes in his open incision that are running blood out almost as fast as they're pumping it in, or it looks like that to me anyhow.

He is on a ventilator for breathing due to being sedated. They will ween him off after he has the surgery to close up his chest, and the doctor said they won't wake him up for 24 to 48 hours after that happens, but their main concern now is to get the bleeding under control and keep him still so everything doesn't continue to bleed.

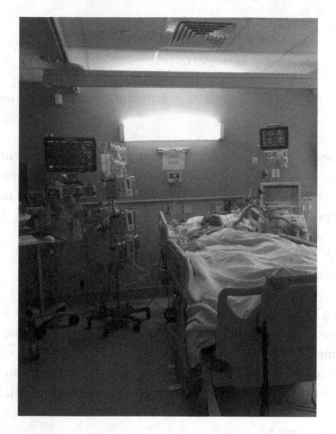

6a.m. June 11 2019

I just got home Dr. Knight told me to go home and rest that I won't be any good to him if I'm wore out. He said Sonny will be sleeping all day. I hope the kids won't be upset at me for coming home, but I just had to. I want my own bed, my own home, and I have my dog and cat to take care of too. Sonny is getting the best care possible. There is nothing more I can do but keep on praying.

I'm going to close my eyes for a bit and I'll give the hospital a call at noon to see if they've made any progress on controlling the bleeding and how he is doing and then I'll go up early tomorrow morning.

His surgeon says he's going to be OK it's just going to take some time.

UPDATE Tuesday JUNE 11 6:20p.m.

I just talked to his day nurse Alex.

He said Sonny is stable and they are bringing him off the sedation a little at a time.

He said they want to wake him up a little bit to check his neurological responses, to make sure all extremities are working on command, then put him back in the medical coma. He said the ventilator will stay in for a day or two longer because they will be taking him back into the OR to close up the ribs and chest.

They expect that will happen tomorrow or Thursday.

One thing I noticed, what they tell me they are going to do and what they do change all the time from hour to hour depending on how he is doing at the time. Most of the time even in his induced sleep he does what is not expected of him, like breathing over the ventilator, and moving his head. To me that proves he is fighting and has not lost his will to live.

Wednesday June 12

I was able to get a little sleep last night and am feeling worried, but hopeful.

Summary of the last few weeks in short version

I had been two days with only two hours of sleep.
Yes, he is in Strong he has been in the hospital since May 27, first Noyes in Dansville and then Strong in Rochester.
On Monday they did open heart surgery.
They had to replace his aortic artery, and his aortic valve they were infected and deteriorated and leaking blood was pooling in the bottom chamber of his heart.

I'll back track a bit here

He got listeria food poisoning over the last week in May. The listeria and septic infection invaded his blood, body, and brain. They got the fever under control right away and the septic blood infection took about a week to get under control due to his low immune system from the chemo.

The listeria took up residence in his heart and destroyed his aortic valve. The only fix was to replace the valve and artery, which he was scheduled for long before listeria took hold.

Surgery was Monday night. The actual heart repair only took four and half hours and all was going well, very good actually.

But his body then had massive bleeding with in the surgery site and they could not stop it They worked on him until 2:30a.m. on Tuesday June 11 to stop the bleeding. He was getting every conceivable clotting medication and blood product there is. Blood was being administered as fast as it was coming out.

There was no single one source of blood loss. Every blood vessel they cut through for the surgery bled and many could not be stopped.

They could not close the ribs or his chest after surgery so they packed him with sponges, surgical gauze and taped him shut.

They sent him to cardiac ICU. By noon yesterday the bleeding was under control.

They are keeping him sedated and on the ventilator. They need him to stay still so the clotting medication can be affective.

His vitals are good, his condition is listed as serious but stable.

Basically, it's going to be a long hard road, but Dr. Knight said his prognosis is hopeful, just a long recovery time.

It has been a very difficult few weeks for Sonny, me, and our kids, but especially Sonny.

We have not made this public information on FB in order to protect Sonny's dignity and respect for him, due to how awful rumor mills can be and are.

That is a brief account of a long reality story of the last month and a half.

Wednesday June 12 11:00a.m.

When I arrived at ICU this morning like every day so far, he is sedated and unresponsive. I'll be glad when they wake him up and he is off these machines.

I hate the eerie sound of the ventilator whooshing, and the other beeping machines with Sonny laying so motionless. It is haunting and I can't fix it!

The doctors and nurses are very attentive and very good to him and me, but I just want to scream at them, "you don't know him, he is still a man, he is someone's dad, he is someone's son, he is my husband." He was once a very strong man and cancer has diminished his strength but it has not diminished his spirit and determination.

A very good report on Sonny this morning

The doctors were here shortly after I got here.

All his vitals are normal.

His skin color is good

They woke him up overnight and did a neurological test and he understood them and followed commands and they told him about his surgery and where he was and what was going on.

Then he tried to pull his ventilator out and became agitated. They were able to calm him down by explaining to him why he needed it.

Then he calmed down and was ok.

He is sleeping now under sedation in a medically induced coma.

They don't want him moving due to the chest still being open. As is pure Sonny style he has movement anyhow!

They are going to take him to the OR sometime this afternoon to close up the ribs and soft tissue They put the ribs back together with wire and chest soft tissue with internal stitches and glue on the outside instead of stitches.

The doctor said he's going to be ok and right now things are good and are progressing like they should. It's just going to take time and will not be a fast recovery.

Bonnie and Lenny G. stopped by Sonny's room. Clearly Lenny was moved, very emotional to see his friend Sonny unresponsive in a coma.

That is exactly why I don't want our kids here to see him like this. I want to protect their hearts from hurting. On the other hand, I know all I have to do is say the word and they would be here in a heartbeat. Some might think I or they are being selfish but we are not. I'm the mom and I will protect them in every way in every sense always.

Today I found out we have a big problem.

The hospital lost Sonny's hearing aids. The evening of the surgery an OR nurse gave them to security, to keep them safe until they could return them to Sonny. They were supposed to bring them to me in the waiting room or take them up to ICU.

I went to Security office; they do not have them. Security sent me to the cashier's office, they do not have them and told me to go back to pre op area and ask if they are being held there.

They are not in the pre op area, and I have checked with everyone in ICU offices, they are not in ICU.

No one knows where they are. I have been all over the hospital looking for them. Every search I was being redirected to yet another place or another office. I must have walked two miles with in the hospital.

I don't know what to do now!

Sonny is going to be so mad when he finds out. First of all because he won't be able to hear, and second of all the cost of replacing them.

I may have to call his audiologist, Sue N. and have her order another set.

They are very expensive over $3000 and insurance does not cover them.

I am just sick over this with anxiety and I know Sonny will be too.

3:05p.m.

He is on his way to the OR to be evaluated so Dr. Knight can determine whether to close his chest or if he has to wait a little longer.

I was told this should take about three hours.

One of the OR nurses was able to locate Sonny's hearing aids. Praise the Lord. We will be forever in debt to her. God bless her always.

He was back in his room in ICU by 5p.m. amazing! Closing the chest went better than Dr. Knight expected.

He is all back together, bleeding has stopped, he is safe and sound being cared for by his wonderful nurses, Mike, Alex, and Nad.

They are the best male nurse team I have ever seen in action.

They take very good care of Sonny with so much dignity and respect in caring for a man who cannot respond to them.

They talk to him as if he can hear them and answer them. They tell him everything that is going on what they are doing. They tell him how he is doing; they speak only positive words to him.

It is a level of professional care that is very sincere.

They never talk about him or his medical condition while in his room, they talk "to" him.

On the other hand, the rumor mill of Avoca is flying faster than a jet rocket headed for Mars!

I won't even address that, it's so hurtful.

When you live in a small-town other's know more about you than you know yourself. The things they are assuming about Sonny are just awful.

Thursday June 13

I've been awake since 3:15a.m.

Already on my second cup of coffee. My mind won't let me sleep no matter how tired my body is.

Unfortunately, I had heard rumors too about Sonny.

I don't usually swear but it's exactly shit like that that makes me mad.

People would sooner rather believe terrible news than think positive or believe good news.

Yes, Sonny was in serious condition but I refused to accept that he wasn't going to be ok. I believe in the power of prayer, great doctors, family and friends. I will not give up hope!

I never gave up on any procedure he ever had, every improvement, no matter how small, is what I ran with and hold onto.

Yes, things looked dire at times but I refused to dwell on those things and dwelled on the man he used to be, and still has a chance to be once again. I refuse to give up.

I knew if I fought hard enough, I believed in answered prayer, and know he is a fighter he will pull through this ordeal same as every other one before this. Maybe he would not physically be the strong man he once was but he is a fighter, a never give up spirit is always with him.

Because of the man that he is and to protect his dignity and reputation and respect for Sonny

I only let our family and a few of our closest friends I could trust know what was going on.

People who I know would stop the rumor mill from spreading untruth.

Avoca has a pretty awful rumor mill, not just about Sonny but other community members as well.

They don't stop to think before they open their mouths about how much it hurts our family. All family's when they talk of what they do not know!

I am always trying to protect my adult children and my grandchildren. I want to stay positive for them.

I don't care if the rumors are out to hurt me, or talk about me, they can say all they want about me I don't care. But it breaks my heart when they hurt my kids with the god-awful lies and rumors.

It breaks my heart and makes me cry for what my kids are going to go through to try to get the rumors stopped.

It shouldn't have to be that way. Family's like ours are trying their best to stay positive and look for and believe the best is going to happen and ya know what? It will. We trust the Lord and our good doctors to pull us through.

Screw the know-it-all asses of the infamous small town rumor mill.

Sorry for the language but a person can only take so much!

Thursday June 13 3:05p.m.

I called and talked to his nurse.

Today is a good day for improvement.

They took the ventilator out today because Sonny was fighting it and was breathing above the vent. They tested him by shutting it off and he was breathing on his own. That is very good. That's the fighter Sonny is!

They told me the ventilator was only because they had to keep him sedated until they got his chest closed up. His progress is very good.

They are weening him off the fentanyl and propofol so he can become more awake and aware, he will only be on fentanyl patches

He is making progress and he is still considered, post-surgery stable.

He is not fully awake but the nurses say, he is breathing on his own and seems more comfortable.

Amazing, I am very happy for him

I will see him tomorrow.

Friday June 14

I took our little dog to the groomer and Libby is picking her up as I headed for Strong to see Sonny. I had no idea what to expect, but what I saw was both good and not so good.

He was lying in bed, his eyes were open, but he had no expression of happiness to see me.

His eyes were pale, and blank. I kissed him and said "hello your awake" he just stared at me.

I quickly got his hearing aids in his ears so he could hear.

That didn't seem to be the problem, there is something wrong, Sonny is not there it's his body but it's not him, he's so far away.

Throughout the day nurses were asking him questions to see where his mind is.

What is your name? He knew this.

What is your date of birth? He knew this.

What day is it? He didn't know, he had lost track of time due to being in a coma for so long.

What year is it. He didn't know

Do you know where you are? He said, "hospital"

Do you know what hospital? He said "St Joseph in Elmira"

I don't know where that came from because he has never been in St Joseph's.

They got him all settled and I tried to talk to him but his words were slurred and he was disoriented, frustrated, and confused. At least he is making an effort to respond.

He had wet his bed and gown, the nurses came in and cleaned him up.

They may put the catheter back in. He knows when he has to go, he just can't hold it until the nurses get there to help him get up out of bed. He can't get out of bed to go on his own, they won't let him, and I was told not to help him up either. The nurses tell me loss of bladder control is a normal result for some people due to the long sedation, his body senses and functions are not awake yet. They told me this was normal and promised me in time he will improve.

Dr Knight came in and said Sonny is very weak it will take a long time for him to get his strength back. He will probably be in the hospital six weeks to two months.

He said just keep encouraging him and keep him talking. He said every day there will be improvements, sometimes by the hour, some big and some small but improvements just the same.

As Dr. Knight left Sonny's room, Sonny asked me, "What the hell did he just say?"

I explained it all again to Sonny and he very loudly expressed,

"How the hell can I get stronger laying in this bed all day?"

Yep, there's the spunky, soft spoken ha ha, Sonny I know. He hasn't gone anywhere; he was just held up for a bit. He never was one for lying around!

Shortly after that a nurse came in and got him out of bed.

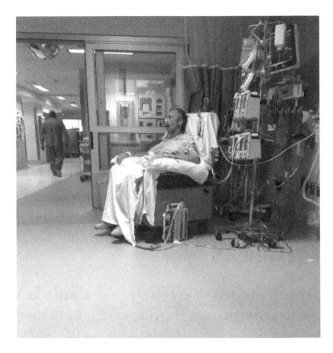

He was happy to get out of the bed. He sat there for about an hour and asked me if "I liked the ass wipes?"

I said "what do you mean" he repeated "do you like the ass wipes?"

I said "I don't know what you're talking about."

Turns out because he can't take a shower, he gets bed baths with warmed wet bath wipes and he said "they hurt like a bitch!" the cloths are warm and soft but his skin is very sensitive and very dry.

Every word he speaks I have to listen closely to and sometimes ask him to repeat, because his words are slurred, due to being on a ventilator so long, his throat is sore, and his projection is weak.

I hate to see him like this. It seems his dignity is slowly getting destroyed. At times he is very childlike with wetting himself and not having control of his bowels and having to wearing adult diapers. This is a great embarrassment for him.

The nurses assured us both this is normal after a long sedation and again promised us he will improve within days. "Please don't worry he will be ok, it's an effect of being sedated for so long, his body functions will return."

We have our history and don't always get along and sometimes he treats me like a no body, insults me, swears at me, at times it feels like he hates me.

Even so no matter how bad he treats me; I know in the last six years it has been because of chemo brain and having to deal mentally with a cancer knowing very few survive with. I don't like seeing him go through this. I know he loves me and I love him. Life has not been easy for either of us no matter what it looks like to others.

For the first time in my married life, I feel like I don't know how to take care of him.

Me the caregiver! I was not prepared for this. The nurses and doctors say it's just temporary, they assure me once again this is normal, he will be ok, just give it time. Time, it's all we have.

How awful for Sonny to go through this ordeal, just heartbreaking.

Will he get better I really don't know I'm not a professional. Dr. Knight says yes but it's going to take a long time. That much I have to believe.

I don't want our kids to see their dad like this. I know they would break down. It is not pretty to see a 66-year-old be so childlike at times.

A man who was once so strong and healthy who can only now breathe, work on regaining his body functions and thinking. Basically, just exist from the bed to a chair. Who at times, doesn't have much orderly thought process and has lost his dignity.

On a good note, Dr. Louis and Dr. Aftar from infectious disease unit came in and said there is no more listeria growing in the blood cultures, but the procedure from here on out for a while will be to keep him on the ampicillin and the Gentamycin for six weeks after the surgery as a precaution in case there are any listeria micro cells that linger and start to grow.

As of right now they are telling us he will go home with an IV and will be on it until the middle of July. Then they will remove the arterial lines.

Saturday June 15 2019

Sin no more and I will bless you

Someone screamed at me as I was waking up from a dream.

Where did that just come from and what have I done?

Am I not a sinner?

Yes, I am, we all are. That little white lie, that cheat when you got too much change back at the store, or you parked in a handicap spot just to be closer to the door in bad weather, because after all you'll only be a couple of minutes. Maybe the gossip we spread. Maybe we swore using Gods name. It's a fact we all sin.

I cannot get back to sleep. It is 2:45a.m.

A bad dream and the voice woke me up. It has to be God.

I got up started some laundry, made coffee, and tried to sooth and quiet my mind. I read my daily devotions, actually, several days devotions since I was so far behind. With all that is going on with Sonny I haven't been able to do much reading.

It's really hard at times to put into words what I am going through.

Others can speak encouragement to me and their words are sincere but my mind and heart can't be calmed or soothed by words. It's not that I don't appreciate their effort and time, I really do. It's just that I want my husband back, whole, healthy and home.

It is very hard; my thoughts and emotions are all over the place. Going at a hundred miles per hour at times. Exhausting.

First, and foremost are concerns about my husband and how am I going to take care of him

Second, I have to worry about my mom who is an unsafe driver and is supposed to surrender her driver's license, but refuses to and it's going to cost her big time.

I just can't deal with her, and I get no help from my siblings because they all work or live to far away to help. For now, mom will have to deal with it on her own. Sonny is my priority!

Third, Sonny's mom is not good, her dementia is getting worse. Lori, like me has her hands full as Mary's caregiver. Up until Sonny got so sick this spring, I was able to help her, whenever Lori would call me. In between Sonny's appointments and helping my own mom.

Since May, everything else in my life has come to a halt except taking care of my husband.

He is my priority.

I am dealing with a lot of guilt about our moms. I know I shouldn't, but I'm just hard on myself, I don't know any other way.

A lot is going on in our life and in my mind. If only you could spend a day inside my mind!

Our youngest child Libby and her husband are building a business and as much as we want to be involved and help her get things done it is physically impossible for us to be there like we want.

I feel so bad about not being able to help much.

The best help I can be at times, is to take care of her children so that she and Derick can be there working on the building without having to keep an eye on the kids.

Thing is I really don't know if Sonny will ever be able to help them. I know she is disappointed because he was able to help her brothers build their businesses and be hands on. He was much younger and healthier than too. Thing is now he can't even be hands on or even give advice in the mental state he is in.

I help as much as I can but it's not enough, I know.

Right now, in my life and all that's going on, I just want to stay in my house, lock the door, not go anywhere, not let anyone in, cover my head and pretend like nothing is wrong. I want to believe that it's just a dream I'll wake up from. I just want to be alone behind these walls and not answer to anyone. I don't want anyone here I don't want anyone in. I want to be left alone.

I'm sure no one would understand that, and think I was being selfish.

I fixed my coffee around 4a.m. then soon as it was day light I got dressed and took Maddie dog for a walk around the pond. There was a beautiful sunrise, it was going to be a warm day. As I walked, I looked at everything that we built, our home, our barn, our property, the well-manicured lawns, the pond, our vehicles, the yard equipment, motor home, pavilion, the business. I felt like I was looking at it with clearer eyes. Everything all just material, all just worthless when we can't enjoy or share it all together with each other.

A life time of accomplishments, all can be replaced, all can be walked away form. The most precious part of our lives is our four successful children and their spouses.

We are proud of each of them.

As I walked around the pond and our property, I cried out to God for forgiveness of any and all sin I have committed. If it is anything I have done to cause Sonny this ordeal in his life, if it is I never did so knowingly. I would not hurt him ever in any way, no matter what he has done to me. I cried and cried, sobs came from my lungs and stomach, my heart breaking for all the pain and suffering Sonny has had to endure the last six years. It is unfair because if ever there was a man who would help anyone, friend, family, or stranger, it is Sonny.

He has been close to death many times. How can he keep pulling out of it every time I wonder?

I tell myself over and over again Sonny must be favored by God, he has been through so much.

I hurt because I keep thinking one day, he won't be so fortunate, one day we will have to face the inevitable of life without him.

It's hard to put into words what I was feeling this morning on my walk I just know I needed that cry. I needed to scream at God. It was like a release. I just don't know what of, I can't put it into words!

By the time I got back to the house my shoes and feet were wet with morning dew but my emotions felt a little lighter. I felt relief and was suddenly hit with extreme exhaustion. I'm not sure how the rest of the day will go.

I tried to nap today; it didn't happen. I am very tired, a physical and emotional tired. I have a head ache, probably stress or dehydrated from crying and not eating right. Just wore out or a combination of it all.

I'm sure it could also be from sleep deprivation and all my worry about Sonny, his mom and my mom.

I don't know if any of them will make it another year. Sonny's mom has skin infections on her legs from skin cancers that are open draining ulcers, and her dementia. My mom should not be driving, and she is unwilling to give it up even for her own safety. I just pray if she has an accident, she doesn't hurt someone.

4:45p.m.

Our daughter showed up to give me a card signed by all our kids and inside was a Visa card with a huge sum of money on it for gas and food while going back and forth to Rochester.

I really appreciate it and can use it. I would never burden them with any money issues.

Financially, I'm good so far but this hospital stay has been an expensive ride and it is far from over.

We have no money coming in except our Social Security and the check from the shop. I really have to cut corners and spend more wisely with all the trips to Rochester.

This was so generous of the kids and appreciated more than I have words for. We raised some great children we are both proud of.

Tonight, I am going to take a hot bath some Tylenol PM, a heat pack for my forehead and go to bed early.

Sunday June 16 Fathers Day

I went to bed last night by 8p.m.. I took a hot bath and literally fell into bed and went right to sleep.

I woke up around 12:45a.m. let the dog out to pee, got a drink and fell right back to sleep, that never happens.

Honestly, that never happens. I was awake again at 2:48a.m. I told myself I'd get up in an hour that this was too early, and dosed back off.

The next thing I know I look at the time it is 4:48a.m. and like yesterday I was woke up by a loud voice. I believe it's the voice of God. Loud and clear, saying to me **"sin no more and I will bless you"**

How can I do that I am human I am not perfect I make mistakes I am a sinner, we all are. I try so hard to be good. The Bible tells us **we all fall short of the glory of God, because of our sin.**

I got up made coffee, had breakfast and headed to the hospital to spend Father's day with Sonny.

Today Sonny was unplugged from a lot of tubes and wires. They removed the arterial line in his left arm for internal blood pressure, the incision drainage tube, the nasal oxygen tube, and they took out the two arterial port lines in his neck.

I'm sure he will be a lot more comfortable and sleep a lot better tonight with all the hoses and wires gone.The only foreign lines he has left are the feeding tube, the two port arterial lines in his right arm, and the catheter!

He still cannot control his bowels, and it's very embarrassing for him, because he is more mentally awake and aware of what is going on now. The nurses assure him it's just a side effect from the coma sedation and in a short time all of his body functions will wake up and return to normal.

I have to go back to Strong again tomorrow because Sonny is having some testing done and the surgeon will be in sometime between ten and eleven to let him know what the next progression and steps will be in his care.

Monday June 17

I'm headed back to Strong today, hopefully to more improvement and Sonny a bit stronger to be able to hold his own phone.

9:30a.m. I arrived at the hospital.

First thing he said to me was "you need to get on line and look at furniture stores and get me a lift chair and a walker. I can't call and I can't get up out of a chair because I can't use my arms, they don't want me to push with my arms because of the heart surgery until the ribs heal back together," he is angry, very angry at his confinement and inabilities.

I understand his upset, but don't start barking orders at me like that, soon as I walk in.

No hello, how are things, just barking orders, I guess he is feeling better!

I tried to get him to understand that they told him he couldn't use his arms for pushing himself up for six weeks and that as of today he only had five weeks left. It's not forever. That he can use his arms to feed himself, and to stop making the nurses feed him!

Then he says "I need a walker, because I don't want to fall." I understand that, I don't want him to fall either.

I told him that Dr. Knight said the more he walks the steadier more balanced he will get that he won't be using the walker for the rest of his life.

That pissed him off. I'm just trying to stay positive and encouraging for him.

I told him I'd get him another walker. We gave his other one away to a family that needed one. We didn't think he would ever need it again after his first knee surgery.

Sonny is quite angry about some things today. For some reason he thought I would be taking him home today. His feet are very swollen as is his right hand.

His cognitive, logical thinking is still off at times. When they asked him if he knew where he was, again he said "St Josephs Hospital." I don't understand why that is stuck in his thinking.

I don't get it; he has never been in St. Joseph's. Funny, the things he is confused about and other things he's very clear about.

He keeps on complaining about hearing a radio that never shuts off. He hears music coming from a radio all day and night. There is no radio playing I don't know what he is hearing. He has complained about that since he woke up from the coma.

He's mad at me for not admitting I hear it too. He tells me to Stop fucking with his head!

Today they will increase the Imodium for the diarrhea and decrease the diuretic medication called Lasix. That should help his control of both his bladder and bowels.

10:30a.m.

He had a swallowing evaluation to determine if they can remove the feeding tube. They gave him three different consistency's, a pudding, water that was thickened with a gelatin, and plain water.

At first, he took too big a bite of the pudding, followed by water and he choked.

We had to get him to slow down and take small bites and not gulp the water.

He did fine after that, no choking at all. They ordered him a meal tray for supper time.

He has to eat at least half of his meals when they come to him over the next twenty-four hours in order to get the feeding tube removed.

He is no longer peeing without control and they let him use the urinal. Now he has to master control of his bowels. The doctor said he is doing so much better that they are going to try to get him transferred to a regular room today too. Out of ICU, yes, that means one step closer to home.

Neurological testing that was done proved he is doing well and will continue to improve as the days go by. Some brain fog, and moments of forgetful interruptions is to be expected because his body has gone through so much in the last four weeks. Between the fevers, the infections, the surgery, the medical induced coma, being on the ventilator, medication and the blood loss there is bound to be brain fog, and some relearning.

11:30a.m.

He is drinking some ice water just staring out his window and he said

"Something must be wrong outside; someone just ran by the window"

I said "I hope not you are on the fourth floor" but just then I saw it too.

What we saw was a reflection of someone running down the hall, and it reflected on his window.

It was good to hear some sense of humor still exist in him

One of the medical supply stock girls came in his ICU room to restock the cabinets with IV lines, line flushes, gauze, tape, etc, she had a flat cardboard box in her hand full of supplies.

Sonny said to her "oh you brought me doughnuts"

She said, "You know better we can't let you have doughnuts here."

he told her "Ok, so you can't bring them to me, I know DD is across the street, get me outta here, well both go!"

Cracked her right up!

Tuesday June 18

I talked to him on the phone a little while ago and he said he is all wired up with an alarm system

If he leaves his chair it goes off.

He said he didn't know why they did that. But my guess is he must have tried to walk out on his own after I left last evening.

Imagine that!

There's a hospital cleaning lady who came into ICU yesterday and she said

"Hi Sonny, do you remember me?"

Sonny said "yes, you're the one who woke me up." (From his coma)

When the nurses were bringing him out of sedation she was cleaning in his room.

The nurses were calling "Paul........ Paul......... wake up, open your eyes Paul, wake up" he wouldn't respond, wake up or open his eyes.

The cleaning lady who had been there every day saw the sign that I hung over his bed since the day he was admitted that said

> **"My name is Paul but everyone calls me Sonny........I am not ignoring you.........I am deaf, I wear two hearing aids but without them I need you to please speak up."**

The cleaning lady walked over to his bed and asked the nurses, "can I try?" and they let her.

247

In a very loud voice, she said

"Sonny wake up, wake up Sonny, do you hear me, open your eyes."

He did and she told him "good morning handsome" she winked at him and smiled and went back to her job.

After that the nurses called him Sonny, and talked loudly.

Wednesday June 19

Today I did not go up. Today I took my oldest grandson birthday shopping since I missed his actual birthday because Sonny was so bad then. His birthday is June 9th.

Today the feeding tube came out. He is very happy about that. I hope he continues to improve.

Doug is going to go see him tonight I hope Doug finds him in mental clarity and doing well.

The last thing I want to do is to have my kids worry about Sonny or me. It's not their job, we are the parents.

Thursday June 20

Today held much promise. Sonny is showing improvements every day.

He is weak and tires very easily. All of that could be much improved if he could get food he could eat. But he doesn't have a choice. He gets only diabetic hospital food. He hates it and he eats very little because it is tasteless and also salt free.

Dr Knight his cardiologist came in today, first time Sonny had seen him in three days.

Sonny told him he wanted to go home. Dr. Knight said if things keep going as well as they are that he can go home on Monday. I pray this is true.

Dr. Knight told him he needed to start eating more in order to gain his strength. Sonny told him "the food was tasteless and in very tiny portions that even a bird couldn't live on what he is being sent to eat even if it was worth eating."

Dr. Knight left the room and came back a few minutes later. He told Sonny "from now on you can order anything you like off the menu, straight from the kitchen here's the phone number." No more diabetic menu food for Sonny. He's a happy man.

Today I was home by 3:30p.m.

I had things to do at home, I had to clean the pavilion tables, floor, and bathroom because it is being used by the Avoca Baptist Church for their senior citizen picnic on Friday.

I just started washing the tables and Roy stopped by to see if I needed anything done at the house. I told him no I was good.

He picked up the garden hose and cleaned the cement floor of the pavilion and I finished the tables and cleaned the bathroom.

I went home and Sonny called later to ask me to go check out lift recliners at HFO tomorrow. He called them they have three. I'll go check them out.

Libby called and I had to hear the same old stuff of her trying to manage my life and my home like I didn't know what I was doing. I know she's just trying to be helpful, but she has enough on her plate as it is, she doesn't need to worry about us too.

Libby: "Do you have any projects around the house that you want done?"

Me: "no, I'm all set, nothing going on that I can't do myself."

Her: "well we can help you"

Me: "We know that, and if we need anything, we will ask you."

I know the motive behind her words is she doesn't want anyone else helping Sonny and I she thinks we should only ask her and her brothers, and not our friends.

Yes, we have children, yes, we would call them if we needed them.

Thing is Sonny and I have been in the shoes of every one of our kids. They have businesses to run, their own homes and children to take care of, we understand that better than anyone.

When you work for your own profit you can't take time off, and when you get done at night your tired.

They don't need to travel one and a half hours both ways to visit Sonny, or come to our house and property to work. They have their own businesses and homes, children, and property to take care of.

If I'm not capable then we have plenty of retired friends who Sonny has spoken with about helping out and they do nothing all day long. They are retired too, and are willing to help us.

They offer all the time, Dick, Roy, Ken, Dave, all of them looking for something to do to break up their days and feel useful.

We are good with that and so are they, and we don't have to burden our kids or call them away from their jobs.

We definitely would call our kids if there is anything at all we can't do. For now, I am pretty self-sufficient and for the most part I don't even need any of the friends to help either. With what I know and with Sonny's advice and guidance there isn't much I can't do. We are both stubborn independent people!

Friday June 21 Today I went to HFO and got a lift chair for Sonny to use until he gets stronger, they will deliver it tomorrow. His walker came in today too.

I didn't go up to the hospital today.

He had a lot of visitors today. Roy went up, Dave and Joyce. Then a bunch of the guys from the farm came to see him, he had a nice visit with all of them. Lots of laughs and good conversation. That was good for him. Made him happy and done his heart and attitude a lot of good. Best medicine he has are his family and friends.

His sister Barb called him but she felt bad she couldn't talk very long. She told me she could hardly hear him, he had the TV turned up so loud. I don't think it was that the tv was that loud, it's just that the sound for the tv comes through the same hand held bedside device that he uses to call the nurse and he probably had it right beside his head near the pillow. She will call him again when he gets home.

Saturday June 22

I had to be there this morning by ten, because they thought I would be getting the training on taking care of his IVs at home. Turns out the home nurse who was going to go through the set up with me won't be there until he gets discharged on Monday.

I only stayed until 3p.m. today because my friend Lillian and I are going out for Chinese supper.

He was doing much better and is getting in and out of his chair to go to the bathroom by himself. They won't let him walk the hall by himself or even with me. There has to be a nurse there.

He is eating much better since he can order his own food from the regular menu.

I won't be back up until 8a.m. on Monday. He will be discharged then and I need to be there for the orders. I hope we are not sitting there all day waiting for doctor discharge orders!

Today I need to go get a bunch of groceries. Sonny wants my macaroni salad when he gets home. I haven't really restocked in the last six weeks. I have only gotten just what I needed. There was not much sense in cooking meals just for me.

I also have to do my laundry, clean the house, and change the bed sheets make the whole house as germ free as I can.

Cheryl D. and Mark D visited with Sonny today. Mark is a cancer patient at Strong too, he and Sonny went to school together. She sent me a message and a picture. He looks like he's doing really good. He is ready to come home and ready for a hair cut. Just two more days.

Sunday June 23

Today I will be sanitizing the bathrooms, cleaning house, cooking and baking. That way when I get him home, I will have less to do and be able to take care of what he needs until we get into a new routine.

This afternoon I have an acrobatic recital to go to for our granddaughter Trinity!

I got up a 4a.m. same as any other day. I made coffee, started the dishwasher and sat down with my tablet.

There was an I-message from Sonny sent at 12:40a.m.. He said he doesn't know what is going on but his BP is very low and has been dropping. It was 80/44 at that time. I don't know why he didn't call me and only messaged me I never heard the message notification.

When this happened before it was the automatic blood pressure machine that was at fault. They tried a couple of times with the machine, then they did it the old way with the pressure cuff that needed pumped up and stethoscope and got a better reading.

I'll wait to hear from him later instead of calling this early.

Monday June 24

I was told to be at the hospital by 10a.m. for training on his IVs.

Well, it didn't happen.

Sonny asked when he would be getting unhooked from the heart monitor and they said just before you go home at 4p.m.

We were both upset at this change of plans. Seems no one really knows or can give a straight answer. He just wants out of the hospital.

This is unacceptable, at times they seem to have no care. We have an eighty-five-mile drive home

I am in tears, Sonny is upset, we have both been misled about the time of his discharge. Our expectations crushed.

I can't ever believe anything the nurses say. But then again maybe they are at the mercy of someone else on his discharge. We are so disappointed and angry. We were so excited to know we'd finally bc on our way home.

Then to top everything off a cardiologist came and said we have to send him home on insulin shots!

Unbelievable he absolutely flat out refused to do the shots he told them no that they were wasting his time and theirs. He was on a pill, metformin, for years at home and that's what he's going back to.

A diabetic nurse came in and told us she would teach me how to give the insulin shots.

Sonny told them "say what you want I'm not doing shots at home or ever."

She also told me how and what to prepare for meals. Like I never cooked a meal in my life. Sonny was getting fisty. He told her "save your breath, my wife is the best cook in the state she knows how to cook for me"

A short while later a lady from cardiac PT came and lectured Sonny about PT and how he needs it. He refused PT also! It will cost us forty dollars in copay every time he goes and they want him to go three times a week. He said "Absolutely not, taking care of my home and property daily is my PT!"

At this point Sonny and I are ready to scream, our emotions, patients, and nerves are shot! When you anticipate something, an event, a happening, you look forward to doing what your told about or what is going to happen. But, when over and over it gets changed or taken away, it becomes hard to believe the one who is in charge of making things happen. Are the doctors calling the shots and making the nurses tell us? We have no idea at this point.

Now we were told, VHNA (visiting home nurse association) called around 2p.m. they won't be here until 5 or 5:30p.m. they got delayed!

This is beyond frustrating. To say we are both upset is putting it mildly.

To us it seems like have no respect for the patient and the family and what they are enduring or have endured.

I don't have any words right now except cuss words and I'm even to mad to cuss, but Sonny has plenty of them and doesn't hesitate to use them!

The teaching nurse from VHNA is finally here but the medicine and pump are not.

They have been delayed! OF COURSE, THEY HAVE!

We finally got out of the hospital around 7:00p.m. and home by 8:45p.m.

Both of us are exhausted!

Tuesday June 25

His first day home after six weeks away.

He slept very well last night for the first time in months, happy to be home.

No wondering, no grumpiness, no waking me up. At this point even if he woke me that would be ok, I'm just glad to have him home.

The VHN came today at 11:30a.m. It was a long visit. She had to go over all of his discharge orders and medications, and do all his vitals. She had to watch me hook up the IV antibiotics to make sure I knew what I was doing. She was here about two hours.

Kylie and Oscar stopped by for a couple of hours. While they were here Libby and the kids stopped by, we all had lunch together.

Our hair dresser Sue came to the house and cut Sonny's hair. His first hair cut in months. He really needed it. She is the best. She has been so good to us through all of Sonny's cancer routines when he was unable to go to her salon, she came to us.

Derick stopped by after he got out of work and put our sunroom air conditioner in the window, but not without some attitude from Sonny telling him how to do it.

Yup my bossy Sonny is back!

He was not patient at all. He never takes into account that Derick had not done this before and only Sonny knew how the extra window panel went in on top of the air conditioner because he was the one who designed it. Between us all Derick got it installed.

Sonny can be so rotten sometimes in how he treats others. That's how we all know he's feeling better!

Roy came by and fixed the hitch on the yard roller because Sonny wanted me to roll the playground and pavilion area this week.

While Roy was doing that Doug saw us all standing outside by the equipment. We were watching Roy.

Doug pulled in and was visibly upset that his dad was outside by the equipment. He thought Sonny was working on something. Sonny was not working or doing anything but standing there watching Roy. Doug calmed down before he left when he saw his dad was not actually doing anything.

Sonny asked Roy to mow from the barn driveway to the pond hydrant.

He told me to get the house lawn mowed, since it was a good drying day.

It's been a very wet spring and early summer. We have to mow when its dry and when we get the chance.

I finished mowing in about an hour and half. When I came in the house, he wanted supper right away and was bitchen at me about supper not being ready. Not even considering I had been outside mowing for the last ninety minutes!

Oh yea, he's feeling better, barking orders and demands proves it! I am glad he's back. That is not a sarcastic remark either, I truly mean it. When he's fisty then I know he's feeling much better. Welcome home Sonny, we sure did miss you!!!

It took me about half an hour to get supper on the table.

He is glad to be home and I'm glad to have him home and to not drive to Rochester. Maddie hasn't left his side. She's very happy to have her daddy home.

I have to remind myself his hands are tied right now and he is very limited in what he can do. That is very upsetting and frustrating to him, so he lashes out at those who do.

Wednesday June 26

What a miserable night.

He fell asleep in his chair right after supper, sometime after that I went to bed. At 9p.m. he came into bed. I did not hear him come in.

About 11p.m. he gets up from bed to go to the bathroom, I heard him get up. Next thing I know I heard him yell "Oh My God, Shirley help"

I jumped out of bed and went to see what was wrong, there was blood all over the bed, the bathroom floor, and his arm. About ten inches of IV tubing was hanging from his arm with a blood clot stringing from it.

In the living room in his recliner was the black bag that held his IV pump and bag of antibiotics and the rest of the IV tubing that is supposed to be hooked to him. The antibiotics were being pumped onto the carpet through the broken tubing.

Apparently when he woke up in his chair and went to bed, he picked up the IV bag set it in the seat of the chair then simply walked away without it and when he did the tube broke. He never noticed and went to bed and the tube bleed out onto the bed as he slept and until it formed a clot.

Could be he was not fully awake or walking in his sleep. Later when he got up to use the bathroom, he realized what he had done.

Turns out the blood on the bathroom floor was already dried on, which means the blood was flowing when he went to the bathroom before he came to bed.

He was so out of it and tired that he was not even aware of what he had done when he came to bed.

At 11:30p.m. I was changing the tubing and cleaning up dried on blood from his arm and the floor.

We were both so tired that I laid a towel over the bloody sheet on the bed and changed it in the morning.

He was able to go right back to sleep. As tired as I was, I laid there tossing and turning and worrying until well after two!

I had a dentist appointment today at 9a.m. I was gone until 11:30a.m. I had to get two fillings. My mouth is very sore. I hate the dentist.

When I got home Jack T. was here visiting with Sonny. It was nice to see him and even nicer to see Sonny in a good mood.

After we had lunch, we were getting ready to go roll the lawn at the pavilion and play ground with the RTV, when our son Scott stopped by. We had a short visit with him and then he had to get back to work.

We went to roll the yard and I drove and did the rolling all the while being instructed by Sonny.

I could tell by the way he was treating me he was not happy with how I was doing it. He yelled and cussed at me about how I was driving the roller, or how I was shifting the RTV. Nothing new but I still don't like it and I'll never get used to it.

I really wanted to yell back, but I know what that would have got me!

Again, I have to put myself in his place, to sit there and have someone else do your work when you are a doer is very hard and frustrating.

Terry and Margret, our neighbors stopped down and brought us some homemade chocolate chip cookies and stayed to visit for a while. She makes the best cookies. Still warm and so chocolaty and gooey good, right out of the oven!

Today was not quite as busy as yesterday but just the same our day was full. Sonny was mean, demanding, and hurtful. I know he is just frustrated by his situation. I try to make him feel helpful and useful. With time everything will get better, it just has too.

Later he took a two-hour nap got up and he went into the bathroom

Came out with his shorts in his hand and said

"Good morning" I just gave him a wired look. He said "are you friken happy, you always want me to say good morning" I told him "I never said that, and besides it's afternoon."

He argued with me that it is not.

Then he went to the kitchen and asked me why I didn't make coffee

It told him it's 3:30 in the afternoon, do you want me to make coffee?

Then he screamed at me and said

"you're a miserable bitch, knock it off or I'll send you to the middle of next week"

Here we go again, I don't know what or why the switch was flipped but he is confused and angry. I think a lot of the mean outburst must be a side effect of medication. He was fine before he took a nap.

A short while later I received a text from Vanessa asking if we were home that she and the kids were stopping by. Then he believed me it was afternoon!

He is quite confused at times, he doesn't understand the simple day to day things.

He asks me for things, no, he demands I get this or get that, and gets pissed because not every demand can be solved instantly.

Just like telling me to go mow the lawn and then soon as I walk in the door from mowing, he wants supper on the table!

He treats me like this all the time when it's just him and I, but if others are around, he speaks to me like he cares! Hurtful, all of it.

I'm tired, very tired of being on call in an instant! I try to put myself in his place but no matter how I try I just don't understand it.

He had anger issues for as long as we have been married, cancer only made things worse.

June 27

4:15a.m. My day begins.

A very long night. He was up wondering around, turning on lights, tv blaring, using the bathroom, changing his shirt and underwear. Every hour to hour and a half!!

I am beyond exhausted. I am so tired my tired is tired.

He doesn't know the difference between night and day and wondered why I wasn't making coffee at 1:30a.m.

At 3:15a.m he was changing his clothes again and I was sleeping in the living room in my recliner because he was in and out of the bedroom so much, I couldn't get any rest.

He came out to the living room to get dressed and turned on the light because he couldn't figure out how to get his underwear on.

Thing is he had a tee shirt in his hands and was trying to put his legs in the arm holes of his shirt. When I told him that was a tee shirt, he told me I was full of shit and why do I always fuck with his head! He was pissed and He went back to bed

He has no clue sometimes if it's day or night. I know the nurses warned me this is normal after being in a coma and on a ventilator and especially being in the hospital for so long! When you're in the hospital lights are on 24/7. There are all kinds of activity nonstop with nursing and custodial work. They try to normalize night from day by closing your door but then come in every two hours for vitals or to administer medications, or IV alarms go off. You really can't get any rest in the hospital unless you are sedated!

I guess even knowing it is normal and it will pass, still does not prepare you for how exhausting it is when its actually happening.

He is very bossy, demanding, and mean. I know no one will ever believe me because they don't ever see the worse of it, only a glimpse occasionally but never to the extreme that I have to put up with. I'll be darned if I will share this with my kids or family, they will insist I take him back to the hospital. I cannot and will not do that again. He made me promise not to ever take him to the hospital again. I promised him before and broke my promise.

He doesn't want to go. One thing he told me to promise, was to never take him again. He just wants to die and was pissed about Strong putting him on the ventilator when he has a standing DNR and DNI order. He questioned Dr. Knight about being put on the ventilator after surgery. Dr. Knight said it was because Sonny was still considered a surgical patient because the surgical site, his chest, was still opened and he was prepared to go back to surgery to close it up.

Sonny said if he can't ever work again then he might as well be dead.

I just wish he would make this known to the family so I don't look like the bad person, when actually I am just giving him what he wants. I can't do anything with him. He does not listen to me.

I hate when he says he just wants to die. I understand people who are terminal get sick and tired of being prodded and poked and laying in a hospital bed when it seems like they have no purpose in life. It hurts me too when I think of living without him.

Guess I'll just see how the rest of the day goes!

The nurse VHN showed up around 11:30a.m. took his blood and did vitals and changed his port lines and bandages.

He has slept a lot today so I bet any money he will be up all night and neither of us will get any sleep!

He wanted to go get ice cream today so we went to twin kiss he got an upside-down banana split and ate the whole thing.

We drove around the country for a bit and stopped at Eric's shop to visit and came home.

Coming down Jacobs Ladder Sonny said to me "I wonder why everyone has their yard lights on"

I just appeased him and said "oh, I didn't notice" because I know no one had lights on in the middle of the day in bright sun shine.

As I pulled in our driveway and he told me to;

"Just park in the drive way to the barn and I'll unload the hay wagon"

I asked, "what are you talking about?" He said "never mind I guess I need my head examined"

He says such random things I don't understand where they come from or why and neither does he.

About 7:30p.m he had a nose bleed. We could not get it stopped; it was awful!

He went to bed about 9p.m. thinking if he laid down the bleeding would stop. However about 10:45p.m. he got right up out of bed and headed to the bathroom in a hurry.

Made it as far as the sink and puked up blood and blood clots. Apparently, the blood just ran down his throat and pooled in his stomach, and made him sick.

He cleaned up and laid back down, for now the nose bleed seems under control.

Friday June 28

1:15a.m.

The same thing happened all over again. Puking blood clots and blood. After that I told him he better sleep in his chair to keep the blood from going down his throat.

His BP was good 118/80

We don't think there is internal bleeding.

He has an appointment with Dr Parker this afternoon so we will see what he has to say about it.

He went to his chair with a towel across his chest and a blanket across his legs. He fell right to sleep and I cleaned up the massive blood mess in the bathroom and did laundry.

I had an awful headache but it had to be done.

Three nights now and not much more than a few hours of sleep for me.

After cleaning the bathroom, I took some Tylenol and a heat pack and fell into bed exhausted.

I woke up about 5:15a.m. let Maddie out and made coffee, he was still sleeping.

He woke up around 6:20a.m. and immediately soon as he moved his nose started bleeding. I got him an ice pack to put on the back of his neck, as he held a cold wash cloth on his nose.

He again vomited blood clots this morning. I fixed him some dry toast and his protein drink

He was doing a bit better after he ate and the bleed seemed to stop for now.

He went to his appointment with Dr. Parker today. Everything seemed to go well. Dr Parker told him to cut back on the blood thinner, Warfrin, to take it once a day instead of twice. He didn't seem to concerned about Sonny's nose bleeds.

On the other hand, his weight is up to 171. I'm pretty sure it's because of how good he is eating now. Hopefully he is on the tract to getting some energy and life back.

Monday July 1

His feet are always swollen he is up about every hour all night long and naps a lot during the day, always with his feet elevated so we don't understand the fluid buildup in his feet.

He has been going to the barn to clean his tool box and tools up. He gets quite upset if I mention anything about getting rid of some of them, even though he often mentions selling some of his tools.

Thing is I know he is not going to be taking the big box to the farm or anywhere else. I know his boys would all like to have some of his tools. He doesn't need to keep them when he won't be working on any heavy equipment. I suppose it's just the security of the only life he has ever known

Dr Parker's office called and they changed his warfarin dose to two times a day and changed his diuretic to two pills, two times a day, until he is off the IV medications, because the IV antibiotics flow through massive amounts of fluid so his system is on it constantly and causes water retention in his extremities. Sonny says he's not going to take any more medication, period!

Tuesday July 2

Today we went out to breakfast, at the Sunrise in Dansville and then took some tools back to Schumacher's Farm that were not his, but in his tool box.

We went to Libby's gym because the equipment came in and Sonny wanted to watch them unload it but, he got very bossy with them. They didn't seem to mind, or they just ignored him. He needs to mind his own business I just don't want him pissing everyone off being so bossy. I guess it's his nature to tell people what to do.

Sonny's IV pump isn't working right. I'm supposed to change out the medication bag every twenty-four hours Which is around 8:30p.m. every night.

Today it was completely dry by 2p.m. I called the pharmacy and they sent out another one and it was here by 6p.m. I hooked it up right away.

We will be glad when he doesn't have to do that anymore, he hates it.

Wednesday July 3

He doesn't sleep very well at night; he is up about every one to two hours because of the fluid and having to go pee. His feet are so swollen and his knee is hurting him pretty bad.

Medical carrier brought antibiotics today. Other than that, it was a quiet uneventful day.

Thursday July 4

No festivities for us, no fireworks show Sonny isn't up to it. VHN came today to take blood and vitals It is very hot, 90+ and very humid, miserably humid!

Brian and Brenda stopped by to visit. They are here for the family reunion this weekend.

Friday July 5 2019

Another hot and humid day, ninety plus degrees again

Many folks from Indiana came around noon to help put up the big party tent at the pavilion. It took us three tries, then we called Scott to find out what we were doing wrong.

After we talked to him, we got it figured out and up. Finally!

I sweat so much and for so long my heart was just pounding out of my chest and my face was very red, I dehydrated very fast in this heat everyone did.

Sonny supervised but there is no way he could have helped in this heat. Maybe next year he will have his strength back, and be thinking clearly.

We came home, cooled off in the AC, and ran the IV treatment, and he napped

Friday evening, we had quite a few people show up for potluck reunion dinner and it rained. Actually, it was a torrential down pour for about half hour. The yard and driveway at the pavilion flooded very quickly. It was raining so hard it was actually deafening on the metal roof, you could not talk to anyone even standing beside you.

We left for home around eight. Sonny was exhausted and needed rest, I was pretty tired too, the others stayed at the pavilion.

Saturday July 6

Ritter Family reunion day.

Another hot sweltering day on the 90's and we are expecting heavy rain again today.

A very busy day for us. Sonny stayed all day he was unable to do much physically but he visited with a lot of people. That was good for him.

We Came home about 5:30p.m. and he crashed in his recliner tired but happy to be strong enough to go to the reunion. Everyone was glad to see him. Next year he will be able to be more involved in the set up and the tear down process.

Sunday July 7

Reunion breakfast at 8a.m. at Libby's.

We got back home around eleven. Sonny and I worked on getting the motor home back in the barn so it's not sitting outside being bleached out by the summer sun. He actually let me back it on the barn for the first time!

After that he had a nap, and I cleaned up from the reunion.

Around 3:30p.m. we went to Walmart he stayed in the car with the air conditioner running, and I got the things we needed. Then we went to Country Kitchen for early dinner.

I was exhausted from the busy weekend, I took a bath and was in bed watching tv by eight thirty, I woke up and turned tv off at 9:45p.m.

Sonny was sleeping comfortably in his recliner. Maybe it will be a good night for both of us.

1:30a.m. The alarm on the IV pump woke me from a sound sleep. I got up and just turned it off. I had to in order to get the doses on a schedule that we can do, and not middle of the night changes. The alarm never woke Sonny he slept right through it.

I restarted a full bag of antibiotics at 5:30a.m. by all reasoning it should need changed in twenty-four hours 5:30 a.m. tomorrow morning. It's a twenty-four-hour drip.

Monday July 8

VHN Kristin came today. She changed his port covering, took blood, and vitals.

His temp was 100.7 so she called infections disease doctors and left a message.

They called Sonny back about half hour later. They suspect that the antibiotics might be killing the good bacteria in his body as well as the infection causing ones.

They want a sample of his bowels! He is not happy about that! I don't think he will comply.

Nope, he isn't going to do that; they have invaded his body and privacy enough. He said "the only way they are getting a stool sample from him is if he shits his pants and he has no intention of doing so". He flat out told them absolutely not.

It's over ninety degrees outside naturally a person is going to be warmer than normal! He feels fine.

Tuesday July 9

Today he decided go out and mow the lawn around the pond. I don't think it's a good idea but I am not one to stop him. He wouldn't listen to me anyhow.

I have no doubt about the no pain from the surgery but his knee is pretty badly swollen and causes him a lot of pain. Matter of fact most of his right leg is swollen from his toes to his thigh. He doesn't see the orthopedic until the eighteenth of July, another nine days.

Wednesday July 10

One month ago, today he had his heart surgery, ended up in a coma on a ventilator for five days. It is quite remarkable that with all his issues and problems that he had going into and coming out of surgery that he is even here to talk about it. Just one month ago the heart surgeon said he'd be in the hospital about eight weeks. I guess they really don't know my husband, and his determination.

I don't know what the future holds, I would not even dare guess. I just know we are in it together; we are not quitters.

We are hoping this is the worse it gets this year and for a very long time. He has had enough, he just wants some quality of life, some enjoyment, not all doctor, specialist, and medications.

Today he has two appointments one with the oncologist Dr Passero and one with the cardiac surgeon Dr Knight.

We are hoping for some changes. One is no more Revlimid, chemo he doesn't want to take it anymore. He said he will refuse it. Yes, it has helped control his cancer, but it has also destroyed other parts of his body, his immune system, his heart, liver, kidneys, nerve damage with neuropathy. Those are only the things we know for sure. He wants no more chemo and hopes it's not too late to save or restore the health of his vital organs.

Two is no more blood thinners or at least cut back on them.

He has question about his DNA after so many blood transfusions during and after heart surgery. He wants to know does he have his own DNA or that of the many blood donors? He was given over thirty-six units of blood.

We found out today that Sonny can be seen in Hornell starting September. He does not have to take any more Revlimid, chemo. It is indeed his choice and that will be medically recorded as his choice! He is very happy about that!

At over $18000.00 for a month's supply, I'm sure our insurance company is happy about that too.

We also found out it takes three months before his own blood has completely regenerated in his body and replaced all the donor blood until then he has a mix of DNA, his and donors from his heart surgery.

Cardiac surgery team has discharged Sonny and he was told he could resume all activities with no restrictions. He is very happy and once again positive that all is finally going in his favor.

It was very good and positive follow up on cardiac and oncology. We are pleased with all we were told today.

Thursday July 11

Today the VHN came and did vitals and blood draw, we hope for the last time.

She said if the arterial lines come out tomorrow, they will come back Monday and write the discharge for Sonny to sign.

Our hope and prayers are that Friday the infectious disease unit will agree to pull the lines and discharge Sonny as well.

Then maybe he can get on to a somewhat normal life for at least a month before going back one last time to Strong, Wilmot Cancer Center. As they say time will tell.

Friday July 12

What a big waste of time.

Today he went to infectious disease appointment thinking he was done with IVs, but no, two more weeks of being tied to the antibiotic routine and excess fluid in his feet and legs, from the IV's. He is not happy at all! He is a very angry man right now.

I for one feel very bullied by Dr. Ted Louis and Dr. Attar.

They said it's because of the rare infection of listeria and that it infected his heart and he had to have surgery to replace the aortic valve due to the listeria.

I jumped right on that letting them know that his valve had been leaking for years and the surgery was already planned long before he even ended up in the hospital with the listeria.

Their argument was the listeria made it worse and if it weren't for the listeria, he would not have needed the surgery. That is totally not true and I informed them of that! He had seen Dr Knight and knew his transplanted heart valve from 2010 was leaking long before the listeria infection. They just were not listening to reason or what I was saying. They hate it when a patent is right!

Again, I told them both it was leaking for years before the listeria and he was already scheduled for the surgery in June before he ever contracted the listeria! They are bullies!

Sonny was pissed at how they were talking down to us, he spoke up and said to them "just shut up a minute and listen to my wife, she can explain it better than I can, and she speaks for me." Still, they refused to believe me.

I also questioned them about the fact that they told us four weeks ago when Sonny was in ICU that there were no listeria bacteria growing in the blood cultures.

Then they go off on a rant "well he has MM and the treatment compromises his immune system and he needs two more weeks of IV antibiotics."

We are not happy at all, not only are we both tied to taking care of the IVs, but it affects his blood sugar numbers, and fills his system with fluids therefore causing frequent bathroom trips, diarrhea, swollen legs, and feet, and a greater chance of congestive heart failure.

It seems to us like a no-win situation. If it were not for the chance of bleeding Sonny said he'd take the lines out himself.

I'm not really sure if he will do the whole round this time or stop it on his own.

They should not have bullied us and used scare tactics to force him to keep the arterial lines.

That is so wrong! Not once did anyone say we understand your situation, or we're sorry.

So many things Strong did to us this time that we're wrong, and unlike any way we have ever been treated before. We were never treated this way by anyone in the last six years, ever! This last ordeal has been absolutely awful. To many inconsistencies with too many doctors and specialist each calling the shots and never communicating between each other, and bad treatments.

They say surgery is at 10:30a.m. then don't take him until 6p.m.

Told me to be there by 10a.m. to take him home then to find out the arrangements to receive the medication we're never made until that afternoon and discharge was after 7p.m. just to name a few.

Sonny and I should have a very big ulcer with all the waiting, all the hope all the anticipations, the gut aches, the going without food and drink, feeling hopeful one minute, then disappointed, and depressed the next.

At the end of today I feel resentful once again!

I hate myself for feeling like this!

All my thoughts are going back years. Back to when I was so sick or had a migraine that would last for days yet I had to work and take care of my family. All the times I thought I could go to the doctor or at the very least stay home and take care of myself, and I couldn't because he would not let me! I had to tough it out!

I am feeling very resentful because he was and is always taken care of by me.

I guess most men are not nurturers by design!

I better leave that thought right there.

I know cancer is no comparison for my past health issues, but we both took the oath "in sickness and health" I guess today I'm just very tired and disappointed. Wearing my feelings on my shirt sleeve is not good, but this journal is real and truthful. I love him with all my heart and I'd do anything for him. I guess I'm just very tired!

Saturday July 13

Sonny had an appointment with Dr. Varon his cardiologist

It was another long wait and a long appointment but very worth it.

Dr Varon was very impressed with how far Sonny has come. He said his heart was doing very well, and strong, and there were no concerns that he could see or hear. He took him off all heart medication and put him only on Eilquis.

His heart is still in Afib but he told us that is nothing to be concerned about so soon after surgery and it can be fixed in about six months if it does not correct its self as his heart heals. Sometime next year, around January or February of 2020 if he still has Afib.

Sonny is very happy about that. The side effects of always being physically exhausted due to medication are awful.

In August he will have Sonny wear a heart monitor for twenty-four hours after he comes in for an EKG just so they can have a comparison and keep a check on things.

Dr. Varon said if after six months if his heart is still in Afib they will schedule up a heart shocking appointment to get his heart back in rhythm, and that it usually works after valve replacement. Over all things are going well.

Now if only he could get his strength back and his knee healed or fixed, he'd feel pretty good and almost normal.

Wednesday July 17

Back at Wilmont in Rochester to see the oncologist Dr. Passero

This was to get information about transferring to Hornell for follow ups and or treatments if needed.

This was Sonny's request due to travel to and from Rochester every month, he didn't want to do that anymore. I support that as well.

Turns out Hornell cancer center does not have an infusion center at this time. Nor do they have MM oncologist specialist.

Their oncologist is general in their specialty. Meaning the oncologist, whoever they are treat all cancers, straight across the board. One oncologist might have several patients during the day. One patient for lung cancer, one for breast cancer, one for prostatic cancer, ect. They do not specialize in any particular cancer.

At Strong you see the oncologist of your specific type of cancer, and Strong being a university hospital has all the latest treatment that are available.

It turns out Sonny will stay at Strong and with Dr Passero and Cheryl B He will go to follow ups every other month with blood draw at Noyes on the in between months, with emails on his health and condition. That is doable and less stressful for us. Sonny agreed to that schedule.

One more big concern is his weight went from 174 two days ago to 166 today. They don't know why because he eats really well. We are wondering if someone just recorded his weight wrong.

Something to keep an eye on. It might be his body eliminating the fluid from all the IVs. That seems the logical answer according to Dr Passero. Still, that seems a lot for a two-day loss of eight pounds.

Thursday July 18

Today he went to the Orthopedic in Dansville and saw Dr. Fiendman

The conclusion after exam was that yes there is fluid in the knee, and a whole lot of arthritis. He will need knee replacement eventually. His other doctors have to sign off before it can happen, the oncologist, the primary, infectious disease team, and the cardiologist. Just like any other surgery he has to get all that consent for.

Dr. Fiendman drew some fluid off the knee to send in to be cultured, and Sonny has to go back next week to get the results.

He is still in a lot of pain and is hoping the doctor will draw off all the fluid next week.

Saturday July 20

Today his weight is 162pounds, so still losing. We are a little bit concerned and I don't know what or why he is losing.

Another thing every time he eats a meal it goes right through him. Often, he has to leave the table to go to the bathroom before he can finish his meal. It goes straight through him.

Monday July 22

This should be the last week of IVs and in-home nurses' visits! He is glad about that.

He is having a lot of knee pain. It interrupts his sleep every night, ice packs help the most. They numb the pain.

He does however nap a lot during the day, hours at a time due to the amount of pain medication he is taking for the pain in his knee.

Thursday July 25

Today is the end of the IV antibiotics, we are both so glad!

Friday July 26

Today Kristen the home nurse came by and took out Sonny's PICC line.

She had a measurement of comparison, 43cm when it was put in, it has to measure the same when she pulls it. But when she pulled it out it was only 42cm.

There is a bit of a concern about the 1cm that is missing.

Was it never there in the first place? Did someone just record the in going length wrong?

Was it really forty-two but the two looked like a three when the technician wrote it?

Worst case scenario, there is 1cm of PICC line inside his heart.

After many calls to his cardiac team in Rochester they decided to give benefit of the doubt.

We have faith, and are trusting that it was just written wrong, and nothing is left behind. After many phone calls they decided to just record what she actually drew out and know in good faith that the forty-three was just a miss print.

Monday July 29

Today he went back to the orthopedic. The doctor drew a little more fluid off his knee, as much as he could. He said there is fluid in there that he can't get because the tissue has a consistency like a sponge and he can't draw the fluid out of it.

Sonny asked for a cortisone shot and the doctor told him he has too much antibiotics in his system. That being said the cortisone would only make things worse. We don't understand that, but it must be a side effect of cortisone.

That explains why his knee got worse from the shot he received in the hospital. At that time, he was on four different antibiotics.

Basically, bottom line is, he has to suffer with the pain until he can have knee replacement, in six to twelve months, sometime in the spring of 2020.

That can't come soon enough for him. I feel bad for him, he just gets the clear for not doing chemo, gets his heart all fixed and healing well, then the knee is so painful!

Seems like this man can never get a break!

August 21

It has been almost a month since I wrote. Sonny is acting kind of strange.

He is on edge, snappy, rude and mean.

He had a cardiologist appointment today for an echocardiogram and had to have a twenty-four hour heart monitor put on. While waiting for his turn he proceeded to read the photo on the wall of 1890 tree sale and prices. He read them out loud, very loudly so everyone in the waiting room was looking at him. Very odd behavior for someone who doesn't like to draw attention to himself.

On the way home he just spouts off about random things and gets upset with me and yells because when I ask him what he means or what he was talking about

He says I "wasn't paying attention to what he was saying."

I was paying attention, it's just the things he was saying didn't make sense so I was asking questions.

August 23

He is absolutely crazy and I don't look forward to today. He has been up wandering around the house and going to the bathroom every hour sometimes every twenty minutes. I wonder if he has another UTI.

It has been two nights now with very little sleep for me and for him

When he does settle down it's constant talking and humming that drives me and Maddie nuts.

His hand tremors are bad. I don't know how to help him. I feel helpless, I'd like to go to the ER with him to find out if there is something, they can do for him. Is it just his medication, or something else going on? He made me promise not to take him to the hospital ever again. My heart is breaking.

I have an appointment today for my car service and he is supposed to go to the gym to re wire the water pump but I'm not sure if he is mentally capable.

I know Libby will want him to go to the doctor, or hospital, but no matter what he is going through he made me promise not to ever take him to the hospital again.

When he gets done at the gym with the water pump, he has plans on going to the farm to visit.

I know when Elizabeth sees how he is she will be all over me. There really is nothing I can do when he won't let me notify his doctors, and I can't go behind his back. I won't, I have to respect his wishes.

I made a promise to him and I already reneged a couple of times on that promise, if I keep doing that, he will never trust me again when it comes to his care.

Do I live with him granting his wishes and the promise I made him, or do I give into my selfishness of wanting to keep him living?

Turned out he was mentally in a good place to rewire the water pump and was doing well the rest of the day. He had a nice visit at the farm and everyone was happy to see him.

August 30

He had his cardiac follow up from wearing the monitor. Dr. Varoon said he has moments of elevated heart rate and added an extra heart pill, metoprolol.

Sonny does not want to take it; he told the doctor he didn't need any more pills.

Also, the dr. told us that his mitral valve and tricuspid valve are both leaking now. We don't get it, all was good and no leaks after the surgery, now three months later two other valves are leaking?

Sonny does not want to have another surgery, so he told the doctor he'd take a chance and live with it. Dr Varon told him he'd see him back in six months.

September 3, 2019

The past week Sonny has been so unpredictable, explosive, and mean to me.

I hate that no one sees this side of him.

No scratch that, I'm glad no one sees that side of him! At the same time, I know it's nothing he can control. Pain makes people mean some times.

He is in a lot of pain with his knee and I am getting the brunt of it. I try to make him comfortable as I can doing everything for him so he doesn't have to move.

Today he goes for an MRI. I hope there is an answer for his knee pain in the MRI.

Yesterday we went to Scott and Lorrie's 25th anniversary party. It was a nice time with good food, good friends and family. Sonny did very well, he stayed and visited with many, he ate a good meal. He did go home early due to his knee pain and being so exhausted.

I wish more of Lorrie's family would have showed up but they didn't.

For the last two weeks he has been having a lot of bladder issues.

He has many urinary accidents throughout the day, and changes his underwear about four times every night and has to wear adult men's disposable underwear.

He has dizziness throughout the day and has now gone back to constantly clearing his throat, singing, humming, and talking in his sleep. I am so sorry he has to go through all of this, I wish I could change it all. I guess I will never understand this part of what he is going through.

My heart breaks for all he is going through. I wish I could fix it, all of it

Sonny went for his MRI on his knee. We will have the results on September 11th. I sure hope it's something that can be fixed and he can be without pain again. He would feel pretty good over all if his knee didn't hurt so much.

It really sucks that he has to deal with so much pain.

I don't know how he does it, most people would have given up through all of the crap he has been through!

Thursday September 5

Grandkids went back to school today.

Sonny called from the farm at about 8a.m. Dr. Fienman the orthopedic called him and said he needed to see him at 9:30 today to discuss the results of the MRI. We don't have to wait until the 11th. I'm not sure if that means good news, and they can fix it right away, or there is something more serious.

Turns out the two large bones in his leg, the one below the knee and the one above the knee both had fractures "old fractures" that already healed, as well as torn meniscus that never healed.

We believe that happened in May when he fell off the scrap metal trailer at the recyclers, when he took the load over for Schumacher's Farm.

He had been in unnecessary extreme pain since then and no one, no one would listen to us or investigated beyond saying it was arthritis! This could have been fixed a long time ago if "they" (all the doctors) would have just listened to us.

Why the hell don't doctors listen to the patient? We know our body's, doctors don't live in our body, so listen, just listen to the patient please! It works both ways, we hear you, we do what is recommended, so why not listen to our concerns too?

Now the plan is to get clearance from the cardiologist, the oncologist, infectious disease team, and the primary care doctors so he can have surgery to repair the damage and free up the knee and pain he has had for over four months now!

Such incompetence in all the doctors is all I can say right now! We are so angry, its beyond words!

Saturday September 7

Another sleepless night for Sonny and me.

He is back to clearing his throat all the time, coughing, humming, talking in his sleep! Mentally confused at times, unable to think, he can hardly walk because of the pain. I hate he has so much pain and confusion and I can't help him.

I am so tired; I just want two hours of uninterrupted sleep.

I got up at 2:15a.m. after hearing him every stinking hour trying to walk around turning on lights, turning on tv, moaning, humming, singing, talking, very disruptive to me, not restful for him either.

I gave him some quick release morphine for the pain, and an ice pack for his knee, after about an hour he fell asleep. But still humming and talking in his sleep.

Last time I looked at the clock it was after 3. I finally dosed off.

I finally got up at 4:15a.m. and made coffee. He slept until 5:30a.m.

He woke up very mean. First thing he said to me was

What time did you get up? I told him and then out of the blue he said

"I don't know why I ever loved you" I told him "that wasn't a nice thing to say." As I choked back burning tears

He said "but it's the truth!" again my heart is broken by his words. Words I know he would not say if he were in his right mind.

He cranked tv up so loud the neighbors could hear it. I asked him if his hearing aid blue tooth wasn't working, he said "ya it is." I asked him "how come you have tv cranked."

He said "just to piss you off" so I got the remote and turned it down and he laughed and cranked it back up! He is such a childish ass sometimes!

This is not the man I married. Life has done us both wrong in the last six years, very wrong!

Then I went to my office/library to work on a funeral service I had in progress for Butch M. A longtime friend and neighbor, that I will be officiating this weekend.

He is being really mean and irritating this morning. Humming and part whistling through his teeth, laughing out loud uncontrollably at times. It's like he's slowly going out of his mind.

I am very worried about tomorrow and his behavior at Butch's funeral service.

Sunday September 8

The funeral/memorial service went well. It was the biggest crowd I ever had to speak in front of. Sonny was very good, well mannered, he was sociable, and did well the whole day.

September 16 2019

Tuesday

A very sad day in our family. Our brother-in-law Tim F. died at a hospital in Kentucky after suffering a massive heart attack on Thursday September 12, 2019.

He was an avid marathon runner and always seemed in good physical health.

Though he had a bad heart attack about five years ago he recovered amazingly.

He did have a history of high blood pressure and cholesterol problems, even so he was the picture of good health and it was totally unexpected and very sad.

His services will be this coming Saturday Sept. 20 at the Methodist church in Bath.

He leaves behind his wife Lori, his daughter Courtney and his son Mitchell.

Sonny was taking it very hard at first. When I told him all he kept saying was, "damn you Tim, that was supposed to be me, damn you Tim"

I went to see Sonny's mom and sister yesterday, and he went to the farm where he works.

My bet is he will not go see his mom or his sister until he sees them at the funeral.

I guess everyone handles death differently.

Many times, he has said he doesn't want to be here. He wants to check out, he's tired of the fight of cancer, the doctor appointments, of the daily medication just to live in a body full of pain.

Every time he turns around there's a new symptom, a new unexplained pain in his bones somewhere. Yet he pushes on persevering every day, for that we are all grateful.

Could very well be as his wife I am a bit selfish because I do want him here to grow old with me. I don't like it when all he talks about is "checking out" of this life. I try to understand all he has been through and all he has yet to go through. I'm hoping when he gets his knee fixed, he will have some good quality of pain free or minimal pain life. He deserves a life without pain.

He is a fighter, I think deep down he doesn't really want to die, he just wants the pain to be gone and death is the only way he knows will achieve that.

He has told me a few times, when he is himself and of sound mind, if it were not for me taking care of him, he would not be here, he would have stopped all his medications a long time ago.

Deep in his heart I know he does love me and appreciate me.

He has cut his hours back at the farm to half a day, I think that is good.

Saturday September 21 2019

Today was Tim's funeral. It was a beautiful tribute to him. Good music and speakers.

Sonny wondered why when someone dies, they are always made out to be a saint?

By listening to these speakers today Sonny said they made Tim sound like a saint sent from heaven who was sent to save souls, and now returned.

Not just Tim's funeral but many we have been to, the speakers always do that.

Sonny told me "do not do that to me, I am not a saint, I'm an ass and I've raised hell, tell them the truth."

One thing about today that really pissed Sonny off was to see all the pictures of family get togethers that included his mom, his sister's and their families, cousins, aunts and uncles, but that we were not invited too, nor were our children.

He said "I can count on my fingers the times we were included in my family gatherings." He was quite angry and says screw them all.

He was pissed to have his sister Barb say to him,

"I don't know what our little sister is going to do now"

I don't know why that statement made him so mad but it did. He really dwelled on that for some reason. He is not handling Tim's death very well.

Sunday September 22

Today on his Facebook page Sonny saw photos of a get together memorial hike for Tim at Mossy Bank Park. He said he could not have walked the hike but he could have sat with his mom while everyone else went walking and hiking. We knew about the hike but didn't know that his sisters were going to take their mom. She doesn't really understand everything any more, and we could have helped. It is what it is!

As they say it's all water under the bridge, none of us get do overs when it comes to life's moments.

Monday September 23

First day of fall, not bad outside a warm eighty degrees and a bit cloudy.

Sonny told me this morning that last night he passed out and fell in the sunroom around 1:30a.m, when he let Maddie outside.

He said he remembers getting very dizzy and falling but he doesn't know why or what happened.

When he came to and got himself up, he went to the kitchen and checked his sugar glucose number and it was 220, so it was not because his sugar was low.

I guess we will have to keep an eye on how he is and what is going on. I'm glad he didn't get hurt.

He has an infected finger that he keeps draining puss out of.

A few weeks ago, he had a metal sliver in it and he dug it out with his pocket knife. No big deal he does that all the time. Not very sterile but it's what he has always done. Every farmer, carpenter, or mechanic has a trusty pocket knife used for everything. Like its some kind of multi tool.

Every day since then the finger has been sore. He cleans it with peroxide, puts drawing salve, or antibiotic ointment on it and a bandage.

Every day when he changes the bandage it drains puss and smells really bad. Rotten like dead animal along the road smell. I want him to go get it checked out. He says it will be ok he doesn't need to go to the doctor for every little scratch and cut. It would only give the doctors a reason to send him to the hospital for "tests" then slap his ass in a bed. His words. He doesn't trust them!

Wednesday September 25

Today is our youngest sons fortieth birthday

Wow I can't believe it. Where has all the time gone.

Never in my wildest dreams did I ever think my grandma was right when she talked about time going by so fast the older you get. She always said "the older I get the faster time goes!"

Sonny is losing more physical strength all the time, though he seems to be eating good once again.

He has cut his work hours at the farm to half days. Well as of last week he did. This week they are chopping corn and he is driving truck to and from the field, so he is working quite late every day. So much for half days, but it's not strenuous work. He loves it, it's in his blood.

He comes home in quite a bit of knee pain, but he won't tell John he can't work. Work is his life, work is Sonny Obrochta purpose in life.

When he gets home, he eats supper takes a shower, takes his medication, ices his knee, he is asleep in his recliner within an hour of sitting down.

Today he complained of awful burning mouth pain, pain in his knee, and muscle cramping on his hands and legs. He said his mouth feels like it's on fire, so he's sucking on ice chips. He also holds ice packs in his hands to stop the cramping of his hands and fingers.

He is being very mean in his talk. I'm sure it's because of the pain. The thing that stinks about that is, everyone else sees the good side of him, I am the only one who sees and gets his wrath.

When others are around, he will speak to me in a decent tone but soon as it's just him and I, he turns into the devil.

I think it's how he handles pain I have to constantly tell myself to not take it personally and know it's only because of the pain.

Sunday September 29

5a.m. Well, he's in a lovely rotten mood

I wasn't even done with my first cup of coffee and he said:

"Are you going to mow today?"

I said "it's been raining most of the night, if it dries out, I'll mow, if not I'll do it this week."

He yelled "You better get it done before we go out with John and Debbie for dinner"

I said "what the hell, what's the big hurry, and why the hell are you so pissed?"

He just grits his teeth, clenched his fist, and glared at me.

It's going to be a great day! Not!

Every day I tell myself, "this isn't him, It's just the pain, it's just the pain, it's just the pain!"

My heart is breaking a little more every day to see him go through this. I am trying to be patient but sometimes I just have to yell back. Then hate myself for how I reacted.

He went out to mow grass around the pond at 9:30a.m. and didn't come back in until 2:30p.m.

When he got back, he said he just couldn't get it all done.

He had to mow slowly because the ground is so rough, he couldn't tolerate the bouncing, due to the pain in his knee. He said he will have to call Roy to mow the next time.

We went out to dinner at Texas Roadhouse with John and Debbie. It was nice to visit with them. Sonny didn't socialize much, but I think it was because he only has one hearing aid, one is at the audiologist for repairs and can't really hear all that good with just one.

We got home and again he was on me about mowing around the house.

He asked if I was going to mow. I told him I'd do it this week but it was getting dark out now.

Then he said "ya know what?" I said "what?"

He said "I don't give a flying fuck if the grass gets up to the windows."

Then he got his pajamas on, sat in his recliner, and turned tv on.

Monday September 30

1:45a.m.

First thing I noticed was the strong presence of Arlene. I got out of bed and soon as I walked to the living room, it smelled like I had walked through the door to her house.

Is she here or is my house smelling like her house did in her last days, the days before a person dies? Is there an odor of death? I don't know. I just know I'll never forget the way her house smelled every time I went there in the last year of her life. A musty, leftover food smell. Like the windows needed to be opened.

Sonny has been up every hour to go to the bathroom

He is having a lot of difficulty walking. A lot, he doesn't, or can't even lift his feet. He just shuffles along at a snail's pace.

I went to the garage and got his walker at 1:45a.m. so he doesn't fall again. If he falls there is no way I could get him up on his feet again without help. We had put the walker away some time ago when he started to use the cane instead.

He is not sleeping well, again with the humming, talking nonsense, the gurgling in his throat, just like back in May all over again, and it worries me, thinking maybe there is another blood infection that is affecting his brain.

I cannot sleep because of the noises he makes, and worrying about him falling when he's up wandering around the house.

He is still losing weight he now weighs the same as I do, according to our scales. Thing is he eats very good.

I am so tired, even though I have been in bed since 8:30p.m. I turned tv off at nine, I have been laying here over four hours, I should have been sleeping but my sleep has been interrupted about every half hour to hour with Sonny shuffling around going to the bathroom or his noises in his sleep.

As I write this, I am so tired, but unable to sleep. Sonny doesn't sleep well either, so it's not just me.

I know I complain or comment a lot about being tired and not sleeping, but this is our reality of living with and caring for a cancer patient. It's so hard on everyone.

5:15a.m.

He is awake and wandering around, and out of his mind. Saying strange things and commenting on the news, things that make no sense at all

291

Like: "what the hell are we going to do about all the snow," (it snowed in Montana this weekend) he saw it on the news, and is thinking we got a lot of snow.

He has closed caption turned on because he can't hear very well with only one hearing aid. As he is trying to read the captions, he is complaining that he can't pronounce the big words, that they don't make sense to him.

A news story about kids with peanut allergy was being reported on and his solution is, make them go to a peanut farm and pick peanuts, then he laughs.

Sometimes his humor is still intact.

He stood up to go get his coffee and he stood in front of me and said"

"Shoot me please, I'll stand right here!"

We are both so tired. I'm sure he will sleep a lot today then not sleep tonight, but me, I'll still have to take care of him and the house.

Thing is I know tonight will be a repeat of last night, and the night before that, and most every night, of interrupted sleep! I am getting awful headaches lately. I'm sure it's from lack of restful sleep.

He doesn't have a clue, he doesn't even remember getting up every half hour to go to the bathroom or just walking around the house, he has no clue he was gurgling, humming, or singing all night long!

He just laughed at me when I tried to tell him! I can't even put into words how tired I am!

Roy stopped by this morning to see us and see if we needed anything done around the house, but we are all set for today. He's a good friend to us both, but sometimes we are in no mood for company or talking.

Tuesday October 1

This morning I slept until 4:15a.m, ahhhhh blessed sleep.

I heard Sonny out in the kitchen making coffee.

Yesterday he could hardly walk, walking only with the walker, he didn't sleep hardly at all on Sunday night and today walking with his cane, and feeling pretty good.

I'll take it. I just wish he had more days like this. I guess some days are good and some days are bad!

He fell again this morning in the kitchen and cut his knee. He doesn't know how or why he fell.

This is the third or fourth time since May he has fallen. Just out of the blue, fell and gotten hurt, not seriously, just scrapes and bruises.

He still felt the need to go to the farm today!

I just don't get it. Yes, I do, you can take the man out of the job but you can't take the job out of the man. He lives to work.

Wednesday October 2

Today we go to the cancer center for his regular appointment.

He can hardly walk and will need a wheel chair when we get to the hospital because it's too far for him to walk.

It was a very long night once again with very little sleep for me.

He was up a lot and when he was sleeping, he was moaning, talking, humming, coughing, just driving me crazy with his noises and being up shuffling around the house, TV on and off a lot of interruptions all night long. I know he can't help it. It just happens.

Right now, it 4:45a.m. I am on my second cup of coffee; he is sitting in his recliner covered up with a blanket because he is cold and it's seventy-eight degrees in the house. He is humming and talking nonsense. I wonder if he has another infection that is affecting his brain.

I think it's going to be a very long day and a long drive on only a few hours' sleep. I don't know how long I can keep this up before I'm the one who collapses from exhaustion.

I am so tired, he was up being a miserable ass, turning on the lights, cranking up the TV, talking loudly to the TV, humming, moaning with pain. Trying to walk but dragging and thumping his feet. I hardly got any sleep at all and now I have to drive eighty-five miles both ways!

I got up at 3:30a.m. and made coffee. He drank a cup of coffee and then slept in his recliner and was still talking and humming in his sleep! It never ends!

I told him to go take a shower three times before he did it and each time, he told me

I was a mother f**r and to shut my mouth he'd do what he wants when he wants, I'm not his mother. If he would only realize how much his words hurt. But he never remembers even saying those hurtful things.

He is shaking very bad, and he is not thinking clearly. The way he's acting I'm not sure he will be coming home once his oncologist sees him today. They might just put him in the hospital.

I know he doesn't want that and made me promise he wouldn't go to the hospital again. On the other hand, I know when his doctor sees him, he will be very concerned for Sonny.

We got to Strong and as soon as he got out of the car, he dropped his pants and pissed in the parking garage!

I was mortified! He said "when ya gotta go, ya gotta go" then he laughed.

We saw Dr Passero and he was very concerned about Sonny falling so much, and the fact of his extreme weight loss. Today he had a low-grade fever too.

Dr. Passero had him admitted to the hospital and put on IV antibiotics.

Here we go again. I can't even begin to tell you how pissed off Sonny is right now.

Sonny made me promise after the last time, that I would not take him to the hospital again. But I wasn't the one who did it. The doctor did it at his office visit.

Dr. Passero said it would only be for a couple of days.

I for one don't believe it, neither does Sonny we have heard this before. Just a couple of days always turns into four or five or even more who knows.

I'm the one who has to make that hour and a half drive every day, to sit there and do nothing for six hours then drive an hour and a half back home. Only to do it all again the next day and every day until he gets discharged.

I'm tired, I'm run down, I want a pain free life for Sonny and normal life for both of us.

Thursday October 3

Today they did a bunch of ex rays on his finger. That is the cause of the infection this time.

I arrived at 9:30a.m. and brought him his clothes, hearing aid, toiletries, his I pad, ect.

It was a long day, he slept most of the time. He hopes to come home by Saturday.

I hope so too.

I left around 3:30p.m. to come home and take care of the cat and dog and get some rest myself.

He called me from the hospital about 6p.m. and told me a hand surgeon came in and numbed up his finger, cut it open, drained out the infection and cut out the infected soft tissue and flushed it out. Then she packed it with gauze, no stitches, the wound has to be flushed and repacked every four hours. They want it to heal from the inside out so it will not be stitched up.

Friday October 4

I don't think I will go up today unless he is going to come home. I have been up since 3a.m. quite sick and very weak. I have bad congestion, sore throat, and explosive diarrhea I need to stay close to the bathroom. I hardly slept at all last night and I need to just take a day to take care of myself. I think I'm just run down and its starting to catch up with my health. I need a day to rest and recoup.

Ya know what? Like he always tells me "You're a big girl you'll figure it out"

He's a big boy he can take care of himself for one day!

How about all the times he dumped me off at the hospital to have babies, or have my gall bladder out, and not come back until the day I got discharged!

Oh yes, he did! No matter how much begging I did for him to come and sit with me, he did his own thing. Starting with our very first child being born.

But hey, I'm supposed to be attentive and be there for him every stinking minute!

I am unbelievably exhausted!

Saturday October 5

I talked to Sonny this morning and he told me I didn't have to come up. As far as he knows all that was happening today is more IV antibiotics.

I am still under the weather and the drive would have done me in. I stayed home and napped on and off most all day, until round three this afternoon.

Then I felt I had a little more energy and not so run down.

I mopped all the floors and vacuumed all the way through the house.

Turned out today the doctors took Sonny to the OR and opened up his hand just below his infected finger and washed the infection out and cleared more of the infected soft tissue to try to stop this infection from going any further in the hand. They said it was MERSA and was eating away at his finger and into the soft tissue of the palm of his hand.

Sunday October 6

Dr. Passeros' couple of days has now turned into four days and two hand surgeries.

He really wants to come home, and I really do not want to keep up this hour and half dive each way. It's just too much, especially when he can take antibiotics at home and all the blood cultures and test are coming back negative. The only infection test to be positive was the culture they did on the drainage from his finger!

He was discharged this afternoon.

Monday October 7

5a.m.

It feels like we are at our breaking point. As a caregiver I am completely exhausted. I don't know where I can get any more strength than I already have. As a cancer victim Sonny is in constant pain. It is heart breaking to see him go through this every day.

Damn Cancer
We Really Can't Fix This

A lot of how angry he is, is all because of the pain. I have to remind myself all the time, it's the pain, it's the pain!

Maybe I'm just being to brutally honest! Or maybe he's right, no one would care!

I want to run away from all of it, leave cancer on a shelf, live under a bridge in a tent.

Yes, I feel bad he is so sick and in so much pain, but he doesn't need to be ungrateful, mean, disrespectful to me. I'm doing the best that I can. I'd fix it if I knew how I really and truly would. It's just the pain, I know it's just the pain. Pain makes people do hurtful things.

I remember when my outside interest used to be my reprieves, my escape. My Bible studies, my continued education, college courses, my part time jobs, my family and friends, my ministry. Every interest I had; I was only allowed to do for a short time then he would become so demanding that I had to let most of them go.

I'm sure everyone thinks I am a quitter. I am not a quitter. I just had to give in to what his wants, needs, and demands are!

8a.m. He is eating ice cream direct out of the half gallon container! For Sonny any time is ice cream time.

He has refused to walk with his cane. He acts like a really old man. He uses the walker and will not pick up his feet, he shuffles where ever he goes. Even the doctor told him to make a conscience effort to pick up his feet and that could help him to keep his balance and to keep from falling!

Around 11a.m. I asked him if he felt up to looking at the door lock on the barn. The combination door lock wouldn't always work.

He took his cane and went to the barn. He took his time and he was able to fix the barn door lock.

All afternoon after that he has been using the cane and actually is trying to pick up his feet as he walks. Very slow but at least he's using the cane and trying not to shuffle. I think his attitude changed when I asked him to fix the door lock on the barn. He knows I still need him, he felt useful.

He even went to the shop this afternoon to hang out. He saw John S. when he was there. John was dropping off a truck for repair.

John told him he'd feel better if he didn't come back to the farm until he was healthier and stronger. Not because he didn't want him to be there, but because he doesn't want him to get sick and get an infection again.

The risk of infection from all the bacteria on the farm is quite high because of the dirty equipment and environment Sonny works in up there.

He reassured Sonny that they would remain friends and he could visit anytime he wants. That regaining his health was the most important to everyone right now. He reassured Sonny that when he gets to feeling like himself again that he will have his shop supervisory job waiting for him.

Sonny has kind of mixed feeling about not going back to work. On one hand he knows its best until he regains some strength and get his knee fixed. On the other hand, it's like cutting off his life line to not be able to work.

Thursday October 10

He had an appointment with Dr Passero and the blood test showed low sodium and high potassium so the doctor wanted to send him to infusion center for an IV of sodium and a potassium lowering fluid, plus a water pill.

Sonny told them he didn't want to go because he felt it was their way of getting him admitted to the hospital and Dr Passero assured him it would only take an hour for the IV and then he could leave.

By the time they took him back for the infusion, did another blood test half way through the IV. Then finish the IV it was past 5p.m. Several hours later!

By the time we got dinner and got home it was time to go to bed. We were tired and frustrated. Again, feeling bullied by the doctor.

Monday October 14

It was a very busy weekend with grand kids, lawn mowing, and going after apples.

I don't know all of what is happening with him. I try to pretend he's ok, because I don't want him to know how worried I am. That I really think he's not doing that well.

He is thin and very weak. He can no longer fill the pellet stoves or water softener. I do most of it, because he cannot lift the bags. The bags weigh forty pounds. Roy and Ken take care of a lot it when they stop by, but mostly it's up to me. I'm ok with that. I know once he gets his knee fixed, he will be doing much better. I just know it.

His knee causes him quite a bit of pain.

As much as he puts me through, I do love him and I hate to see him go through all of this.

He is scheduled for knee surgery on the twenty-nineth. I hope it helps with the pain.

Sometimes he's a little confused and I don't always mind as long as it's just him and I and he's not mean and hateful.

I don't want the kids or anyone else to know. I cover up for him quite a bit. Simply because I don't have the answers as to why he is this way.

Like today when he woke up from his nap around 5p.m. he told me I needed to get to the barn and get the cows milked!

We don't have cows, but he sounded just like his dad use to when Paul would talk to his mom about going to get the cows milked!

Monday October 21

The weekend just flew by. John M. a carpenter friend of the family came on Saturday and started prepping to build a ramp in our back room to the garage because steps are so hard for Sonny to navigate with his bumbled-up knee and overall weakness.

He has become very slow in his movements; he doesn't need to be falling, he can't afford any broken bones. Besides that, the ramp will come in handy in our old age when we both have trouble walking up and down steps. HaHa

On Saturday Roy helped Sonny run water lines to the back yard. This had to be done before the ramp goes in, because of the placement of the water lines in the room where the ramp is being built. We finally have a water spigot out back. Something we have wanted for thirty years!

Also, we moved the water holding tank and water softener.

Sonny unknowingly screwed up the water softener when he pulled out the drain tube and cut it off much too short.

If he was thinking like he used to he never would have done that. We had to put in a whole new drain tube and Roy had to crawl under the house and reinstall it into the septic drain pipe because Sonny didn't have the strength to do that. We are very grateful for Roy's help. He has been so good to Sonny.

The water lines and softener all had to be moved because of the location of the ramp we are having built.

Yesterday Sonny had called Roy to stop by and help get the motorhome winterized.

What should have taken an hour for Sonny turned into a four-hour ordeal. He has done this for years and years and it never takes over an hour. There was a time he could do it without even thinking about it.

This time he was confused on how to do it. Sonny couldn't remember exactly what the steps were. He filled the motorhome holding tanks with water and he should not have done that. When I questioned him, I was told to shut the F up.

I finally got the owner's manual out so it would be done the right way. I needed to know myself how to do it.

Sonny could not drive the motor home he was to unsteady. I pulled it out to work on it and then and backed it in. It's all winterized and hopefully mouse proofed too, with plenty of mouse repellant and moth balls.

I don't know what this week will hold. I can only imagine what I'm going to have to deal with.

I hope he does not go to the shop because I know with his mental state, he doesn't need to be offering advice to anyone.

I hate having him home all the time. He is lost without a job to go to everyday. Work is his life.

He thinks I'm his personal slave

"Get me this, get me that, do this, do that, really you have to vacuum right now,

Turn the radio off, turn the music off, I want this or that," he is angry and demanding.

I can't do a darn thing I want. I can't even eat a hot meal without having to get up and get him whatever he demands.

He eats fast, chokes a lot because his bites are huge. Then when he's done, he starts with the demands. "I need my pills, the stoves need pellets, the dog needs to be let out, I want the water treatment to soak my finger and hand."

I don't mind helping him or taking care of him but I hate all the demands and no gratitude!

I am trying to be patient and understanding. I tell myself that it is his state of mind due to his inability to work anymore, and due to his health.

"Lord hear my prayer, please bless me with an overload of patience and understanding." Amen

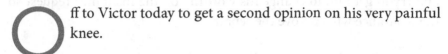

To High Of A Risk

October 22 Tuesday

Off to Victor today to get a second opinion on his very painful knee.

He saw Dr Kaplan, an orthopedic.

Unfortunately, this doctor only does knee replacement and they won't do that on Sonny.

He's **too high a risk** for infection. So frustrating to know no one will help him with his constant knee pain.

Well, he got another pill!

Meloxicam for the arthritis.

The doctor he saw today just confirmed what we already knew. "Oh, that's a bad meniscus tear" but "Unfortunately, with low immune system, you're **too high of a risk** for surgery"

Basically, their way of saying they won't operate.

They don't seem to care anything about relieving his pain short of another pill!

No immune system, blah blah blah. We have heard this so many times.

Here's our thought, suppose someone with immuno-compromised system was in an auto accident and required surgery to live? Would they say but with your immune system, or lack of we can't do anything for you. If you weren't immunocompromised, we could save your life!

We both know they would operate

Dr. Kaplan told us that Dr Capecci should do the meniscus removal, and only by arthroscopic surgery

Now it's back to Dr. Capecci, his orthopedic in Dansville on Thursday and try to get him to change his wording on the insurance request so the insurance will approve the repair!

Dr Capecci says he did report the tear in the meniscus and the insurance company flat out denied the surgery. Sonny **is too high of a risk**.

He offered Sonny a series of injections that will put a gel type cushion under his knee cap to help relieve some of the pain.

But once again we are at the mercy of the insurance company and have to wait for insurance authorization.

There was a time in this country where doctors could go ahead and treat a person and insurance companies would pay. Not any more now it's the insurance companies that tell the doctors what they can do. This country is so screwed up!

Tuesday October 28

Last week we had a ramp built in the back room. Steps are so hard for Sonny to maneuver. Even two steps are too hard.

John M, Roy, and Arron B. all worked on it, under Sonny's supervision.

The ramp is beautiful and very nice and very well built.

One of the first times Sonny came down the ramp when it was completed, he fell. Tore the skin off his left elbow. I'm not exactly sure how he fell. I was taking care of tools.

Roy was here he was cleaning up wood pieces and hardware from the construction work on the ramp.

He helped Sonny get up. Sonny was very embarrassed. He said he got too confident and walked without the use of the hand rail, lost his footing and went down, plus he had his slippers on. That probably didn't help. I will get grip type skid strips and put on the ramp so neither of us fall.

I don't understand what is going on with him. Sometimes he walks without assistance and other times he needs the walker.

He is having the shakes and tremors again in his hands. He has very little strength I have to put his socks and shoes on for him and pour his beverages. He can't even lift a gallon of milk. I take care of the stoves because he cannot lift the pellet bags. I know it bothers him, but I really don't mind.

Today he went to the shop early in the morning to pick up Rick C. to go to Schumacher's Farm with him to get a transmission for one of Johns trucks.

Rick told me Sonny fell asleep twice on the way to and from Cohocton.

Doug told me his dad was acting confused and very repetitive in his conversations.

I hadn't noticed much confusion at home today. That doesn't mean anything because at times his mind set can change hour by hour.

The only time I notice it is when he first wakes up in the morning or even after a nap. It's usually off the wall things about milking cows, or whatever is happening in the news. Sometimes I discourage him from even watching the news because he takes everything so literal and personal.

Not sure why but cows are his favorite subject when waking up. When he was a youngster at home, he hated the cows.

His elbow is still bleeding from the fall. He actually tore the skin off it when he fell so it has not scabbed over. We keep it covered with antibiotic ointment and a bandage. He doesn't need another infection.

His finger with the MRSA is healed over and looking much better, finally.

I don't think there is any infection that would cause the confusion, so I'm not sure what is going on with his cognitive ability. I'm sure it's not the chemo because he has been off that since August.

He sleeps a lot during the day, he often talks about not wanting to live because he doesn't have the life he wants. He can no longer do what he enjoys which is working.

His feet are swollen to three times what normal is. Not sure what is going on with that, or why he is retaining fluid.

Tomorrow he has an appointment at Wilmot Cancer Center for his monthly appointment.

I guess we will see what they have to say.

Wednesday November 6

Today he had an appointment with Dr Capecci to start the gel cushion injections in his right knee.

But the doctor took one look at his knee and decided there was too much fluid to do the injections so he drew some fluid off and even that did not go well.

The fluid was thick and had grainy crystals, so he had to send it on for cultures and testing. If there is infection he will have to be on antibiotics before he can start the injections.

We are very disappointed because he can't stand the twenty-four seven pain!

Now he has to wait another week. I feel so bad for him and the pain he is dealing with. Just heart breaking! No wonder he is so angry all the time. I would be too.

Friday November 8

Very early this morning we had to be in Rochester at the imaging department on River Street. He had a PET scan. By the time he got out he was miserable with pain. He had no coffee, his medications, or breakfast.

We got out of there around 9a.m. We went to breakfast and he took his medication and it kicked in on the way home before he got any relief from the pain.

Now we wait for another week for the results.

We arrived home around 11:30a.m. after the PET scan and breakfast at IHOP

Around 1p.m. Dr Capecci from Dansville called. He said Sonny needed to get to Hyland hospital due to a rare yeast infection in his knee. That he will need surgery to flush out the infection and a drainage tube put in and to be put on IV antibiotics. He really didn't want to go to the hospital ever again, but since this was not for the cancer he agreed to go.

Off we went back to Rochester

Hyland Hospital admitted him, X-rayed his knee every which way that is possible.

I came home this evening to take care of the stoves and the animals. I'll go back up tomorrow to see what is going to go on, and what the results are. He is supposed to be seen by the orthopedic team and the infectious disease team.

He really doesn't want to stay, but they told him he needed to at least give them the weekend to try to get the infection under control, and help with the pain.

On the other hand, good news from his oncology nurse Cheryl B. She called and said his PET scan looked good for no new multiple myeloma cancer lesions.

She said there was a nodule in or on one of his lungs but it was too small to worry about at this point. They would check again in six months.

Sunday November 10

We are home

He checked himself out AMA

Earlier today, one of the orthopedic doctors came in this morning and Sonny asked her when they were going to start the IV antibiotics, so he can have the surgery on his knee. Right now the only thing he is getting by IV is fluids and pain medication.

She told him "maybe tomorrow, but probably not until sometime this coming week"

He told her he wanted to go home that there was nothing they were doing that he could not do at home.

The orthopedic charge doctor said "you're not going anywhere" and walked out.

Sonny called the nurse with his bedside control and told her to take the IV out or he will take it out himself, that he was leaving.

Well wouldn't you know it within minutes three doctors come out of the woodwork from nowhere.

Sonny told them:

"I want to know why the hell I am here? I have been here since Friday and not a damn thing has been done. I have seen several so-called specialists and no one can make up their mind as to my treatment or what you're going to do."

"All I'm doing is laying around and being served my meals. I want the hell out of here. Either discharge me or I'm taking my own IV out and walking out of here"

The doctor in charge for today looked at Sonny's chart and saw that our local orthopedic recommended Sonny have the arthroscopic surgery to flush out the "rare yeast infection" and put in a drainage tube.

But the doctor in charge said all cultures came back negative, and that is why they never put him on any antibiotics!

Sonny went ballistic, he told the doctor; "I'm here on a false alarm and have been since Friday, I'm going home one way or another. All you have done for me, the testing, the bed, the meals could have all been done at my local hospital as an outpatient and I could have been in my own home, not two hours away taking up a bed for someone else more serious than me"

They told him "we don't advise it." Sonny said "I don't advise you stopping me, I'm leaving it's not your choice, I'm out of here, no more argument."

They then got him his AMA paper he got dressed and we came home!

We agree something has to be done with his knee and the pain he is having.

We feel if they would have operated on it and removed the fluid and the torn meniscus months ago, he would have had relief a long time ago, and wouldn't be going through this right now.

But no one will listen to him.

Also, Hyland hooked him up to a heart monitor because of his irregular heartbeat, Afib

They wanted to add more heart medication for it. Sonny told them, no he wasn't taking any more medication"

He told them "I have had Afib for over a year, even after my heart valve surgery in June, to leave it alone, stop throwing fuckin pills at me!"

Every time he got up to go to the bathroom the nurses came running, because according to his monitor his heart was racing yet he had no symptoms, just the reading on the machine that told the nurses what was going on.

The mechanic came out of Sonny. He told them their machine was defective. That his heart was not racing. There was something wrong with their machine.

Finally, he got a nurse who believed him. He said to her "pick up the monitor halter" which is the exact motion he makes whenever he gets out of the chair and sets off alarms.

She picked up the portable monitor from Sonny's pocket, when she stood it up it went crazy like Sonny's heart was going to explode. Of course, that set off alarms at the nurse's station. Many of them came running.

She laid it back down and it went back to normal

Turns out the monitor was defective, just like he told them.

All Sonny said was: "And you wanted me to take more medication, another fuckin pill!"

Sonny and I wondered what happens to those who don't speak up, or can't speak up.

Are they medicated unnecessarily due to ineffective equipment? Has the unneeded medication caused even more harm to a person's body because a "machine" says there is something wrong with that person?

Not only had he been in the hospital since Friday afternoon but, he never once was allowed to take a shower. He even asked a few times for a wash cloth and towel so he could at least wash up. No one even brought him a wash cloth. He used the paper towels in the bathroom to wash and dry with. Totally unacceptable!

First thing he did when he got home was take a long hot shower.

What a god-awful night He was out of his mind!

He was fine until around 7:00p.m. then he was talking to the tv saying random stupid stuff, singing, humming.

Just hours before he was so clear headed that he told off the hospital staff.

He had ice cream, not unusual but over the time span of two hours he had three large dishes of ice cream, not remembering he already had ice cream.

Around eight he decided go to bed in our bedroom. He hasn't slept in a regular bed for months.

I wasn't ready for bed, so I stayed in the living room to knit and watch tv and he went to bed, or so I thought.

After about twenty minutes I went in to see what he was doing because he was talking to himself and I couldn't understand what he was saying.

He was sitting on the edge of the bed with the adjustable bed control in his hand trying to plug it into the handle on his cane.

I asked him what he was doing and he said "plugging the charger in" he thought he was plugging in his hearing aid stringer to the charger. I did it for him.

Then he changed his mind about going to bed. He came out into the living room and was back in his chair watching tv and nodding off.

I went to bed about 9p.m. he decided he was going to watch tv for a while.

Next thing I know he's singing and talking to himself about recalled meat from the grocery store.

Then the light on his table beside his recliner was going on and off repeatedly.

I got up to see what he was doing and he said he was looking for his dish, he needed his dish.

I told him it was time to go to sleep he didn't need a dish. He decided he wanted to keep watching tv.

I said "that's fine but don't keep messing with the light."

I thought I had him all settled and I went back to bed. I no sooner got back in bed and I hear his motorized lift chair going up and down, back and forth over and over. He was playing with the controller. I got back up and asked him what was wrong. he said he "wanted to turn tv off but his chair was moving so he couldn't."

I showed him the tv remote and fixed his chair so he could recline it back.

I got him some of his quick release morphine and ice pack for his knee he settled down and fell asleep and I went back to bed.

He slept until 1:30a.m. I heard him up walking around slowly because of his knee, but every step he thumped the cane and his good leg very hard and loudly. He made it to the bathroom then instead of going back to his chair he walked straight to the area beside his dresser where his walker is parked.

Next thing I kept hearing a bang, bang, bang, I grabbed the flashlight beside my bed and he was trying to walk with the walker but pushing it up against the window thinking he was at a door way. I asked him "what is going on? he said he "can't get the door open."

I told him it was the window and it was still night time to go back to bed.

He decided to go to bed in his bed, he adjusted the head of the bed as high as it would go, got in and covered up, then all the noise started, singing, talking, and humming. By then it was 2:30a.m. I was wide awake.

It's going to be another very long miserable, exhausting day, that I have to smile and pretend once again I am fine, all is good. In sickness and health, I will always take care of him.

Monday November 11, 2019

Today was the grand opening for our daughter and son in laws new gym, Project Iron.

I hope Sonny is well enough to go.

We went. They got a lot of visitors to check out the gym, and a few memberships in person and some on line.

As for Sonny his knee was very painful as usual but his mind seemed to be on straight compared to last night. He was very happy to see the gym finally open.

He said that's all he wanted to live for, once they were operating, he didn't care what happened to him, that now all of his kids are self-employed and successful. We are proud of all of them.

The orthopedic called this morning and I have to take him back to Hyland Hospital in Rochester tomorrow at 6a.m. He is going to have surgery on his knee sometime late morning or early afternoon. We are hoping it is in out same day surgery, we don't know for sure. At least no more than an overnight stay.

When we got to the hospital, they told us he has some kind of bacteria, mold, or fungus. That is growing inside the knee joint. It needs to be scraped, flushed out and a drain tube put in. Which is the reason he was sent their last weekend. When they did nothing but slap his ass in a bed in a room!

Tuesday November 12

Very cold and our first snow of the season. We left the house at 4:45a.m. and arrived at Hyland at 6:45a.m. The snow-covered roads did hold us up and slow us down a little.

After he was finally admitted he was sent to a private room on the 6th floor.

We talked to several people, the medical team, the infectious disease team, the surgical team, and the surgeon.

Turns out there is a mold/fungus in the knee culture called Aspergillosis.

It took over a week to grow the fungus in the lab from the fluids drawn from his knee over a week ago. For that they wanted to keep him in a bed in the hospital until the cultures were determined. Yet doing nothing for him except bringing him his meals. Makes no sense at all why they wanted to keep him. That is why he checked himself out.

The fungus will be treated with and anti-fungal IV in the hospital and a pill when he goes home called Voriconazole

The surgeon came to see me around 3p.m. everything went well. She cleaned out all the visible fungus and affected tissue, put in a drain tube that is exposed externally. When I asked about the meniscus repair, she said she did not see the meniscus in the area of the fungus. Somehow, I really don't believe her, the knee isn't that big of an area that she could have not seen it. Especially knowing the meniscus was damaged and causing him pain.

She said they will monitor the drainage for a couple of days and if everything looks good, they will remove the drain and he will go home on anti-fungal medication in a couple of days.

8:30p.m. I am home now. The roads were not bad and I made it home in a little over an hour and half.

When I left, Sonny was still a bit confused and drowsy from the operation. When they brought him back to his room and the charge nurse was getting his vitals and checking his paper work from the OR. He looked at her and said:

"You might as well wipe your ass with that paper cause we don't have any bacteria in our milk"

In his medicated mind, he was at the farm and this lady was the milk inspector.

After that he dozed off again and I explained to the nurse what he was talking about.

Wednesday November 13

I slept pretty good last night; I woke up a couple of times but was able to go right back to sleep.

Even though I feel rested I'm still tired. I think it may be an emotional tired, trying to keep up with all of his medical appointments, treatments, keeping him comfortable, not to mention the house work, laundry, meals, etc. When I do sleep my mind never shuts off.

I probably will not go up to Rochester today, depends on what is going on with Sonny when I talk to him this morning.

Thursday November 14

I did not go up to see Sonny yesterday. I will not go up today. He is not coming home until tomorrow so he told me not to come up. He seemed a little bit confused sometimes when I talk to him, but he was very tired too.

I have quite a cough today. Probably allergies, post nasal drip. I'm feel really run down. I took a decongestant and napped on and off throughout the morning.

Friday November 15

I arrived at Hyland Hospital around 11a.m.

He will be going home sometime today. We are both happy about that. We hope it is not to late when they discharge him, I hate driving in the dark.

He got discharged around 3:30p.m. From the hospital we had to go to CVS pharmacy on Mt Hope in Rochester. They are the only place that had the medication he needs for the fungus in his knee joint.

On the way home Sonny wanted chicken wings for supper.

I called the cafe in Avoca and ordered chicken wings to go. We picked them up on our way home and we arrived home around 5:15p.m.

I let him out of the car in the driveway like I always do, because he can't open the car door all the way once I'm in the garage.

He got out of the car in the driveway, and I pulled the car into the garage. I got out of the car and started to grab our dinner and other things from the back seat. I heard him yelling for me to help him.

I came to the back of the car and he was laying on the driveway. He had fallen he could not get up. I tried to help him, I could not get him up. He told me to go in the house to get a cushion he can put under his knee so he can brace his knee against it to get up.

I came in to the house to get a cushion he asked for. When I went into the house to get the cushion, I called down to the shop for some of the boys to come help me. I knew I wouldn't be able to lift him. When I got back outside to Sonny, Mary a neighbor had stopped because she had seen Sonny laying on the driveway.

Rick, Cameron, and Joe showed up right after that and helped to pick Sonny up. They had Sonny sit on the seat of his walker and they pushed him up the ramp into the house.

He skinned up his right elbow even though he had his winter coat on. He also landed on his right shoulder and is now red swollen and looks like it will be bruised. His skin is so thin it tears easily.

We finally ate our supper and he settled into his recliner.

He flipped a switch; he went from being lucid and talking sensibly to being confused.

I really believe most of his confusion is from the medications he takes. Most of his confusion always comes at night after he takes his evening medications.

We will have to discuss this with the doctor at his next appointment.

He was watching tv and started playing with the remote, pushing buttons and ended up signing the whole tv off line! I got it straightened out and explained the channel selection to him and how to use the remote.

Saturday November 16

I thought for sure he would sleep well seeing that he is home.

Wrong, so very wrong.

I went to bed about eight last night and watched a little tv and he was settled in his chair and watching tv in the living room. I turned off my tv around 9:15p.m.

9:35p.m. he was banging around the bedroom because he couldn't find the door way to the bathroom.

I turned on the flashlight so he could see the open-door way. He went to the bathroom and then went back to his recliner. Of course, now I am wide awake but very tired!

9:50p.m. He was in the living room yelling about the Democrats and what they are doing to our president. I came out to the living room and asked him what was going on, he said he was just discussing the impeachment.

Then he yelled at me for not having any lights on. Mind you the hall light is on and the light over the kitchen stove is on as well as the bathroom night light.

He said his knee hurt pretty bad, so I gave him some of his quick acting morphine and got him an ice pack. I think he has taken the morphine so long (6years) that it doesn't even work for him anymore.

10:45p.m.

I went back to bed, about fifteen minutes later he was talking very loudly telling someone how to drill holes in the cab of a truck so they could wire it up. I told him it was time to go to sleep he could fix the truck in the morning, he said he wanted to watch tv.

I turned it on for him, I think he went to sleep for a bit after that.

11:30p.m. he came into the bedroom and was banging into everything with the walker. He said his head is telling him he needs to go to bed.

He sat on the edge of the bed and proceeded to tell someone how to mix the feed for the cows.

I begged him to please, please go sleep. The cows are fed and he can take care of it in the morning, I was very tired and I can't sleep when he is doing all this.

He told me to "go get fucked it's his house, his cows, he will do what he wants if I don't like it, I can get out!" I know it's just his mental state talking, yet the words still sting.

Then he totally switched from farming, to talking about how to weigh and measure road millings. Again, I told him "go to sleep. I'm tired, you can take care of it in the morning."

Again, he responded "fuck you, I'm just doing my job!"

I got up and went to the living room to my recliner with a blanket. Not comfortable at all, even though I am so tired. As of now I have had forty-five minutes sleep tonight.

He has had a yogurt, a peanut butter sandwich, and two popsicles and left the whole mess on his chair side end table in the living room. He has turned into a midnight muncher. That's all fine and good. He does need to gain some weight.

12:10a.m. He is back up clunking around with the walker.

I told him I need some sleep I'm very tired he needs to go to sleep too, either in his recliner or in the bed.

12:20a.m. He heads for the bed and sat on the bed telling someone how Hyland hospital is safer than Strong Memorial because of the hand rails in the halls so no one falls, on and on. I am so tired but I don't dare go to bed because I don't know what he will do, will he fall, will he get into things that he can get hurt on?

1:10a.m. I am getting angry because I am so tired.

I know I shouldn't be but I think exhaustion and pain both make people angry. I'm angry for several reasons. Mostly because here you have a strong hard-working man who is now resigned to someone I love, but yet someone I don't know him.

I am so angry because I know he will sleep all day and I won't and tonight I will do this all over again.

I ended up going to the spare bedroom at the other end of the house to try to get some sleep.

At 3:10a.m. he came through the living room and down the hall with the battery-operated hurricane light on his walker yelling

"Shirley, Shirley, are you here, are you in the house? Maddie needs to go out"

I got up and took Maddie out and he turned on every light in the house. I guess he's up for the day!

My goodness, I am so tired! I made coffee and he wandered around with his walker

I don't know how today is going to go, but I do know I am not going to let him sleep much. I'll try to keep him busy and awake so he can sleep better at night. 4:50a.m. He is sleeping soundly in his recliner!

He got up around 5:45a.m. and had a bowl of Rice Krispies and his morning medication.

Then again around 8a.m. he ate another bowl of Frosted Flakes cereal, Yogurt, Oreo cookies, milk, I'm glad he's getting his appetite back. It should help with his strength.

2p.m.

He has had a couple visitors today. His cousin Dick stopped by briefly, he had some questions on a tractor he was working on. Sonny was clear minded enough to talk about that.

Roy stopped by and Sonny could not stay awake as they were talking. He told Roy he was worried about whether Maddie would live very long because of being out in the parking lot when he's at the gym. She doesn't know to look out for cars. Thing is Maddie doesn't go to the gym with us, she never has.

He told Roy about his fall in the driveway when we got home from the hospital yesterday.

He told Roy "Mary stopped to help when she saw him lying on the ground and next thing ya know there was military men everywhere with guns, and the guys from the shop showed up, he didn't know if there was going to be a fight or what was going on."

He does seem to remember what happens but the details are not always clear. I already gave Roy the heads up on his confusion.

One thing about Roy is he always is so kind to Sonny. He makes sure whenever he helps Sonny that he always preserves and looks out for Sonny's dignity. He has the utmost respect for him. He knows just how to help him by letting Sonny make the decisions on all that Sonny ask him to do.

Doug stopped by but Sonny was sleeping in his recliner so we didn't wake him.

I don't want the kids to know how confused and crazy he is sometimes. It's just easier that way because I don't have the answer as to why he does what he does or how to make it better.

Many times, I went against Sonny's wishes and took him to the hospital because I can't help him and I know he needed medical help. Then each time he comes home, he makes me promise to never take him again.

The visiting nurse association is supposed to show up any time now. They called and said they would be here between two and two-thirty this afternoon. I hope he's not too crazy when she is here.

His VN was very nice. She had been here before when he got home from his hospital stay from the listeria infection and heart surgery.

Tuesday November 19

He had to go back to the orthopedic surgeon to have his stitches out. So, we thought. Turns out it was to take his drain tube out and no one at the surgeon's office was told it came out before he left the hospital.

Another wasted trip to Rochester with over an hour of just sitting in the waiting room. He has to go back next Wednesday, the day before thanksgiving to get the stitches out.

Wednesday November 20

Today was a hectic day.

Our water softener crapped out and water went everywhere in the mud room.

We ended up getting a new water softener. Roy came to help Sonny install it because of Sonny's knee. He is pretty limited in his movements and coordination.

I emptied the salt out of the old softener this morning so that could be unplumbed and taken out. That was quite a job, very time consuming, heavy, back breaking job.

Sonny had a very good day. I would even say excellent. He was clear minded, kind, thoughtful, walked most of the day unassisted, no cane, no walker. He felt great. It seemed like heaven to have him more like himself.

He got the new water softener installed and programmed. He seemed back to himself again that was nice. He was very happy, feeling great, mind on right.

Maybe, just maybe things are finally looking up, he's feeling better, his strength is good today and so is his mind.

My fingers are crossed that prayers have finally been answered and things can only get better from here. It's so nice to have him back to himself today.

This afternoon I went to Ginger's father's funeral. Cousin Sis officiated and did a great job.

I got back home around 4p.m. They were still working on the water softener.

I fixed supper for Sonny and Roy around 6:30p.m., when they were done and cleaned up from the water softener install.

By eight Roy was gone and Sonny was ready for bed. His knee was hurting a bit, but he had been on his feet all day. He went to bed happy, pleased with his accomplishment and his self for once.

Thursday November 21

Sonny is having a very confusing morning.

He was trying to remove everything in the living room because he wanted to make room for the bed, we are not getting a bed for the LR. For some reason in his head, he thought we were.

He asked me for the red paint and brush so he could make the sign.

I asked him what sign? Then he got on his tablet and said he'd find it and I could copy it.

But then he never said anything more about it. Sometimes he makes no sense at all.

He has bad hand tremors today too. About an hour later he asked me if I had all my questions answered I told him "I didn't have any questions."

He told me "you aren't that smart that you didn't need to find out the answers if you didn't have the questions!" I'm beginning to think I'm the one who is confused!

He has a doctor appointment today at 2p.m. with Dr Parker. I hope he is just as confused so that the doctor can see what is going on.

It baffles me, one day he is good, perfectly normal, like yesterday, and the next day he hasn't got a clue on what is going on.

Dr Parker was very concerned with Sonny today.

When he checked him over, he had a mucus rattle in his lungs, a little confusion, whole body tremors and a low-grade fever. He wanted Sonny to go to the hospital for blood work and chest X-rays. I'm sure that is why Sonny wouldn't talk to Dr. Parker. I knew Sonny would refuse to go.

In the doctor's office Sonny wouldn't talk to anyone, not me, the nurse, or even doctor Parker. He looked at us like he didn't understand us, or was just pissed off at us. He sat in the chair and just leaned his hands on his cane, bit at his lower lip, and refuse to say a thing.

The nurses and Doctor Parker helped me get him in the car.

On the way to the ER, before I even got out of Cohocton, I had to pull over and he vomited, after that he was a little more coherent and was able to carry on a conversation, sort of. At least he would answer my questions and voice his opinion on where we were going.

He just wanted a drink of water, I told him I'd get water for him when we got to the hospital.

When he found out where we were going, he refused to go to the hospital, he said "no, if you take me there, I'm not getting out of the car because I know this trick, they send me for blood work and X-rays, then they will admit me and I'm not going to do that again." I explained Dr. Parker wanted him to go. It didn't matter, he just wanted to go home. He was very insistent.

I honored his wishes. I turned around and we came home.

As I pulled into the driveway Roy was right behind us. It was a good thing because Sonny needed help getting out of the car and into the house. Roy helped him and I carried everything else.

He sat in his recliner had a couple Tylenol and a glass of iced ginger ale and went to sleep.

He woke up around 7p.m. had supper and a shower, and got ready for bed. He wanted his nightly ice cream and I got him a dish. He ate his ice cream and shared it with Maddie. His fever seemed to be gone. I didn't check it but he didn't feel warm. He had his nightly medications and laid back in his recliner and went to sleep.

Sonny Gets His Wings

November 22, 2019

4 a.m. I got up same as any other day, I let Maddie out, and I made coffee. Sonny was snoring and sounded like he needed to clear his throat of mucus.

I never heard him get up all night, so I'm thinking he had slept pretty well.

I could smell urine and I knew he had slept so soundly he had peed himself.

I woke him up and told him I was making coffee, to go get cleaned up he had an accident.

He just looked at me like he didn't understand my words. Like we all do at times when we get woke up.

I asked him if he needed help and if he wanted his walker and he never answered me he only shook his head yes.

I placed the walker in front of the recliner and I pushed the button to raise the chair so he could stand, and reach for his walker.

He stood for just a second and he yelled out in pain "ouch" I assumed it was his knee.

But hind sight now says maybe not the knee, maybe a stroke or his heart.

I quickly helped him sit back down and put the chair in a seated position. He immediately closed his eyes went right back to sleep doing that gurgling and snoring.

I tried several times to get him to respond, to answer me, he would not.

I took his temperature it was 99.7 I tried to take his BP but I could not get the cuff around his arm so that it would velcro right and when I inflated it, he said "ouch that hurt", and winced his face in pain.

I called 911 and I told them "I needed help getting my husband up, he won't respond to my voice, he's awake, but can't or won't talk," They asked if he's breathing, I told them "yes, he is breathing but he won't talk to me it's like he doesn't understand me" They said an ambulance is on the way.

I went in to get dressed before the ambulance arrived. I was sitting out in the sun room putting on my sneakers when Eric C from the Avoca ambulance crew was the first to arrive. He is an ambulance personnel, friend, and neighbor.

He asked me where Sonny was, that maybe he and I could get him up.

Eric and I went into the living room and he called Sonny's name and shook his shoulder, "Sonny, Sonny, do you hear me?" No response, Sonny was not breathing.

In the time it took me to tie my shoes Sonny was gone and my heart was broken into ten thousand pieces.

I had already called the kids and his sister Lori earlier to tell them I was calling the ambulance because he wouldn't respond or answer me even though he was awake. I suspect he had a stroke. Now I had to call them back and tell them he's not breathing and has passed on.

Within a short time, Scott, Doug, Libby, and Lori were here. I could not get ahold of Eric his phone was turned off.

Sonny was gone, I was heartbroken. I begged him to "come back, please just one more Christmas." I know stupid of me to say that, but that's what I said to him as he sat there in his chair.

The ambulance people were going to try CPR until they asked for and read the DNR. Instead, they called the State Police, the medical examiner, and the corner.

My cousin Sis and Aunt Nancy showed up. We were comforted and grateful to have them here.

Elizabeth finally got through to Eric and he came.

We were all questioned by the state police and they took everyone's name and phone numbers. They also took all of Sonny's prescription medications. They said to dispose of them. That seemed really odd to me and everyone else. Getting rid of his medications was one of the farthest things on my mind.

Steve, the coroner came and filled out the paper work. He was very kind to me and became emotional when we talked. He had known Sonny for years and he was heartbroken too.

The BCI investigator was even called in. When he came he had to take a report and take pictures. I just lost my husband to death, talk about being made to feel like a criminal on top of everything else! BCI officer Jeremy H explained that because I was the only one home with him when he died and it is considered an unattended death.

We all said our good byes to Sonny. The Avoca Funeral Home came and took Sonny away.

Sonny is gone. Gone with his dad, his grandparents, his baby sister, brother-in-law Tim.

He is gone, and with him is a wealth of knowledge that no one will ever know.

He leaves a legacy in his children, his family, all who knew him, everyone he worked for, all the employees we ever had and everywhere he ever worked.

Monday November 25

Friday the twenty second was hard, very hard and a whirl wind of visitors and loud deep grief I felt it in my mind, my heart, and my gut.

My mom and my daughter stayed overnight with me on the day Sonny died.

Saturday I was numb, my body felt so heavy so very heavy it was hard to move. I was completely exhausted yet I had not worked for even one hour.

A lot of people in and out all day, a lot of food brought in, flowers, and phone calls.

Sunday a repeat of Saturday except I felt a little more peace. I could smile today, even laugh at some of the memories when people spoke of him.

I walked around my house room by room looked at all we built together. Our family photos that hang on the walls. I see love in the photos. I know there was love between us like no other we each have known. Even though it was so hard to express these last few years in our day to day living with cancer, multiple appointments, the treatments and medication side effects. But right now, in my heart I feel nothing but love for the man who was and always will be my husband. He is my heart. I pray he knows that.

Today Monday 4:30 a.m. I am all alone the house is quiet. I made coffee checked emails, and Facebook. Reading all the private messages and FB condolences melted my heart.

Suddenly a meltdown of emotion hit me.

I knelt by his chair and tried to pray. All I could do was cry and beg forgiveness from a man who is no longer here. Forgiveness for me being so tired, for complaining about never enough sleep.

I need his forgiveness for me not doing enough to keep him alive. I feel like I failed him. I was his caregiver he needed me and I feel like I failed him.

I am dealing with a lot of guilt. My sorrow is horrendous. I don't know what to do. The last thing I tried to do for him to help him stand and get to the bathroom and I ended up hurting him. His last voice of utterance I heard was "ouch, that hurts" when I tried to take his blood pressure.

I feel like I didn't love him enough. I didn't love him like Jesus did or he'd still be here with me.

Funny thing about cancer or any terminal illness, it kills your life before your even dead. Looking back in the last few months he clearly lost his life long before he died.

The pain of his physical body and the chemicals he was taking for the last six years totally destroyed any form of personal life we had. Oh, we still loved each other very much. But married life changed drastically. Intimacy was out of the question for years with chemo and pain. We accepted that. We still had each other, until death do us part, as hard as it was sometimes, there was never any question or doubt.

We have actually lived more as partners or caregiver and patient than husband and wife for the last seven years. Maybe too much personal information here, but if you have cancer and you take those "helpful poisons" you know what I'm talking about.

I became the care giver and he became the one I cared for. We took a vow in front of God and family "In sickness and health forsaking all others."

I'd do it all over again too because I remember why I married him in the first place. It was because we were in love, we really were. Cancer turned us both into people we never wanted to be.

Tuesday November 26

I woke up at 2:22a.m. with the sound of the most beautiful music. I couldn't tell where it was coming from. I laid there and listened to it. It was not guitar, piano, organ or harp, or any instrument I recognized. It was like nothing I have ever heard, there are no words to describe the sound. It was very comforting, soothing, easy listening, and very nice.

I lay there listening to it. Running through my mind where it could be coming from, no tv on, no radio on, possibly from my neighbors or a car on the side of the road.

As I laid there listening, the music started to fade and became softer and was harder to hear, farther away. I had to strain my ears to hear it, I got out of bed to go find where it was coming from. As soon as I got out of bed at 2:40a.m. the music stopped.

Throughout my day I mentioned this music that woke me, to some of my family and friends. Everyone said it was Sonny's way of telling me he was ok; he had arrived on the other side.

I now believe it was divine heavenly music. Imagine, Sonny gets to be soothed by that all day long.

As I reread some of this journal that I wrote a few years back. I was reminded that Sonny once heard music that woke him up. He was the only one who heard it. It also left him very happy and peaceful the night that he heard it. I wonder if it was the same music, I heard last night?

He died on 11-22-19 and I was soothed awake at 2:22a.m. with beautiful music, just saying.

Today was the worse day yet for fatigue

I have been tired beyond feeling before from too many hours of physical labor and stress, but I have never been or felt this kind of tired.

There is a heaviness in my body that makes it hard to even move my feet and legs, they feel like lead weights.

I think it's my soul and breath that is so tired.

I'm trying to stay strong for my children because that's the only way I know how to help them. I don't want them to keep on hurting, I want to fix their broken hearts.

Today I met with Pastor Berre and I feel I should have been more prepared. I should have known what I want for a service. Officiating funerals for others is what I do. Today my brain was blank and at the same time all over the place in thoughts.

I could not put things together all I could do was talk about my kids and Sonny. I found myself rambling and sometimes making no sense. I could hear myself, I was there in person, yet I wasn't really able to focus.

I will have to keep this in mind the next time I have to serve others. I now know firsthand what others are going through when they meet with an officiant for a funeral or memorial service.

Today I donated Sonny's hearing aids so that the actual computer inside can be made into aids for anyone who cannot afford to buy new aids.

Thanksgiving 2019

Just six days after Sonny's passing and already, we have to celebrate a holiday. I think I'm ok with it, I'm really not sure how or what I'm supposed to feel.

We all gathered at Libby's house and she was in a bad mood. I understand her missing her dad, and the first holiday meal without him. I don't understand why she has to take it out on the kids and everyone else. She asked me to say the blessing that was very hard, I cried through it.

But I finished it too.

After we ate, we went through the boxes of family photos that I brought with me, and pulled a lot of them for the photo boards at the funeral and the slide show Eric is putting together.

As hard as it was I loved being with my family today. Libby seemed to lighten up once we started looking at photos and reminiscing.

I'm glad to be back home. Our home, the place Sonny and I made, my safe sanctuary.

November 29, 2019

My 67th birthday and one week exactly since Sonny died.

It has been a very busy week, yet one day runs into the next.

Just one major/minor issue in the house and that is with the pellet stove in the back room. It's not burning right.

I have to keep clearing the burn pot because it fills up with pellets and doesn't burn. As Sonny always told me, "you're a big girl you'll figure it out!"

This afternoon I headed to Tractor Supply to get a pair of welding gloves that fit me. Sonny's' are to big. I need to stop burning my hand when I reach into the stove to clear the ashes. It's the first public place I have been since Sonny died.

While I was there, I ran into John and Connie, Sonny's cousin and our neighbors. I talked to them for a few minutes. It was black Friday so there were so many people in the store. I just couldn't breathe; my heart was racing like it was beating out of my chest. I wanted to run out the door before I ran into anyone else.

The hell with the gloves, I can't do this, I'll get them another time

On my way out of the store I ran into Sandy Y at a register in the front of the store.

She stopped me and hugged me so tight. I guess I needed that. I didn't know it but I did.

When she released me from her hug, we talked a bit, but still my mind raced for me to just get to the safety and solitude of my car and back home. To the house that we built. My security!

I went to Libby's again tonight for my birthday dinner. She had pizza and cake. That was plenty after a big thanksgiving meal yesterday. All my kids were there except for Eric's family. They we're having thanksgiving at Vanessa's parents.

Also, my best friend Lilian and our friend, Roy came to share my evening too.

Again, it was nice of the kids to do that and it was even better to get back home to my solitude and quiet house, the house that we built. My security.

Sunday December 1

We have had freezing rain and sleet all morning.

Libby and the kids, Jill and Aidan, Vanessa and the kids all came over in the late afternoon and put pictures on the poster boards for Sonny's services this week.

Everyone left around 6:30p.m. and I soaked in a hot bubble bath.

Took a NyQuil and went to bed by 8:30p.m.

Monday December 2

Today I woke up to eight inches of snow and no desire to go out and clear it.

Truthfully, I was mad at Sonny for not being here to take care of it. To clear the drive way.

Something is wrong with me. I should not be mad at a dead man, but I was.

My electric went out around 7:15a.m. I had such a time getting the generator started and power to the house. After about 45 minutes of messing around in the deep snow going to the electric pole and then to the barn, I finally got it. Thing is I have done this before. I knew how to do it, but today it seemed like an impossible task.

Again, I was mad at Sonny for not being here. I'm sorry, maybe I should not admit that, I wonder is something wrong with me to be mad at him?

Four men from Doug's shop showed up and shoveled and plowed me out with both the Kubota and the tractor with the bucket. That was very thoughtful of them and I really appreciate it.

Power came back on after three hours.

December 3

Another early morning call of another family death.

Sonny's mom passed away early this morning.

Bitter sweet because of her mental condition. No matter when I saw her, she always looked like Mary, but Mary was not in her eyes and thoughts. Dementia is an unforgiving disease.

Today is also my oldest granddaughter Kylie's eighteenth birthday. Mary's first great grandchild and our first grandchild. A mile stone birthday she now has to share with the death of her great grandmother.

There are many dates in our family that hold double events of births and deaths.

Sonny died on Tim F birthday. I believe he would have been 50.

We have now had three deaths in the last four months.

Though we all knew she wasn't good and death could happen at any time, I was sad and very overwhelmed when I heard about Mary death this morning.

Then as wrong as it was, suddenly my sadness turned into resentment.

I probably should not even say this, but this is my journal so I can be brutally honest if I want to!

It's not fair that Mary got to live to be old and Tim and Sonny died too early.

Forgive me Lord for such thoughts! Sonny and Tim should have been afforded that much life too. I'm an emotional mess. Our family hasn't had time to grieve even one person, but yet someone else dies. How is a family supposed to handle that?

I picked my 4-year-old grandson up from nursery school today. As we pulled into the garage at home, he said:

"Papas not, here is he?"

I said "no he's not"

"Papa's dead, isn't he?"

With a lump in my throat, I said "yes, he is Jax"

Then Jax said

"I don't have any papas any more but I still have a grandma."

"Yes, Jax you still have me honey, you still have grandma."

Kylie our oldest granddaughter, had a special bond with her grandpa. She and Sonny had a standing date twice every year. One was the RC plane air show at her parents place every June.

The other was the car demolition derby every August at the Steuben County Fair. She loved when she got old enough to drive and she could take him to the fair. He loved going it was an interest they both shared.

Today she got her first tattoo in honor of her grandpa. He never had any tattoos but I know he would smile ear to ear to see hers.

December 5

Today is Sonny's best friends' birthday and I'm sure he will miss Sonny today as he goes to his birthday breakfast minus one friend. The ladies at the Howard diner "Birdy's" are making Roy a cake. Today he gets cake for breakfast. Sonny had always gone with Roy on his birthday and Sonny's birthday for breakfast for the last few years. I hope he has a fabulous day of memories with his friends sharing their memories of Sonny. He misses Sonny as much as we do.

December 6

I have been awake since 2:15a.m. I laid in bed until 3:30a.m. I am tired but I cannot sleep. Too much has happened to our family in the last three months.

Today are the calling hours for Sonny at the Avoca Methodist Church.

> *Lord hear my prayer:*
> *I pray Lord for your protective arms of warmth and peace over my whole family. From my youngest grandchild to my oldest child, their spouses and every one in between. Please Lord bless us all with sincere comrade that it will be carried through from this day forward of siblings who stay connected and helpful to each other, both in my family and in Sonny's family. May those who knew Sonny keep his memories close at heart and in their minds.*
> *Father God I give you all the glory for ever and ever*
> *Amen*

I feel like my heart is sedated and numb, unable to feel. My eyes are open and I'm breathing. I'm going through the motions of everyday living and coping. My heart has not beat for me since the morning of November 22, 2019.

Calling hours went well tonight. I was told over 300 people came through the line. Family, friends, former customers of ours who are now customers of all of our sons. There was family here from all over the states. A lot of tears. Tears of sadness, tears of joy at seeing many lifelong friends and the ability to hug them close once again.

The flowers were beautiful from so many people and groups.

I saw more men in tears tonight, that I thought could never have any kind of emotion except to be funny, full of it jokers. Big tough burly men who hugged me tight and cried with me.

Many women with tears of sympathy and a fear in their eyes that said:

"God I'm so sorry for you and I pray I never have to go through what you are"

I hugged them very tight and said "this is the hardest thing I have ever had to do in life, and I pray to God you don't have to go through it either"

In my heart, I know death of someone we love is something we all will have to experience.

There is no shield or armor we can wear to protect us.

Tonight, I am beyond any kind of physical tired and it's only 8p.m.

I was at the church at 2:30p.m. this afternoon and never once sat down until it was time to go home at 7:30p.m.

I pray sleep and a quiet mind as well as restorative rest will overcome me tonight.

Tomorrow the celebration of life and then on to the final chapter of this book.

Tonight, as I lay here thinking about this journey neither one of us asked for. I remember six years ago December 13, 2013 when we were given this life sentence. Christmas was just days away and we didn't feel like celebrating. We felt no joy only numbness and heart ache. Not knowing where any of this was going to lead, hoping beyond all that we were that "they" were all wrong about the diagnosis.

Well, here I am, December again full circle of six years and its Christmas time again. Once again, no joy in Christmas celebrations, just going through the motions with a mask of smiles, and choking back sobs.

Just one thing different this year Sonny, you're not here to share this journey. I love you dearly and I miss you even more. I always will. No matter what we went through you were always my husband and I was always your wife.

Also feeling a broken heart is Maddie. She doesn't understand why you don't come home. I often find her sitting by the door just watching. Ears alert, tail wagging in anticipation when she hears a pick up pull in.

Your obituary was truth and honorable. Elizabeth and I wrote it together.

Paul E Obrochta Jr. (Sonny)

After fighting a long battle of health issues, Paul E. Obrochta Jr (Sonny) passed away peacefully at home with his wife Shirley (Baroody) Obrochta by his side early Friday morning, November 22, 2019 at 66 years old. He was born on May 9,1953 in Bath N.Y. to Paul E. Obrochta Sr. and Mary A. (Coots) Obrochta. Sonny was raised on Knightsettlement Rd. on his family's farm.

Sonny and Shirley shared 47 year of marriage, married on January 8,1972. Sonny is survived by his wife, his children and grandchildren: His sons: Scott (Lorrie) Obrochta of Bath N.Y. and their daughter Kylie Obrochta, Douglas (Jill) Obrochta of Cohocton,

N.Y. and their children Trevor, Ariana, and Aidan Obrochta, Eric (Vanessa) Obrochta of Bath N.Y. and their children Gavin, Evan, and Trinity Obrochta, and his daughter Elizabeth (Derick) Nadjadi of Avoca, NY and their children Kendal and Jax Nadjadi.

He is survived by his two sisters Barbara (Steve) Strzpek of Ormond Beach, Fl. And Lori (Tim dec.) Fuller of Bath, NY and many nieces and nephews. Sonny is also survived by his close friends, John Schumacher of Cohocton, NY, Dave Hall of Cohocton, NY, Roy Shiloh of Howard NY, and his cousin and good friend Richard Hargraves of Bath NY. Sonny was predeceased by his father Paul E. Obrochta Sr. and his brother-in-law Tim Fuller.

Sonny attended and graduated from Haverling High School, Bath NY. Over his lifetime he was involved in many different organizations like Avoca Fire Department, The Avoca Free Masons, The Champagne Whirl-A-Ways square dance club, Murphy's Bowling Leagues.

For 35 years, Sonny and Shirley owned and operated Sonny's Service Auto and Truck repair in Avoca, NY. He and Shirley started out in a small two bay garage on Main St. in Avoca in 1981. Within 6 years the business had grown and expanded with an addition of a large truck bay. They then added the heavy-duty wrecker service and was the only one in the area to do so at that time. In 1997 they built a new shop and moved their business to Rt. 70A in Avoca. His hard work and dedication to perfection had paid off.

Over the years Sonny touched the lives of so many people. Customers, neighbors, friends, and family all share stories of how Sonny had helped them at one time of another. From rescuing them from ditches in the middle of the night or just answering their questions when a mechanical issue had them stumped.

Sonny was not only truly gifted with endless mechanical knowledge, but most importantly he was caring and compassionate too. Newcomers to the area share how his kindness made them feel welcome in Avoca. He did not judge or discriminate. He offered a helping hand and was always there when anyone was in need.

Through 35 years of business, Sonny also had many employees, who still to this day appreciate all that they learned from him. "I'll never forget what Sonny taught me" Sonny wasn't always the easiest to work with as he always had a certain way of doing things. But, if you were fortunate to have learned from him, or to have worked alongside Sonny, you know how truly invaluable that time and information is.

In 2013, life as business owner came to an abrupt haul for Sonny when he was diagnosed with stage three Multiple Myeloma cancer. Those who knew Sonny, know how difficult it was for him to step away from the shop and leave the life he had built and knows, but at that time his health became a priority. All three sons have successfully carried on Sonny's legacy and life passion in their own business. His determination, drive, work ethics and care for others are evident in all of his children. Sonny was proud of the accomplishments of each of his children and because of them his legacy will live on.

Scott and his wife own and operate Scotts Tire and Repair on Windfall Road in Bath NY, where he specializes in farm equipment repair and tire sales. Doug and his wife own and operate Sonny's Service on County Rt. 70A in Avoca NY, where they specialize in tractor trailer repair. Eric and his wife own and operate South Main Auto in Main St. Avoca NY, where they specialize in auto and pick-up repairs. Elizabeth and her husband chose to follow Sonnys footsteps by becoming self-employed and opened their gym Project Iron in Kanona NY.

After a brief retirement, to get the cancer under control, Sonny returned to the life he knew so well. As a mechanic on John Schumacher Farm in N. Cohocton NY. On the farm Sonny ran the farm shop, servicing the farm equipment and vehicles. He took great pride in diagnosing and repairing equipment. He also found great comfort and happiness once again being back on the farm.

Despite being faced with constant medical challenges, Sonny was a fighter and did not give up. He continued to work, despite the risk and his wavering physical health and strength. Sonny loved to work and continued to do so. To say he was a workaholic would be an understatement.

He fought courageously to the very end of his life, astounding his doctors with his strength and resiliency to live and always amazed them with his unique health situation he always was able to overcome and get on with his life. He refused to let sickness keep him down or define who he was. Despite a leaky heart valve, an aortic aneurism, open heart surgery, multiple myeloma, a second open heart surgery, countless infections, Sonny continued to live, to thrive, to teach and to help others. Sonny lived his life, not his cancer.

Sonny will be missed by many. The knowledge and skills he took with him is more than anyone will ever know, "He truly was the strongest man I ever knew"

Please join Sonny's family in celebrating his life

Calling hours: Friday December 6, 2019 from 4:00pm-7:00pm at the Avoca Methodist Church

Celebration of life: Saturday, December 7, 2019 at 11:00am at the Avoca Methodist Church

Burial immediately following the service

Luncheon to follow at the Avoca Methodist Church

In lieu of flowers, donations can be made in honor of Paul E. Obrochta Jr. to:

Wilmot Cancer Institute
Blood Cancer/Multiple Myeloma
300 E. River Rd.
Box 278996
Rochester NY 14627

December 7 2019

10 a.m. I arrived at the church. Pastor and the funeral director were already there as well as the kitchen manager for the meal after the service. We made small talk and all was warm, sincere and friendly. Eric showed up and got the memorial video running.

By the way he and Libby did an amazing loving job on the video tribute.

By then people had started to arrive. I should have gotten there much earlier, or made a special time with Pastor Barre to be alone in the sanctuary with God and Sonny.

All I wanted to do this morning was to go in the sanctuary close the doors and have quiet prayer at the alter alone with God. It didn't happen, but then how could it, I didn't ask for it.

The service started about 11:05a.m. it lasted a little over an hour and a half and was a wonderful testament to who Sonny was to everyone. So many people spoke, Roy, John S, Andy H., Dan H. myself, Libby spoke for all of our children, Tim C, Nick P, many others I can't remember them all.

A lot of stories of how he helped everyone, how kind he was, fun, crazy times, and how he was a great neighbor. A lot of tears and laughter. He would have approved, laughed, and liked it.

After the service, Doug carried the tool box urn out of the church. I walked out with our kids. I climbed up into the passenger seat of the big Peterbilt wrecker that Sonny was so proud of. With Sonny's cremations held on my lap in his red tool box urn, we gave him his last ride in the Peterbilt wrecker that he was so proud of.

We drove to the top of Jacobs Ladder road, turned around at the four corners and headed down the hill to the cemetery. What a beautiful sound of the jake brake that echoed off the hills as we slowly approached the cemetery where everyone was waiting. Sonny loved the sound of a jake!

Scott came out to meet us when we parked the wrecker on the side of the road, and he carried his dad's urn to his final resting place.

As we sat there facing the spot where he will be buried the sky was bright blue with fluffy white cotton candy clouds. There was about five inches of snow on the ground. I was thinking this weather is exactly like the day we got married. A thought went through my mind.

Sonny always said "marriage, funeral no difference" Odd that our wedding day ran through my mind as I sat there.

Pastor performed the comital service and we all headed back to the church for lunch.

All in all, there were over five hundred people total who came between Friday and Saturday. We had people from all over our local area, and from Indiana, Ohio, Pennsylvania, Michigan, and New York City. Truly a great tribute to who Sonny was to many.

Sonny please, please, forgive me. I just could not keep it together emotionally, or was physically strong enough to preach your funeral. If I was strong enough to officiate your service this is what I would have said: This is also what I would have needed to hear myself, but I don't often listen to the words I speak for others.

> **Sonny's service that I never officiated**
> **This is what I would have said:**
>
> **"The most profound emotional experience any of us ever have to face in our life time is the death of a loved one.**
> **There is no right or wrong way, there is no certain time set to deal with death**
> **As we all go about our lives it doesn't matter if we are rich or poor, selfish or giving, complaining or complimentary, happy or grouchy**
>
> **Dealing with grief is as individual as we are**
> **At times like this people often say things, not to be hurtful but because they are worried about you, they want you to feel good again**
> **But right now, you have a void in your life and your families lives**
>
> **Grief is a process with no time line, no one person suffers like the next one**
> **We all however possess the power to endure through our faith and hope in God**
>
> **When we wake up each day, we should pray this prayer:**

Thank you, lord, for this day and what I am about to face. Give me strength to get threw one day at a time. I place myself and my weakness in your hands, guide me I pray and protect me always.

Our world has forever changed, our family make up has changed
Right now, I believe that Sonny has found peace, comfort, and absolutely no more bone pain of any kind anywhere, and love in heaven from Jesus and those who have gone on before him.

We cry because he is gone but we can smile because we knew him. Because of our loss and suffering we can look at each other with a new and kinder understanding knowing we share what we all are going through; we are not alone in our grief.

John 14:24 Peace I leave with you my peace I give unto you not as the world gives give I unto you. Let your heart not be troubled neither let it be afraid

We may not feel it today but try every day to feel the peace that God sends us

To everyone with in the sound of my voice, believe it or not some day you will all think about the end of your life and you will talk to someone about what your wishes are.

Anyone who is sitting here and knows Sonny have heard him say threw out the years "when I die bury me ass up so the whole world can kiss my ass. Then he would laugh.

On the serious side he asked me some time ago if I would preach at his funeral. I told him I don't think I can do that, then he said:

One time I heard pastor Armstrong say, "if one believes in Jesus and ask Him for forgiveness you repent and then you are saved and when you die through His grace and the blood He shed, you get a new body with no pain and you are completely healed.".

"I believe and I know I will have a new body complete with ears that hear and if you do this for me, I won't miss a word." I asked him if I do end up speaking at your funeral what should I say?

He said "tell them I was not perfect. I was not always kind. I was a sinner. I was not always compassionate or patient, but God loved me anyhow

Let them know we eventually came to peace with this cancer because we know it really is in God's hands. Let them understand yes, we did get mad at each other and angry at God and scream and cry, but we also knew we were in this for the duration. Side by side no matter how bad it got seeking God when there was nothing else, we could do. Knowing whatever way, it went God never gave up on us." Though honestly, let them know we gave up on God many times.

All of you who knew Sonny throughout the years knew how much he loved old Hank Williams. If Hanks music was on, he'd cranked it up loud. Not because of his hearing issue but because he just loved Hanks music. "I saw the light" was his favorite one.

You have all heard the praises of Sonny and his ability to do just about anything anyone ever wanted. Not only to do them but do them to perfection, because that was his way.

I won't repeat all of that at this time, but in fact I will tell you about some of his imperfections, in the bedroom.

When this man sleeps, he sounds like an old John Deere tractor and an old-fashioned coffee percolator all rolled into one. Putt, putt, glib, glub, snore, putt, putt, glib, glub, every night!

Then sometimes just before drifting off to sleep, to put it politely, he'd often have exhaust issues too. He'd say "catch it honey I just blew you a kiss" and he'd laugh as he fluffed the blankets to make sure "I caught it all."

In the most respectful way, I'd give anything to hear those foul body sounds and smells again before I fall asleep.

Sonny was not perfect, and no way am I perfect either. We had many disagreements over the years. Neither one of us was ever a winner in any argument. We conceded after many years that difference of opinion is ok, it's not the end of the world.

How boring would it be if we always agreed and we all thought alike?

To our beautiful children and their spouses and to every couple sitting out here today. You have beside you your perfect and not so perfect mate. In the end, it will be the small things that you remember, yes even the annoying things

It is my wish that you may forever enjoy all of the imperfect moments of each other well into old age Sonny was beautifully imperfect and I loved him dearly for all that was right, for all that was not right and for who he was

We were in business for over
2+thirty-four years. In those years, we came across quite a few different kinds of people and situations. Some that would really tug at your heart.

Both Sonny and I knew there were some who were very poor, but the one car they drove was needed to get them to a job that hardly put food on their table.

There were plenty of times Sonny and I forgave debts people owed. I don't tell you this to brag, I tell you this because Sonny was that kind of man. That is how we both ran the business.

We agreed that poor people hardly ever pay up because they just can't. Many others have it and pay late or not at all. Some always pay up eventually, he said to always look and listen closely and you'll know the difference.

As you all know Sonny had cancer. We fully expected some kind of remission because though the doctors said there is no remission for Multiple Myeloma we knew our God is bigger than that. We counted on it. He did eventually reach what they called a partial remission.

The hardest part about his cancer was not the pain, as some may think, though it was extremely unbearable at times, the hardest part of this cancer was letting others do things for him. He was a doer, a fixer there wasn't anything he couldn't do. But even Sonny could not fix this battle with the big C.

Let me leave you with this

We all have something priceless that Sonny has left us
His way of teaching life's lessons was not always easy,
gentle, or kind, matter of fact he was at times very
gruff and loud with a mouth like a sailor, if you know
what I mean.

He was always honest, brutality honest at times,
always hard working, and always dependable
What he gave us is not something we can hold in our
hands or put on a shelf for later use.
We can share it and as we give it away it will grow.
Though we can give it way we cannot exchange it for
anything better. The more we give it away the bigger
it becomes and the more value it gains

Even though we have given it away time and time
again, it is with us always where ever we go.
If anyone were to ever take everything we own you
would be left with this very thing Sonny gave you.
It is our memory, all he taught us, our minds priceless
treasures. I have a life time of them.

To each of our four children; to see your Dad once
again all you have to do is look in the mirror. I don't
mean you will all see a physical reflection of the
person he was
But in that reflection, you will see the legacy of hard
work, and initiative that made your Dad who he was.
That is what I see when I look at each of you. You all
inherited so much of him and who he was as a person
in work ethic, morals, and values.

At this point in your lives, you don't have the life
experiences that he did, but you have all inherited his
determination, strength and stamina on his life and
work ethics

Let the seeds of dignity, hard work, and honesty he planted in you and your memory of him grow and flourish and pass them on to your children that way the wisdom and knowledge of this man will live on for generations.

Years ago, he had his big framed strong body, tanned face and arms, he was a very handsome symbol of health and strength for most of his life. I would even say there were times he seemed immortal and I just knew he'd be here forever.

In all ways Sonny was the strongest person I ever knew, not just in a physical way but in attitude, determination, and emotion too. I cannot tell you how many times he stayed on the job no matter how much pain he was in.
He worked without altera motive, he was pure, he simply loved to work or to help others

When he was angry his anger was impassioned by the wrong, he felt
He was angry at the cancer, but he could not just get mad at it, cuss at it and be done with it. He could not cry mercy as in arm wrestling to indicate he was giving up.
He didn't have a choice to put it on a shelf until he could deal with it, because unfortunately cancer was always the boss, ultimately the winner.

He was at the mercy of the doctors, medications, and chemo treatments.
But even bigger than that he had the mercy of God and our faith.
Faith that he often questioned; would God actually protect him from this becoming terminal?

Then one day we read the scripture about putting on the armor of God, and he did. From then on, he knew God was his shield and whichever way his cancer went he knew he would be shielded until the end by God. Either by the end of the cancer and full remission or the end of his life here on earth to a life of eternity with Jesus.

He knew that in the end God would grant him a life more previous than the one he is living here on earth. He conceded either way it's a win win situation for him.

He said tell everyone don't be scared. That when you die because of Cancer you do not lose to Cancer as most people think. We are actually winners because of how we live with Cancer, then by how we die with Cancer.

He said tell them "I may have not been the "best Dad" or the "best husband, but being your husband and our children's dad is by far the best thing I have ever done. You all are not like my work, but you are my life. I love you more than I have words to say."

"I know I will see Jesus light as Hank sings, I saw the Light. I also know the song Tears in Heaven speaks to me too because I too know like the song says I don't belong here in heaven"

YES, YOU DO SONNY, YOU DO BELONG IN HEAVEN

Sonny, if only you had died of old age this would be so much easier, because then I would be that old too. I think about all we have discussed over the last six years. I think about all we have prayed about and prayed for but did not receive. All the expectant years have now vanished, and we all wonder at the mystery of death.

I don't want one more Thanksgiving, one more Christmas, one more Easter, one more birthday or anniversary or any other holiday. What I really want is just one more ordinary day with you.

I will never say I regret the life we had, because all our life, all we have been through, we were just what each other needed. I appreciate everything about us, our similarities, our differences, they were who we were together and separately.
Unfortunately, life doesn't allow us to go back and fix our mistakes, we forgive and move on, it's what we did and I'd do it again in a heartbeat, even knowing how hard this cancer journey was. I'd do it all over again. Love is when you keep coming back to each other's arms and kisses despite the fights and arguments, because in your heart you know you were made for each other.

Sonny, Paul, Mary, and Tim once again united.
RIP my family RIP!

Again, I'm sorry, I could not speak your funeral service, but I sat beside our daughter as she spoke for not only herself but her brothers too.

This is what she said:

"I didn't know if I'd be able to do this. But I have thought about it for a long time. I always thought it was strange to have to think about what you would say at your parent's funeral, especially when they were still both living. But when your parents are as great as

ours, I knew there would be so much I would want to
say to truly honor them

Thankfully for everyone here today I have lost those
countless pages I had started so long ago. But its ok,
I'm never at a loss for words because there are so many
great things to say about my dad. It won't be easy but
I wouldn't forgive myself if I didn't share with you
how amazing he was and how much I loved him. I
will never pass up an opportunity to talk about my
dad. Never.

I just want to say how truly grateful I am for everyone
here today; it truly is a testament to who he was as a
person. He touched so many lives.

I always knew this would be one of the most difficult
days I'd ever face in my life and I knew I would be a
mess, which I am As selfish and crazy as it may sound
it was and still is hard to see other people carrying
on with their lives. I thought the world should have
stopped for him. He was my everything and I thought
he deserved that. But I know he would not have
wanted that. It's the last thing he would have wanted,
actually he would have wanted us to all keep working,
tires need patching, cows need milking, equipment
needs repaired and cleaned up for spring, plows need
to be put on, engines need rebuilt, frames need to be
fabricated, kids need to be kids and we all need to
keep living.

My whole life I have struggled with understanding
my purpose in life as most people do. I constantly
wondered what it was and am I living it. I struggled
with who I was I always thought I was different or
weird because I felt everything so much more than

I could handle. I feel everything a million percent, happy, sad, angry, hurt, everything!

I would often pray that God would take that away from me because I couldn't handle it. I couldn't understand why He would let me feel all of those things so intensely.

My love for things and people is beyond what I thought was normal.

I thought I would never survive a day without my dad I just love him and my mom and my family so much I couldn't imagine a day without any of them. It wasn't until today as I am writing this that I finally understand why God let me feel all of these things, let me love so deeply let me hurt so deeply....

Its because this is who I am and this is my purpose.

I have finally for the first time come to terms with this. He knew my time with my dad would be short be he allowed me to love my dad and get to learn and appreciate him enough for a life time and I know I wouldn't change a thing. I realize now that this was a blessing not a curse, I am eternally grateful for that.

I will continue to love deeply, to feel enormously because here on earth our time is short. As cliché as that may sound it is true, and I want to feel everything and love deeply and be excited about all the small stuff, because they really aren't small, I'll continue to take pictures, to be cheesy, to be vulnerable, to put myself out there, to learn new things, (even if they aren't girly) because that is what I enjoy.

I never thought I'd be able to move to breathe or function without my dad here on this earth with me. He gave me strength I didn't know I had he gave me a sense of self confidence that I could do anything no matter how big or small. I struggled my whole life with self-doubt and anxiety and fear a lot. But when it came to my dad, he would ask me to do something (regardless of whether or not I had a clue on what I was doing, or whether I actually had the physical strength to do it) without hesitation I would do it. Because he gave me that kind of strength.

Because of you dad I know what a walking floor trailer is, I know what a Peterbilt, a Freightliner an International, and a Western Star is. I know that hammer staplers are dangerous and they hurt. I know how to use a chain binder, I can strap down a load on a trailer, I can kind of park your trailer... not very well but you let me try. You believed in me that I wouldn't hit anything. I know how to operate a man lift and got up there despite my fear of heights, because fear of falling was a lot smaller than the fear of disappointing you.

I know the proper way of holding a flashlight when assisting you on any job. I know it's a million times better to get dirty and help than to just stand there. I know that being a workaholic isn't the worst thing in the world. It's not a bad thing at all actually. You've taught me the value of hard work to the highest standard, to be humble, to be fair, but to hold people accountable, you were a man of your word and because of that I will do the same.

I've got a lot of Sonny in me. Adopted or not. And I can't tell you how grateful I am for that. It's an honor and privilege to be his daughter, to be my mother's daughter and my brother's sister.

When I have a bad day and missing you just get to be to much dad, I know I can just go visit my brothers, spend time with mom, hug my kids and nieces and nephews, because I know you're a part of all of us and that will never go away.

I can take a trip on some back roads, watch farmers in the fields and remember how we would ride around and you'd tell me all about what they were doing and how the machines worked. I can take a walk-through Lowes and remember the trips we took together recently. When I feel stressed, I remember how just having you there with me made it all ok. I can go to the shop and breathe in the deiseal fumes, put my hands in something greasy. I can go visit Scott and sit in the service van, hang out inside the big tractor tires like I use to when I was younger. I can go to Erics shop and remember this is where it all started for you. Where you and mom took a chance, took that leap of faith together and built this life for all of us.

I can drive by Polly O and remember the stories of your time there; you would always tell me about whenever we went by. I think of you whenever I see a farm tractor, a Dodge dully, tractor trailers, hear a jake brake, smell diesel fumes, use a hammer stapler or a belt sander. I'll think of you when I eat a dish of ice cream at night, when I sit at my desk that you and I built together and remember how mad you were when we moved it. But you'll never really be gone dad you are so much of who we all are and everything around us.

Because of you I want to be a better mother, better wife, a better daughter, a better sister, a better friend, a better business owner, a better neighbor. I won't give up like I thought I would.

So, Dad I hope your resting in peace, whatever that looks like for you. I know it wasn't something you enjoyed so much here on earth. So maybe you're up there talking shop with Marty Costello and Jim Russo, or talking about farming and tractors with grandpa Obrochta or talking about us kids ok your beautiful wife with all those who have passed before us.

Whatever you're doing Dad I'm glad you are no longer suffering. I hope you're walking tall again and I know you will be forever watching over us all. I just ask on bad days, and I know there will be many, that you continue to give us all the strength, the confidence and the lack of fear to push through like you did while you were here on earth with us.

Libby, Scott, Doug, and Eric

Tomorrow we will honor Sonny's mom and she will be laid to rest as well.

These last few months of 2019 have been a journey of losing to many family members all in one season. I hope I never have to repeat it in any form for anyone.

Our life will go on and we will survive with hope of eternal life in heaven with all those who have gone on before us. The hardest part about losing someone to an untimely death isn't saying good bye, but trying to fill the hole left by their absence.

Final Notes

Sometime in my life between high school, football games, dating, school dances, marriage, homes, children, careers, and cancer, life happened.

There were plenty of times I wished I could have been someone else or someone else could be me.

I didn't know if this was the life I was supposed to have. Was this what God planned for me or did I choose it against Gods plan for me?

I guess the older we get we wonder about the hand we have been dealt or the hand we played. Were we supposed to be more or less than what we are?

I have always been an organizer. I try to plan ahead and prepare as much as possible for what needs to be done. But sometimes life circumstances happen out of my control. I could not ever plane for what we have been through the last six years. Not even in my wildest dreams.

So many wonders in my mind

Did I love him enough? If I loved him more would he still be here?

I know I didn't love him as Jesus does because God took him from me. He clearly loves him more and my love couldn't keep him here on earth.

Do you have any idea what six years of mental, emotional, spiritual, and physical exhaustion feels like?

At times I feel guilty for when I lost my patients from my care givers exhaustion, or got upset with him and his demands. I am truly sorry that I let those feelings rule me at times.

I can't take it back. I don't get a do over. None of us do. Until you have been through what I have all I ask is that you please don't judge me in how I handled situations at times. I promise you if you ever have to go through anything like this I will understand completely.

Someone asked me does my house feel empty now?

In a way it does, but I still have my dog and cat. In the last year he was in the hospital a lot. Many nights I came home to an empty house. Almost like a preparation for him no longer being here, now that I look back.

I find when I have to go someplace, anywhere, I am always anxious to get back home. My home, our home, my comfort, my security, we built together. It's where I want to be.

The end of your life is not about what you leave to your children, it's what you leave in them.

Because if what you leave in them is everything that you were, they can go out in their world and make their own way successfully. What Sonny left in our children is priceless. An inheritance no amount of money can buy.

Life isn't like a movie or tv sitcom. You don't always get a happy ending and you don't get a ninety second commercial break where everything is perfect when you get back to the show.

When your told you have cancer, you hate your life, you hate God.

All of these statements come to mind than........ Life is not fair.......Why me.......Why us......Am I being punished........What will happen to my family.......How will we tell our kids, our elderly parents........What are we going to do now......How can we fix this....... There has to be a way out.......The doctors have to be wrong, it's not really cancer....... What if one of us has to live without the other.

All the hospital stays were overwhelming, all the doctor appointments were overwhelming, but we did them. We did them all with the end goal in mind and that was remission and those two words "cancer free." But we never did get to hear them, we knew we wouldn't. Regardless, we never gave up and never lost hope.

A lot of what I've had to write about in this journal is a brutal honest account of what our life has been like in this cancer journey. If you have never been in our shoes don't judge us.

Some of it may seem mean or uncalled for. Maybe others who are or went through this kind of thing were better equipped for it, or maybe they would never admit their faults like I did.

Truth is, this was our reality, our real life. I did not sugar coat any of it. It was the way we lived, the feelings, and events as they happened and as we experienced. Brutally raw and honest, like Sonny always was.

He was always the strong one physically, he could lift a house, I think.

I could work right alongside of him and lift, push, and carry many times more than a woman my size should. Physical work was our of life, it always had been, we are doers, we don't just talk about doing something we just do it!

I am paying for it now, physically that is. Working like a man but in a woman's body has taken its toll on my female body parts. Wore out before my time.

God's word tells us to "give thanks in all things" to me it's one of the most haunting verses in the Bible.

I had many days of doubt and no trust in God because I could not fathom "how was I supposed to find thankfulness in cancer? How can I be thankful for a husband who is so selfish at times, and mean to me, when others think the sun rises and sets with him?

Just because Gods word tells us to be thankful in all things.

All things, really Lord? Thankful for cancer? This could not be. At first, I was to angry and ignorant, or maybe just not fully informed, to be thankful about anything.

But as they say, put on your big girl panties and move on. Or as Sonny always said to me:

"you're a big girl you'll figure it out"

I found out that I was not only the spiritual strength for my family and Sonny. I was now the mental cheerleader. I was now the one who had to be physically strong. I took over many of the things he use to do. Like cleaning the pellet stoves, carrying forty-pound bags of pellets and fifty-pound bags of water softener salt. I pushed and lifted the snow with a shovel in the winter, and mowed and weed whacked the grass in the summer.

Early on in the cancer journey, after having my melt down with God. I tried to always show my family faith, hope, peace, and love, and hoped those characteristics transferred from me to them and everyone I came in contact with.

Matter of fact the nurse receptionist, Geraldine, on the stem cell transplant floor said to me one day. "good morning Miss Shirley, every time I see you, you're always smiling.

I love it, but, how can you? How do you always stay happy?" and all I could say was

"God is good" and she smiled too!

Yes, this journal or book is all about Sonny's journey with Multiple Myeloma and a little bit about my journey, and what I have endured through Multiple Myeloma and our life in general. Because it truly was "our" cancer. Cancer really does affect the whole family.

Many times, I find myself wishing I could go back to an age of innocence. Days of no responsibilities and no knowledge. Especially knowledge of the kind I have now. I'd like to go back to an age of no worries, days before cancer, back to high school days of dating, home work, and being mad at my parents for grounding me. Days of my youth, few responsibilities, and no worries!

Being a wife of someone who has a debilitatingly painful and terminal illness is not easy. An illness that most of the time you cannot see, but you know it's there, is a helpless feeling.

Especially when both Sonny and I have always been fix it people. One thing we both agree on is we have no time in our life for lazy people. Lazy doesn't fly in our home, ever!

If it's broke, don't complain, don't tell others how it should be done, unless they ask, don't over think it, don't analyze it, just dig in and fix it.

The prognosis never changed. Oh, at times it seemed better, and the all the test will say things are going well, but it will never be gone! We have had fleeting moments of peace and acceptance, and also many fleeting moments of fight and flight modes.

The many varied emotions cause you to grow very thick skin. Sadly, sometimes a hardened heart. For that we were not proud.

Watching someone go through this is pure hell on a daily basis!

It was hard for both of us to look at our lives and see where we were at the moment, and know how this was not part of our plan to be here doing this at this time in our lives, or ever.

It was at times very difficult not to live in the past when he was healthy, and even more difficult to think of the future that would not be there for us together.

The craziest maybe insignificant, selfish, unimportant, part was we would never dance again.

I love to dance, though I'm not good at it, and even though he really did not like to dance, and he didn't really like much of any music that I do, he would always dance with me regardless. It is one of the nice things he always did for me.

That was not to be any more. The last time we were at a wedding reception where we could have danced, we didn't do it. We just walked away from the music that night and resigned that it would never be again. He listened to his country music radio in his truck and I only listen to old time rock n roll, country music, and easy listening love songs, when he isn't around. If he was around, I'm not allowed to listen to it, and if he's with me in the car he turns my music off. Music was just too painful a memory for him in a way that was not a physical pain but mental. If that makes sense to anyone.

It is a strange thing to realize and accept your own mortality. Most of the time it's one of those things you ignore. Days keep ticking by, you come to expect, that they always will. We imagined growing old, grumpy, gray, and wrinkled together.

We found out that life is precious, fragile, unpredictable and that each day we were given was a gift, not a given right, and definitely out of our control.

What a comfort for me to be able to speak in this journal. To tell all you care givers what I am going through, and maybe you are too, or maybe you have. Maybe you're a better care giver than I was. I did my best. As hard as it was, I never ever stopped loving him. There were times I didn't like what he put me through but I still loved him.

What peace to know we are not alone in being caregivers.

I was my husband's caregiver for over six years. His cancer was Multiple Myeloma stage 3, and there is no cure it is terminal.

He was given eighteen months to three years, and he had made it six plus years. He was blessed. Not all of the six years were easy for any of us, but especially harder for him than us.

What have I learned as a care giver:

1. I've learned there are some things I can't fix, but instead I support whatever is happening at the moment. This does not mean I accept what is going on and that I always research how to fix it!

Dr. Ifthi bless his heart, was already doing everything within his medical power to "fix" Sonny and his cancer but it cannot be done. There is no complete fix to Multiple Myeloma. Our thinking was always maybe Sonny will be the first!

2. People are just trying to be helpful, not hurtful when they say things to try to make you feel better. Things like, "I know people who have had that cancer and never made it" or "oh he is strong he will beat this" or "he's a fighter, cancer won't beat him".

My all-time favorite "he doesn't look sick," I often wondered, what the heck does cancer really look like anyhow, what exactly did you expect to see?

3. Regardless of what shape Sonny was in, or what treatment he was going through, I never gave up. It was never about the man he used to be, or the man he would become later, it was always about the man he is at this moment. He and I both knew there would be no "after the cancer," moment for either of us. I can't say we fully accepted it but yet we knew it.

4. Sometimes you find yourself whining about unimportant things such as being stuck behind a slow driver when you're in a hurry, or maybe your coffee isn't as hot as you like it, maybe you didn't sleep very well.

Then your mind goes to thinking about someone facing much bigger issues than what just pissed you off. Someone who is facing a life and death in their everyday living. Suddenly your everyday problems really are not that big a deal.

5. I hear people complaining how terrible their job is, how they hate going to work. How hard it is to exercise. From my view point and that of Sonny's. Just be grateful you are physically able to so those things.

Doing work and exercise may seem trivial, until your body doesn't allow you to do them anymore.

6. Be grateful for every day you don't have pain, be very grateful. Even on days when you have the sniffles, muscle aches, a head ache, sore back, etc. Just accept that and be thankful it's not life threatening and it will go away.

7.Get up early, get things done, Sonny always said "you can't get anything done by lying in bed past sun up" Enjoy that first cup of coffee just watching the world wake up and daylight happen outside your window. Don't take one moment for granted.

8. It's weird to have money in the bank. You can go out and buy whatever your heart desires, except your health and more time.

When he was first diagnosed, I could not pray, or read my Bible at All!

I made it look like I was strong, handling life with positivity. A false front to keep everyone else at easy and not to worry for us.

Many scriptures haunted me because I was looking for the one perfect promise that this too will really pass.

My pastor mentors, told me. "you don't have to pray, we will hold you up in prayer, just know God is by your side and He understands"

There were many times, I walked alone around the huge property we own and I screamed at God and I cried!

You see we had been self-employed for over thirty-four years; we were ready to retire with in four years before the diagnosis. Then became medically forced to sell and retire, due to many appointments and hospitalizations and his ill health.

It wasn't the retirement we dreamed of. All our dreams went out the window and buried under a life we didn't want. Not to mention most of our savings are now gone to co pays, hospitalizations, travel expenses, instead of the dream vacations of our retirement.

Yes, I'm pissed, he was too. Yes, I get mad, I hate the hand that Sonny had been dealt, no one deserves that. NO ONE!

Thing is I never or very rarely show that side of me to others. I know that's not good for me, I hold it together when anyone is around. I stay strong on the outside for my adult children and grandkids. I always want to stay positive, and carry the family burden myself.

I don't want our kids to have to deal with what I am carrying. I will share anything I own, but I refuse to share this burden. It's the toughest thing I've ever experienced in my life!

Life is hard sometimes very hard. But life can be good too. No one is guaranteed a perfect life with all good, all the time, it just doesn't work that way. No one can go through life without being hurt or touched profoundly by what happens along this journey called life with an intrusion of cancer.

As always God gives us much more than we deserve in so many ways. Even when our tears of sorrow turn into tears of hope. We need to remember today and every day we are given is one day closer to heaven for all of us who believe.

I don't care who you are a cancer diagnosis is a frightening thing. Even to a big strong as a brick wall kind of guy as Sonny. When you are told you have Cancer your gut hurts like a lead ball and sinks into the very core of your body.

When a doctor tells you, "you have Cancer," no matter how soft spoken he is, and Dr. Ifthi was, those words are loud. Three little words that ring in your ears nonstop, you cannot unhear them. It's as if they are being shouted at you through a microphone and echoed back repeatedly off deep canyon walls.

The words "I'm sorry but you have cancer" are so loud and yet they numb you and make you deaf to anything else's that is said after that. It's like your ears and mind get plugged and your body is completely suspended in the air, yet weighed down as if you're drowning all at the same time.

You feel like if you leave the doctor's office you won't live to see tomorrow, but as long as you're sitting there in that office, with that doctor, you are protected. Your heart is still beating, you can still breath, you are safe. The doctor knows what to do.

You are weighed down by all the things in your mind, the "what if's." You want answers, you want a cure, you want action, you want to get started right now with treatment, there is no time to lose no time to wait. You feel like you're going crazy in your mind, what do we do next, where do we begin?

How do we give into or even address the possibility of living without our spouse of over forty years?

Simple!!! We won't talk about it and it will go away. We can handle this on our own. We don't need anyone. We will be ok! Sonny is invincible!

Well, that was a first thought, now it's real and now we have talked about the reality of things to come and how we are going to handle it. Life has forced us to talk about things we weren't ready to talk about, things we aren't old enough to talk about.

Sonny asked me to speak at his funeral, to talk to our kids and grandkids, I told him "I'd think about it." Reality is, I knew I couldn't do it.

No one likes the idea or even the thought of any of this, even though we know in the back of our mind death is a real possibility. We just didn't want to address the possibility of death; we were "to young" to think about dying.

Definitely to young to do this kind of end-of-life planning.

About two years after diagnosis, he took care of getting some of our possessions into my name so *"it will be easier for you when I die"* that's what he said. I resisted, because it seemed to me if we did that, that death was a reality I was not ready to admit.

Everyone was fighting for him even when he didn't want to fight for himself. Every little glimmer of hope. Every little light of wellness and possibility, I turned into a full-blown light house, that light of hope, to keep our eyes on so we didn't sink into forever darkness.

At some point after the rage, I knew I had the hand of our Almighty God in my right hand and ahold of Sonny's hand in my left. I was determined the two were going to meet and Sonny was not going to give in to cancer or death without knowing God's grace.

There can be life after cancer diagnosis, or a cancer diagnosis can be the end of your life.

In Sonny's case we were determined to believe that even though there is no cure, he will have a life with cancer. After all, even a healthy person doesn't have any guarantee if there will be a tomorrow either. We decided to live our life the best way we could for whatever was happening at the time. We would adapt and adjust.

Onward we marched into this cancer journey and whole new life style.

We put on the armor of God and the face of determination and a large helping of good attitude, most of the time. Cancer did not have us even though he has cancer. He was determined to live his life not his cancer, his survival attitude was strong most of the time.

We may have had many long nights of tears, misunderstanding, arguments, struggles, extreme fatigue, and fear, only to be meet in the morning with another day, some sunshine, and one more I love you, sometimes one more I'm sorry, and one more chance.

Lamentations 3:22 the Lords mercy and loving kindness are new every day for great is your faithfulness.

This book is our personal journey with our knowledge, and not so eloquent or proper words. But to share, to offer hope, encouragement and understanding for anyone going through cancer or any kind of debilitating terminal illness.

Hopefully you who get to read this, don't take your health and feeling good for granted.

I have poured out some very personal feelings and information here in this journal/book. Not to become famous, especially not to say "oh poor me," but to help others understand everything they feel. Good, bad, or indifferent because we are human, and to know they are not alone.

This is not to diagnose any of you or to take place of your doctor, but only to share our story and to know that if you took the time to read this very personal account of our cancer journey. Know that I love you all and I support you too with my prayers for whatever kind of Cancer you are fighting. We know your fear, determination, and unanswered questions.

Let go and let Gods love and peace embrace you and hold you safe in your journey too.

May God be with you in your storms and your times of peace and goodness. May you rest in God's love, health, healing, warmth, mercy, and grace.

In Christ Love

Shirley Obrochta

Printed in the United States
by Baker & Taylor Publisher Services

Printed in the United States
by Baker & Taylor Publisher Services